IMPROVING MEASURES
OF ECONOMIC WELL-BEING

This is a volume in the

Institute for Research on Poverty Monograph Series

A complete list of titles in this series appears at the end of this volume.

IMPROVING MEASURES OF ECONOMIC WELL-BEING

Edited by

MARILYN MOON

Department of Economics
University of Wisconsin—Milwaukee

EUGENE SMOLENSKY

Department of Economics
University of Wisconsin—Madison

ACADEMIC PRESS   New York   San Francisco   London

A Subsidiary of Harcourt Brace Jovanovich, Publishers

This book is one of a series sponsored by the Institute for Research on Poverty of the University of Wisconsin pursuant to the provisions of the Economic Opportunity Act of 1964.

ACADEMIC PRESS, INC.
111 Fifth Avenue, New York, New York 10003

United Kingdom Edition published by
ACADEMIC PRESS, INC. (LONDON) LTD.
24/28 Oval Road, London NW1

Library of Congress Cataloging in Publication Data

Main entry under title:

Improving measures of economic well-being.

(Institute for Research on Poverty monograph series)
Includes bibliographies.
CONTENTS: Introduction.–Watts, H. W.   An economic definition of poverty.–Weisbrod, B. A. and W. L. Hansen.   An income-net worth approach to measuring economic welfare.–Garfinkel, I. and R. Haveman.   Earnings capacity, economic status, and poverty.   [etc.]
    1.   Poverty–Addresses, essays, lectures.
2.   Income distribution–United States–Addresses, essays, lectures.   3.   Poverty research–United States–Addresses, essays, lectures.   I.   Moon, Marilyn.   II.   Smolensky, Eugene.   III.   Series: Wisconsin.   University–Madison.   Institute for Research on Poverty.   Monograph series.
HC110.P6I47   362.5   76-50400
ISBN 0–12–504640–5

The Institute for Research on Poverty is a national center for research established at the University of Wisconsin in 1966 by a grant from the Office of Economic Opportunity. Its primary objective is to foster basic, multidisciplinary research into the nature and causes of poverty and means to combat it.

In addition to increasing the basic knowledge from which policies aimed at the elimination of poverty can be shaped, the Institute strives to carry analysis beyond the formation and testing of fundamental generalizations to the development and assessment of relevant policy alternatives.

The Institute endeavors to bring together scholars of the highest caliber whose primary research efforts are focused on the problem of poverty, the distribution of income, and the analysis and evaluation of social policy, offering staff members wide opportunity for interchange of ideas, maximum freedom for research into basic questions about poverty and social policy, and dissemination of their findings.

To Jerry, Smitty, and Douglas
with appreciation and affection

Contents

II   An Income—Net Worth Approach to Measuring Economic Welfare   34

BURTON A. WEISBROD AND W. LEE HANSEN

III   Earnings Capacity, Economic Status, and Poverty   52

IRWIN GARFINKEL AND ROBERT HAVEMAN

IV   Aspects of the Variability of Family Income   75

THAD W. MIRER

V   The Economic Welfare of the Aged and Income Security Programs   88

MARILYN MOON

VI   Transfer Approaches to Distribution Policy   111

ROBERT J. LAMPMAN

List of Contributors

Numbers in parentheses indicate the pages on which the authors' contributions begin.

Michael C. Barth (201), Income Security Policy Analysis, Department of Health, Education, and Welfare, South Portal Building, Washington, D.C.

Irwin Garfinkel (51), Institute for Research on Poverty, Social Science Building, University of Wisconsin—Madison, Wisconsin

W. Lee Hansen (33), Department of Economics, University of Wisconsin—Madison, Madison, Wisconsin

Robert Haveman (51), Department of Economics, University of Wisconsin—Madison, Madison, Wisconsin

Robert J. Lampman (111), Department of Economics, University of Wisconsin—Madison, Madison, Wisconsin

Thad W. Mirer (75), Department of Economics, State University of New York—Albany, Albany, New York

Marilyn Moon (87), Department of Economics, University of Wisconsin—Milwaukee, Milwaukee, Wisconsin

John H. Palmer (201), The Brookings Institution, 1775 Massachusetts Avenue, N.W., Washington, D.C.

Robert Plotnick (131), Department of Economics, Bates College, Lewiston, Maine

Maria Schmundt (131), Department of Economics, University of Wisconsin—Madison, Madison, Wisconsin

Timothy M. Smeeding (155), Department of Economics, University of Utah, Salt Lake City, Utah

Eugene Smolensky (131), Department of Economics, University of Wisconsin—Madison, Madison, Wisconsin

Leanna Stiefel (131), Graduate School of Public Administration, New York University, New York, New York

Harold W. Watts (19, 85), Center for the Social Sciences, International Affairs Building, Columbia University, New York, New York

Burton A. Weisbrod (33), Department of Economics, University of Wisconsin—Madison, Madison, Wisconsin

Foreword

Since its inception in 1965, the Institute for Research on Poverty has supported research on the measurement of economic status. This volume is a collection of some of the most important articles by Institute staff in this area. While they have (with one exception) been published elsewhere, taken together they constitute a substantial corpus of Institute work and a significant contribution to the literature on measurement of economic status. In this sense, the whole is greater than the sum of its parts.

The analyses presented in this volume help provide answers to questions as diverse as the following: Have we underestimated the progress we have made against poverty during the last decade by not counting benefits from in-kind transfer programs like Food Stamps and Medicaid? Is a family with a retired 68-year-old head, $3,500 of social security income, and a mortgage-free house, any poorer than a five-person family with a head who works the entire year, earns an income of $7,000, and pays rent? Is a five-person family in which the head earns $6,000 and the spouse earns $2,000 any better off than a comparable family in which the head earns $6,000 and the spouse earns nothing? Does inflation really hurt the poor? All these questions are answered as soon as poverty is defined and its incidence measured.

The appropriate definition and measurement of poverty obviously must derive from the definition and measurement of economic status more generally. In order to ascertain who is poor, it is necessary first to rank families from richest to poorest by some measure of economic status. Then some dividing line between the poor and nonpoor must be established. Much of the public controversy over the definition and measurement of poverty has centered on the question of how high to draw the line. The higher the line is drawn, the more poor people will be included and the more poverty will appear to be a general and severe problem. The political nature of the question is obvious. The papers in this volume do not address this normative issue precisely because the authors believe that how high the poverty line should be is a question of values and politics to which scientists, as scientists, can contribute little or nothing.

The papers in this volume *are* concerned with how to rank families. Given our nation's commitment to reducing and eventually eliminating poverty, pressures exist to provide government benefits to those families and groups of families defined as poor. Thus, while inquiries into who is poorest may appear at first blush to be unrelated to public policy, and perhaps even little more than scholastic disputation, they may have a profound impact on the nature of public policy by changing our perceptions of who is truly poor and thereby deserving of help. The "discovery" of the working poor in the 1960s, for example, was due in large part to the development and widespread acceptance of an economic definition of poverty. Only after poverty was defined and measured was it possible to identify the large proportion of the poor who did not fit the conventional sterotypes—aged, disabled, widowed, or unemployed—but rather worked full time or nearly full time and still remained poor.

As John Maynard Keynes so aptly put it:

> The ideas of economists and political philosophers, both when they are right and when they are wrong, are more powerful than is commonly understood. Indeed the world is ruled by little else. Practical men, who believe themselves to be quite exempt from any intellectual influences, are usually the slaves of some defunct economist. Madmen in authority, who hear voices in the air, are distilling their frenzy from some academic scribbler of a few years back. I am sure that the power of vested interests is vastly exaggerated compared with the gradual encroachment of ideas.

The authors of the articles collected in this volume are not yet defunct economists and, perhaps for that reason, do not yet rule practical men. Yet the ideas and arguments put forth here are, in my judgment, closer to right than wrong.

IRWIN GARFINKEL
Director, Institute for Research on Poverty

Preface

Some time ago Bob Haveman, then director of the Institute for Research on Poverty, noted that a large proportion of research by Institute staff could be viewed as addressing the question "How should economic welfare be measured for policy purposes?" He further observed that even the authors may not have viewed their research in quite this way and, hence, that the relationship of these papers to a common theme may have been missed by the profession at large. Since the topic was important and was being actively pursued by many other scholars, we were eventually asked to collect the relevant work of the Institute and to write a suitable introduction. Accepting the premise that the sum could be larger than the whole of its parts, the Publication Committee of the Institute, with great trepidation, agreed to override its policy of not reprinting published articles.

In nearly every case we have included the entire article even when much of it dealt with only distantly related issues; this was done because we believed the reader would want to know why each discussion of economic welfare took the precise form and content that it did. Moreover, the various uses of the economic welfare measures suggest the array of policy applications.

We wish to thank the authors and original publishers of the various pieces, and also Barry Chudakov, Gini Martens, and Felicity Skidmore, for making this volume possible.

Financial support came in part from funds granted to the Institute for Research on Poverty by the Department of Health, Education, and Welfare, pursuant to the Economic Opportunity Act of 1964.

MARILYN MOON
EUGENE SMOLENSKY

Introduction

Over the past decade, concern with the design and evaluation of antipoverty programs has led researchers at the Institute for Research on Poverty to review critically the existing indices of economic welfare and to develop alternatives. The starting point has invariably been a "cash (or money) income" measure, i.e., income plus cash transfers. To this, other correlates of economic status have been added to make the measure more comprehensive. In this volume, these various and often piecemeal efforts at identifying economic indices that would serve social policy are gathered together. The hope is that others will be stimulated by the papers presented here to a comprehensive reconsideration of this important but still unsettled area.

The papers reproduced here share some attributes dictated by the purposes of the Institute. One of its important concerns is research which will contribute toward achieving static, horizontal equity. That is, the majority of the articles attempt to define who the poor are among the population. A related, and to some extent, inseparable issue is the ranking of families by economic status and the equality of the resulting distribution. Improvements in measuring these attributes, which are especially relevant to vertical equity considerations, via a more comprehensive indicator of economic status also help to guarantee horizontal equity. Finally, while the emphasis is on ensuring static horizontal and vertical equity, some research has also centered on revising measures of economic status to maintain the equality of equals across space, demographic characteristics, and time.

I. THE NATURE OF THE PROBLEM

Interest in the measurement of poverty can be traced to as early as 1890, when the development of a poverty line was discussed by Charles

Booth.[1] However, the related issues of appropriately measuring the economic status of families and of defining the poor remain to be settled. These problems are crucial if we intend to provide similar treatment to families of equivalent economic status. For example, government programs directed at poor families often intend to include all those who are poor and totally to exclude those who are not. When receipt or denial of substantial benefits is dictated by a single empirical index, it is obviously important for that index to conform to a generally shared view of both horizontal and vertical equity. More comprehensive measures of economic status, which better distinguish poor from nonpoor families, increase the likelihood of policy improvements that will treat those whom society views as equals equally.

Cash income is the most commonly used indicator of economic status, but it is widely recognized that this measure is inadequate. Comparisons using a cash income measure may not assure horizontal equity since many other consumable resources are ignored. For some families current cash receipts constitute only a small portion of the available sources of economic welfare. Differing amounts of leisure time, in-kind transfers, and physical and human capital can substantially alter the economic position of families with similar cash incomes, causing them no longer to appear as equals. For this reason other sources of purchasing power are often added to create alternative indices of family status. Moreover, vertical equity considerations—the ranking of families and the equality of the distribution—are also likely to be affected.

In addition, family size, location of residence, disability, income variability, and age are often introduced to modify the rankings that result from using either cash income alone or an expanded definition of economic welfare. For instance, the Orshansky poverty threshold lines use cash income with adjustments for family size and location to determine which families are poor. The individual income tax recognizes age, disability, variability, marital status, and source of income when defining equals (i.e., those in the same marginal tax bracket). This approach to maintaining horizontal equity alters the mechanism used to classify families, rather than changing the measure of economic status directly. Intertemporal equity concerns have also been considered in adjustments to the measure of economic status.

We now turn our attention to placing in perspective and summarizing the papers that follow. Work by other researchers is mentioned, but no attempt has been made to provide a complete review of the literature.

---

[1] For a discussion of the history of the measurement of poverty, see, for example, Eugene Smolensky [25]; and Oscar Ornati [17].

The first section deals with expanding the measure of economic status, while the second section addresses the issue of maintaining horizontal equity over space, demographic characteristics, and time.

II. THE APPROPRIATE STATIC INDEX

In every instance but two, Poverty Institute researchers have proceeded on the assumption that indices of economic welfare ought to be based not on actual levels of consumption, nor on actual levels of income, but rather on the resource constraint faced by the household. The appropriate measure is one that reflects the level of attainable rather than attained consumption of the family. The most explicit and forceful case in support of this view is made by **Watts,** who aptly characterizes such an indicator of economic status as a "property of the individual's situation, rather than a characteristic of the individual or of his pattern of behavior" [30, p. 371]. In particular, categorizing families as equals on the basis of their behavior (e.g., food consumption) is inappropriate if the similarity in behavior results from differences in tastes rather than similarities in resource constraints. (One author who will contest this position in this volume is Watts himself, in a later paper.)

In the remainder of the section, efforts to value non-cash components which enter the household resource constraint and hence affect the appropriate index of economic welfare at one point in time are discussed. Among the elements considered are: the annuitized value of the household's net worth; utilization rates of human capital; private transfers; governmental taxes and transfers; and leisure time and non-market activities.

A. Net Worth

Property income in part reflects the amount of net worth owned by a family. However, asset ownership adds more to economic welfare than is indicated by property income. Some net worth, such as home equity, generates no money income. Moreover, the optimal allocation of that equity over the remaining lifetime of an individual can add significantly to potential consumption in any period while being apportioned so as not to "prematurely" draw down the value of net worth. Thus, an annuitized portion of net worth that effectively incorporates property income more comprehensively measures the contribution of this economic welfare component.

A study by **Weisbrod** and **Hansen** [31] includes this additional component in a measure of economic welfare. The authors assert that the level of assets owned by a household enhances its "economic position"—defined as a function of the flow of services over which the family unit has command. Weisbrod and Hansen claim for their construct only that it will improve upon the inequitable, "single-dimensional money income measure" of economic welfare; they do not view the approach as yielding an ideal or complete measure. Since all groups among the population do not benefit equally from this source of economic well-being, both the absolute levels of measured economic welfare and the resultant rankings of families are affected by adopting this broader concept instead of a money income measure. In another study, Moon [13] uses the Weisbrod–Hansen current annuity measure in a calculation of the economic welfare of aged families. Even within this age group, the substitution of the net worth measure for property income alters the rankings of families substantially.

In a criticism of the Weisbrod–Hansen approach, Dorothy Projector and Gertrude Weiss [21] have claimed that such a measure has only limited value. In particular, they are wary of using this measure either to establish eligibility for public programs or to identify equals of different ages. The implicit assumption in the Weisbrod–Hansen approach, that a family will want to consume evenly over time, is consistent with a permanent income hypothesis, but the constant annuity calculation additionally implies that other sources of well-being will tend to remain stable over time. Families of different ages are likely to have different expectations for the future, particularly for earned incomes. More complicated allocation formulas pose difficult problems, and have not been implemented empirically.

B.   Human Capital

Expected future earnings are an important component of the present value of a lifetime resource constraint. The ratio of current to future earnings is very important for comparisons across age groups. Families with large amounts of human capital can expect to draw upon that source in the future and consequently can consume more today out of current income. In some cases, it may even be possible to borrow against future expected earned income.

Although the importance of human capital has been recognized, no empirical work has directly related human capital to a measure of economic welfare in the same way that adjustments have been noted for physical and financial assets. However, some limited compensations have been made. For example, Michael Taussig [27] has used the human capital concept to smooth out year-to-year variations in earnings as reported by individual workers. By calculating an experience-adjusted earnings figure, he has replaced the actual earnings of an individual with the average earnings of a representative worker having the same sex, race, occupation, and years of experience. Taussig himself points out that this procedure does not solve the problem of classifying those of widely divergent ages into groups of equal economic status.

A more comprehensive approach to the human capital issue similar to Taussig's has been used by **Garfinkel** and **Haveman** [8]. Their measure, "earnings capacity," uses a family's current endowment of physical and human capital and an estimated rate of return on each component to calculate what the family could earn in the current year if it fully employed these assets. The returns on human capital are estimated jointly for years of schooling, work experience, and various demographic characteristics. To the extent that the discrepancy between actual earnings and the capacity measure reflects the individual's preferences, this measure more effectively identifies families who are poor for "voluntary" reasons. An obvious example is a student whose earnings capacity is much higher than actual earned income. This approach adjusts for deviations from full-time work and for the nonpecuniary differences that exist among jobs, but does not incorporate the present discounted value of expected future earnings into a measure of economic status.

C. Variations in Transitory Income

Year-to-year fluctuations in total income cast serious doubt on the use of money income in any one year as the appropriate measure of economic welfare. Permanent income or life-cycle measures smooth out these fluctuations, yielding a more reasonable estimate of what a family could consume in a single year.[2] However, income variability itself may affect the economic well-being of families. If, for example, a family has the same average income for two periods, but its income shows a much larger fluctuation in one of those periods, that family may not feel itself as well-off during the time interval in which income is erratic. If a family is risk-averse, uncertainty about income reduces utility for any given level of permanent income. **Mirer** [12] finds that consumption is negatively correlated with income variability, supporting the claim that well-being is a function of the stability of income.

[2] See, for example, Albert Ando and Franco Modigliani [1].

D. Intrafamily Transfers

Another important aspect of economic welfare, only partially included in measured current income, is aid from relatives. Cash gifts from relatives outside the nuclear family are included in measures of current income, although these may be underreported. More important, however, is *intrafamily* aid, often in the form of an in-kind transfer. Intrafamily transfers occur when two or more nuclear families reside together in an extended family group, thus sharing resources. For certain portions of the population—e.g., the young or old—such living arrangements may have an especially important bearing on the level of economic welfare.

While such living arrangements reflect a wide range of motives, economic incentives must count among the most important. In general, "doubling-up" is a less costly way to provide for needy relatives than are cash transfers or other means. Morgan, David, Cohen, and Brazer [15] found that most people they interviewed disapprove of such arrangements and bring relatives into the family only to provide support. Their study concluded that about three-fourths of the dependent "extra adult units" improved their economic situation by living with relatives, while only 5 percent of those units were worse off than if they had lived alone.

Attempts at estimating the size of intrafamily transfers have been quite limited, with most research directed only at identifying families who might benefit from such transfers. However, the Morgan et al. study actually calculates a measure of intrafamily transfers. It estimates the value of food and housing that a dependent subfamily would receive by living with relatives, and adds to that reported cash gifts to obtain the net intrafamily transfer. This measure provides a conservative estimate of the subsistence needs supplied by the primary family unit.

Another approach of some interest is one suggested by Baerwaldt and Morgan [2], although the authors do not specifically deal with extended families. They estimate flows of income and resources among all family members—which sometimes also includes other relatives living in the household. The study is noteworthy because it attempts to estimate the actual dollar amount of transfers among family members and consequently provides some guidelines for the allocation of intrafamily transfers. For several different variants of income, Baerwaldt and Morgan allocate transfers to family members in three ways: (1) on a per capita basis, (2) in proportion to physical needs as measured by food requirements, and (3) in proportion to needs, with additional assumptions about savings behavior for persons above a certain income.

A similar approach by **Moon** is used to estimate intrafamily transfers within extended family groups, although her research is confined to families with at least one member 65 or older. The allocation formula is based on the size of each nuclear family's resources relative to its needs (the welfare ratio). At very low levels of economic welfare, the transfer is assumed to equalize the welfare ratios of the member families. For families with greater resources, the imputed transfers to needy members become less comprehensive, no longer guaranteeing equal welfare ratios.

In all three of these studies, the transfer measures are based on imputed rather than observed values. Morgan et al. base their estimates on presumed costs of necessities, while the latter two studies use the level of economic status of both donors and recipients to estimate the potential size of the transfers.

E. The Impact of Government

Another important component of economic welfare only partially captured by current income measures is government expenditures and taxes. Cash income measures are not usually limited to factor income but also include the value of cash transfer payments (but without any adjustment for tax payments). However, all government expenditures and taxes influence the level of economic welfare, affecting the family's consumption choices through both income and substitution effects.

After-tax income has frequently been cited as an indicator of economic status, reflecting the amount of current income a family has available for consumption. Moreover, a substantial amount of research has centered on estimating the final incidence of various taxes, particularly the income tax, and in some cases the entire tax system.[3] One of the most recent of these studies, by Pechman and Okner [20], uses a microdata file merged from two sources to calculate tax burdens for each sample family. Using two different incidence assumptions, the authors compute after-tax income for families and then examine the resulting distributions.

In contrast, only a few researchers have sought to measure the total impact of government expenditures. Studies by Gillespie [9], Bishop [5], and Reynolds and Smolensky [22] do examine the net distributional effects of government for 1950, 1961, and 1970, respectively. However,

---

[3] See, for example, Gerhard Colm and Helen Tarasov [6]; R. Musgrave et al. [16]; and G. A. Bishop [4].

these studies are based on macroeconomic data and do not specifically attempt to derive an expanded measure of economic welfare.

There has, however, been some research on government expenditures—particularly in-kind transfers—directly applicable to measures of economic status. In-kind transfers increase a family's command over goods or services, thus shifting out the family's resource constraint. One such study, by **Lampman** [10] is concerned with the transfer process from both public and private sources. His article shows that expanding the definition of transfers beyond the traditional government cash payments has the potential to drastically rerank the preredistribution poor. Lampman does not himself pursue this issue. His direct concern is with an issue in vertical equity: the share of the total transfers, private and public, going to the pretransfer poor. The implication for categorizing equals is, however, readily discernible.

Perhaps as important as the inclusion of noncash government transfers is their correct valuation. It is the recipients' valuation of in-kind transfers, rather than the cost to the taxpayers, that should be included in a measure of economic welfare. However, no clear-cut guidelines exist for determining the value of an expenditure to the recipient.

For in-kind transfers which the recipient could have refused, the expenditure provides a good or service that enters positively into the recipient's utility function. However, when a good is subsidized, the resulting price change will usually place the individual on an indifference curve that could be reached with a smaller cash grant. Measured in dollar terms, then, the value of the expenditure to the recipient is not as high as the cost of providing it. There are several exceptions to this, such as when the indifference curves are either linear (perfect substitution with other goods) or rectangular (goods consumed in fixed proportions). Also, if the subsidized good is granted only in fixed quantities and the quantity is the amount the recipient would have consumed were he or she to receive a cash transfer, the good can be valued at its full market price.

For the more common case, where the value to the recipient does not necessarily equal the cost of providing it, the paper by **Smolensky, Schmundt, Stiefel,** and **Plotnick** [26] develops a procedure for valuing in-kind transfers in "equivalent cash transfer units." This approach requires specification of a utility function and knowledge about each family's level of disposable cash income and the combination of available in-kind programs. From this information, a series of benefit weights for government programs are derived which, when multiplied by the dollar amount of in-kind benefits received, approximate the value of the transfer to the recipient.

In another article in this area, **Smeeding** [24] incorporates federal taxes paid and noncash transfers received into the traditional money income measure. Noncash transfers are estimated at their recipient-valued cash equivalents. Moreover, Smeeding adjusts the Current Population Survey data for the underreporting of cash transfer income by families. These adjustments expand the measure of "full" income by including much of the impact of government.

F.   Leisure and Nonmarket Productive Activities

The final major source of potential consumption to be explored is the value of nonmarket productive activities and leisure time. The output of home-produced goods and other nonpaid but productive activities enhance the level of well-being of a family. Moreover, if leisure is a normal good, then the value of leisure time should also enter the family's measured income. Such a concept of leisure places a value on time spent outside of work without regard to its specific utilization, on the presumption that the value of time is the same, at the margin, in all nonpaid uses. Leisure time—including the value of nonmarket production—is therefore generally treated as a single component of economic welfare. One of the most extensive studies of the value of time is by Sirageldin [23]. Time is treated both as a commodity for consumption and as an input into production. Sirageldin relies on the work of Becker [3] for establishing his theoretical model, and his study attempts to link utility theory with a measure of well-being. He also suggests that adjustments for family size and composition should be included to account for needs.

Taussig [27] also values leisure as part of a measure of economic welfare. He multiplies an estimate of leisure time by the marginal net-of-tax wage rates of individuals. Although leisure time is adjusted downward for those who are ill or unemployed, Taussig makes no attempt to adjust for involuntary retirement. An alternative approach, by Morgan [14] would not attempt to transfer leisure into dollar terms. Morgan proposes to measure "enjoyed leisure" and then multiply this figure by a welfare ratio measure of other forms of income (both money and nonmoney).

Garfinkel and Haveman also indirectly include consideration of leisure time in their earnings capacity study. By calculating a measure of full-time earnings for each individual, the implicit assumption is that those who choose to work less than full time value their leisure at least as much as they value forgone earnings. An individual classified as poor by a money income measure but whose earnings capacity places him much higher in the distribution has a strong preference for leisure. Consequently, when leisure is added to the resource constraint, that person is no longer considered poor.

G. The Static Measures of Economic Welfare Applied

Policy analysts concerned with identifying various target groups, particularly the poor, have been especially interested in the expanded measures of economic welfare. Including a family's important nonincome resources provides an alternative basis for evaluating the horizontal equity of alternative policies. An important issue, therefore, is whether or not these various expanded definitions alter the rankings of families and hence the distribution of the benefits and burdens of public programs among different age, occupational, or regional groupings. Additionally, some have thought that the degree of inequality per se is relevant to policymaking, and they have sought to determine the sensitivity of aggregate measures of inequality to alternative characterizations of the income base.

In fact, most of the studies cited rerank families by the particular measure derived. Weisbrod and Hansen, for example, contrast their income-net worth approach with a simple income measure and find that the distribution of families becomes less equal; furthermore, some groups, such as the aged, tend to gain, relative to others. Families with equal amounts of current income can be at quite different levels of economic status when an annuitized value of net worth is added. This measure can generally be used as a substitute for current income. However, it is sensitive to comparisons across age groups where the size of various components of the resource constraint may vary. For example, the income–net worth measure would do well in capturing resources for aged families but would be less comprehensive for the young. Like Weisbrod and Hansen, Moon finds that adding net worth to the measure increases the inequality of the distribution. However, other included components—public and private noncash transfers and tax liabilities—reduce the inequality of the distribution of aged families. On balance, the resulting distribution is a more equal one. Moreover, the effect on horizontal equity is also important, since not all families maintain their rank ordering when the measure of economic status is broadened. Obviously, this measure has more restricted application since it is calculated only for the elderly, and a comparison with current income measures for younger families would be inappropriate. However, this measure does a better job of capturing long-term expectations of well-being for the aged than does a money income measure.

Changes in the inequality of income are also of concern to Smolensky et al. in their study of in-kind transfers. Adding the simulated values for noncash transfers to either factor income or the more conventional measure of cash income reduces the inequality of the distribution. Actually two components of in-kind benefits are measured, those to taxpayers and those to recipients. The equalizing effects of recipient benefits more than offset the taxpayer benefits (which increase inequality). Although specific beneficiaries are not identified, a measure of income plus noncash transfers could also affect horizontal equity unless all families at the same income levels received equal benefits. The Smolensky et al. approach is certainly applicable across a broad range of policy issues. Whenever cash and in-kind programs are to be compared, this measure is preferable to current income. For example, such a measure would ensure horizontally equitable treatment of families in determining how to "cash out" in-kind programs in favor of an alternative transfer such as a negative income tax.

Rather than rerank all families, some of the studies concerned with economic status simply classify individuals or families into broad groups, such as the poor or near-poor. Garfinkel and Haveman recalculate the proportion of households in poverty for various demographic groups, using their earnings capacity measure. By an earnings capacity standard, more of those at the bottom of the distribution are black and live in large families that have one or more full-time workers than by a current income standard. In other terms, the earnings capacity measure shows fewer old and young persons, farmers, whites, and persons residing alone in the poverty category. These results conform to expectations, since the earnings capacity measure purges the poverty category of those who have few resources chiefly because of low participation in the labor force. This measure would be most applicable to a limited set of policy issues. By smoothing over short-term earnings fluctuations, it sorts out those who are either temporarily poor or poor by choice. Garfinkel and Haveman also capture a reasonable earnings level for an individual working at capacity. Consequently, these aspects of the measure should help to highlight those among the poor most in need of education or retraining programs, for example. On the other hand, this measure is less well suited to determining eligibility for cash transfer programs whose aim is to guarantee everyone a minimum yearly income. The policy relevance of Mirer's income variability measure would have the same limitation; it is most applicable to longer-term policy decisions.

Lampman is also concerned with redistribution to the pretransfer poor as a group. He estimates that from an initial share of 3 percent of all factor income, the pretransfer poor eventually receive 9 percent of postredistribution income. In addition, Lampman examines the demographic characteristics of recipients. Lacking data on all aspects of government transfers, he concentrates on cash transfer beneficiaries. Those pretransfer poor who benefit most from these transfers are not particularly representative of the poor before transfer. The most favored groups are the aged and the nonworking poor. Again, this research can have significant implications for horizontal equity when certain individuals within the poverty population receive greater noncash transfers than others.

III.   MAINTAINING HORIZONTAL EQUITY OVER SPACE, DEMOGRAPHIC CHARACTERISTICS, AND TIME

A.   Space and Demographic Characteristics

Some researchers argue that families operating within the same resource constraint are at lower levels of economic welfare if they have larger family size, live in urban rather than rural areas, or reside in certain regions of the country. One way to operationalize this judgment would be to change the rankings of families through an adjustment to their measured economic status. Moon, for example, standardizes her economic welfare measure into dollar amounts for an equivalent aged couple. This and similar welfare ratio approaches allow families of different size or other characteristics to be examined in a single distribution [7]. The more common approach to the problem has been to make the techniques for grouping people into such categories as the poor or near-poor more flexible. Thus, for example, families of different size are subjected to different criteria for determining their appropriate grouping. Such methods are comparable to adjusting the measure of economic welfare to achieve better horizontal equity. It is particularly appropriate to manipulate the classificatory criteria when the population is to be divided into a limited number of categories. Most of the concern has centered on establishing a poverty threshold, dividing families into two groups.

Initially, the official poverty threshold measure made no adjustments for family size or location. It was a relatively crude measure based only on the cost of a subsistence level food budget. From the observation that families of two or more generally spend one-third of their income on food, the poverty threshold was subsequently established as three times the food budget. Improvements in this measure sought to account for differences in "need" among families. Consequently the Orshansky poverty thresholds, the most commonly used measures, make adjustments to reflect cost differences in maintaining families of various sizes and farm–nonfarm locations [18]. Additional research in this area has sought both to expand the number of adjustments that can be made and to improve upon the equivalency calculations.

A paper by **Watts** [29] offers an alternative means for standardizing across both family size and region of residence. His measure is one of the few in this volume that is based on observable behavior. In the old tradition of the "wolf-point," Watts uses the share of income devoted to particular categories of consumption as the basis for defining equivalence among families. If the fractions of income spent on particular types of expenditures change as economic status changes, then families with equal proportional expenditures on such items (e.g., food and other necessities) are viewed as equally well-off. This approach is similar to the Orshansky measure, which assumes that food represents an expenditure equal to a constant fraction of income. However, Watts determines the income levels at which expenditures on food (and on a group of expenditures corresponding to necessities) constitute equal proportions across both family size and region of the country from Engel curve estimates. Consequently, Watts's method requires an actual subsistence budget calculation for only one "typical" family, after which calculations for families differing in such characteristics as size and residence can be made from observed behavior. Such an approach expands the number of equivalency adjustments that can readily be made.

B. Time

While the variability of transitory income is the principle issue associated with examining incomes over time, there are other related problems that may affect the measure of economic welfare. An approach that uses only current incomes for comparisons among families ignores changes in relative economic status which may occur when inflation and the policies employed to prevent it differentially affect various groups within the population. Unless the effects of rising prices are evenly distributed over all types of goods and services, the level of economic welfare of some groups within the population will change relative to others even if their nominal incomes show no relative differences. **Palmer** and **Barth** [19] find that this has indeed been the case for one group, the officially impoverished, when compared with the nonpoor during the recent past. While Palmer and Barth are directly concerned with an issue in vertical equity, i.e., the relative well-being of the poor during inflationary periods, their study also points to consequences relevant to horizontal equity. Because transfer programs that serve the elderly poor are indexed while other transfer programs generally are not, the impact of inflation on, for example, the elderly is less severe than on the nonelderly. As another example, unemployment induced by anti-inflationary measures affects female heads of households differently from male heads of households.

IV. SOME FINAL COMMENTS

Many behavioral changes that accompany the life cycle have either not explicitly been included in measures of economic well-being or have been entered with the wrong sign. The birth of a baby raises "need" and, *ceteris paribus*, lowers some welfare measures, leaves others unchanged, but never raises any measure of well-being. Similarly, the decision to invest time and money in one's own human capital, or in one's children, to choose home production over market production, to form a separate household, or to take more leisure time leaves some measures unaffected, lowers others, but raises none. Yet common sense and the "new home economics" both say that marriage, childbearing and child-rearing, schooling, and setting up an individual household are, more often than not, utility-raising, rationally made decisions. The challenge is to find ways to incorporate the benefits that attend these decisions, now frequently quantified, into measures of economic well-being in ways consistent with the treatment of the net worth of the aged. Determining permanent income, or the capacity to consume, requires looking forward as well as back in time.

The explosion of hedonic indexes using Lancaster's [11] model leads in a different direction. It provides a way to measure minimum needs by costing out specific nutritional and other requirements, rather than constructing budgets from consumption patterns over commodities. Combined with a programming model in physical units, it would provide a measure of the inefficiency of commodities now available in the marketplace for meeting minimum consumption standards. For those wicked enough to contemplate them, the implications could be profound.

The optimal portfolio theories point in yet another direction. The wolf-point or iso-prop literature turns to consumption patterns for indications of who are equal. Even the poor are, by now, holders of some wealth, and perhaps it is appropriate to examine the size and composition of portfolios, including collectively administered savings like Social Security, for indications of who are the nonpoor and who are the poor.

Finally, with collective consumption at 35 percent or more of Net National Product, it is time to consider the effect of all government expenditures, rather than only transfers and taxes, on the economic well-being of households. It is especially important to recognize that most public goods are local ones, i.e., their benefits vary with the location of the household. It is also necessary to consider that the benefits of expenditures, as with the burdens of taxes, are shiftable and do not necessarily lie where they fall.

The conceptual problems of determining economic well-being are formidable and the data problems monumental, while the policy implications may not be substantial. But as a nation we have a great yearning to know the truth about just how well-off our poor now are when compared to the poor of times past and to more affluent contemporaries.

CONCLUSION

The need for a more expansive measure of economic status for descriptive, analytic, and policy purposes is obvious if equals are to be identified. The papers included here are a beginning, but a more fundamental, comprehensive, and definitive reconsideration of this unsettled area is now in order.

The place to start, perhaps, is with the new theories of household behavior. Nearly all of the measures discussed here draw upon the microanalytics of households as consumers and as investors in human and tangible capital. This underlying body of theory has grown considerably of late, due primarily to the work of Friedman, Modigliani, Lancaster [11], and Becker [3]. Not only do we currently understand more fully how the budget constraint affects the quantity and quality of goods purchased, we also better understand how time is allocated and how family formation and child-rearing decisions are made. Tobin and his students have clarified how portfolio and savings decisions are made.[4] Our next step is to learn from these theoretical advances how better to deduce from survey data on current income, labor force participation, consumption, age, family size, asset levels and composition, and from relative price differentials at different locations just which families face equivalent resource constraints.

[4] See James Tobin [28, especially chapter 34].

REFERENCES

1. Ando, A., and Modigliani, F. 1963. The "life cycle" hypothesis of saving: aggregate implications and tests. *American Economic Review* 53: 55–84.
2. Baerwaldt, N., and Morgan, J. 1971. Trends in inter-family transfers. Working Paper, Survey Research Center, University of Michigan.
3. Becker, G. 1965. A theory of the allocation of time. *Economic Journal* 75: 493–517.
4. Bishop, G. A. 1961. The tax burden by income class, 1958. *National Tax Journal* 14.
5. ———. 1967. Tax burdens and benefits of government expenditures by income class, 1961 and 1965. Research Publication no. 9, Tax Foundation.
6. Colm, G., and Tarasov, H. 1940. *Who pays the taxes?* Temporary National Economic Committee. Washington, D.C.: Government Printing Office.
7. David, M. 1959. Welfare income and budget needs. *Review of Economics and Statistics* 61: 393–99.
8. Garfinkel, I., and Haveman, R. 1974. Earnings capacity and the target efficiency of alternative transfer programs. *American Economic Review* 64: 196–204.
9. Gillespie, W. I. 1965. Effect of public expenditures on the distribution of income. In *Essays in fiscal federalism*, ed. R. Musgrave, pp. 122–86. Washington, D.C.: The Brookings Institution.
10. Lampman, R. 1972. Public and private transfers as social process. In *Redistribution to the rich and the poor: the grants economics of income distribution*, ed. K. Boulding and M. Pfaff. Belmont, Calif.: Wadsworth.
11. Lancaster, K. 1966. A new approach to consumer theory. *Journal of Political Economy* 84:
12. Mirer, T. W. 1974. Aspects of the variability of family income. In *Five thousand American families—patterns of economic progress,* vol. 2, ed. J. Morgan. Ann Arbor: University of Michigan, Institute for Social Research.
13. Moon, M. L. Forthcoming. The economic welfare of the aged and income security programs. *Review of Income and Wealth.*
14. Morgan, J. 1968. The supply of effort: the measurement of well-being and the dynamics of improvement. *American Economic Review* 58: 31–39.
15. ———; David, M.; Cohen, W.; and Brazer, H. 1962. *Income and welfare in the United States.* New York: McGraw-Hill.
16. Musgrave, R., et al. 1951. Distribution of tax payments by income groups: a case study for 1948. *National Tax Journal* 4: 1–53.
17. Ornati, O. 1966. *Poverty amid affluence.* New York: Twentieth Century Fund.
18. Orshansky, M. 1968. The shape of poverty in 1966. *Social Security Bulletin* 31: 3–31.
19. Palmer, J. L., and Barth, M. C. 1976. "The distributional effects of inflation and higher unemployment." Mimeographed.
20. Pechman, J. A., and Okner, B. A. 1974. *Who bears the tax burden?* Washington, D.C.: The Brookings Institution.
21. Projector, D. S., and Weiss, G. 1969. Income–net worth measures of economic welfare. *Social Security Bulletin* 32: 14–17.
22. Reynolds, M., and Smolensky, E. 1974. The post-fisc distribution: 1961 and 1970 compared. *National Tax Journal* 27: 515–30.
23. Sirageldin, I. 1969. *Non-market components of national income.* Ann Arbor: University of Michigan, Survey Research Center.
24. Smeeding, T. 1976. "The economic well-being of low income households: implications for income inequality and poverty." Mimeographed.

25. Smolensky, E. 1965. The past and present poor. In *The concept of poverty*, pp. 35–67. Task Force on Economic Growth and Opportunity. Washington, D.C.: Chamber of Commerce.

26. ———; Schmundt, M.; Stiefel, L.; and Plotnick, R. 1974. Adding in-kind transfers to the personal income and outlay account: implications for the size distribution of income. Discussion Paper no. 199-74. Institute for Research on Poverty, University of Wisconsin—Madison.

27. Taussig, M. K. 1973. *Alternative measures of the distribution of economic welfare*. Princeton, N.J.: Princeton University, Industrial Relations Section.

28. Tobin, J. 1975. *Essays in economics*, vol. 2, part 5. Amsterdam: North-Holland Publishing Co.

29. Watts, H. 1967. The Iso-Prop Index: an approach to the determination of differential poverty-income thresholds. *Journal of Human Resources* 2: 3–18.

30. ———. 1971. An economic definition of poverty. In *On understanding poverty*, ed. D. P. Moynihan. New York: Basic Books.

31. Weisbrod, B. A., and Hansen, W. L. 1968. An income–net worth approach to measuring economic welfare. *American Economic Review* 58: 1315–29.

I

An Economic Definition
of Poverty

HAROLD W. WATTS

INTRODUCTION

This paper starts from the basic model of consumer choice. It stresses the distinction between preferences and constraints, and argues that the notion of poverty should be limited to the more objective constraint side of consumer theory. Poverty then can be defined as a "severe constriction of the choice set" and measured by the family's generalized command over real goods and services. A permanent income measure comes closest to capturing the largest level of potential consumption during a period of time. By contrast, current income has too short a time horizon and ignores some of the important resources available to families, such as wealth holdings and the potential returns on human capital. In conjunction with the proposed definition of economic status, adjustments in family size and composition and location of residence, which will make possible comparisons among families, are specified. The resulting welfare ratio can be used as an input into the evaluation of programs which seek to help the poor.

The discussions of the poverty seminar, whatever else they did or did not achieve, accomplished one thing most conspicuously. They highlighted two radically different approaches to the definition of "poverty": on the one hand, the "narrow economic" definition, and on the other, the "culture of poverty."

Reprinted by permission from Chapter 11 by Harold Watts, "An Economic Definition of Poverty" from *On Understanding Poverty*, edited by Daniel P. Moynihan, pp. 316–29, © 1968, 1969 the American Academy of Arts and Sciences, Basic Books, Inc., New York, Publishers. The introduction has been added.

The economic concept is defined in terms of the external circumstances that condition a person's behavior, especially the behavior he displays in economic transactions: buying consumption items, selling productive services, securing professional advice, etc. The cultural concept focuses on the internal attitudes and behavior patterns that a person brings to any particular set of circumstances. The one locates poverty in the person's condition; the other finds it in the person's character.

A program aimed at eliminating economic poverty will measure its success by the increase in command over goods and services that is induced by the program. A program aimed at eliminating the culture of poverty will measure its success by changes in the complex of attitudes and behavior patterns characteristic of that culture. Any program will, in general, influence both economic poverty and the culture of poverty, but not in equal proportions or with equal directness.

Because the external conditions, given a sufficiently long exposure, can affect the patterns of behavior we term "culture," and, in turn, "culture" can and does influence the nature of the external world a person faces, it is not usually possible to attribute exclusive effects on either "economic" poverty or "cultural" poverty to any particular policy or program. It can be argued, however, that much of the current and widespread dissatisfaction with antipoverty policies is due to a failure to make an explicit choice of a restrictive definition of poverty. In a situation in which each critic can choose from a wide range of poverties—and feels no need to restrict his choice to any single one—it is not a hard task to find all policies wide of some target.

A clear notion of what one is trying to do has always been of importance in the formulation of policies. The advantage of choosing the most efficient means of attaining a specific goal is also no new discovery. However, the recent adoption throughout the executive branch of the federal government of PPBS (Planning, Programming, Budgeting Systems) does indicate a change in the direction of more explicit and coordinated application of these principles. By requiring agencies to state their objectives and to establish priorities among their program proposals according to the degree that the programs serve those objectives, PPBS enforces a tighter correspondence between objectives and policy decisions.

In the language of the model of economic choice, we may take alternative programs (or increments to them) as the set of objects of choice. PPBS asks an agency such as OEO to consider all possible combinations of programs and to establish a preference ordering among them based on the agency's interpretation of its mission or goal. A determinative choice, of course, requires the addition of constraints— financial, political, or what have you—but these constraints are not finally decided at the agency level. When the choices are made by the Bureau of the Budget and ultimately the Congress, objectives of other agencies must be considered and balanced with the antipoverty objective.

Hence, it can be seen that the choice of a definition of that poverty that we want to eliminate *must* be made. And that the choice affects not only the setting of priorities among antipoverty programs, but also the higher level assessment of the relative importance of getting rid of poverty vis-à-vis other objectives of society.

If the problem of poverty is worthy of a distinct name (even of a special agency), then it certainly should be possible to distinguish poverty from the entire collection of social problems. The task of evaluating and ranking programs for their effect on poverty is not responsibly discharged by usurping the presidential-level problem of balancing the claims of all social objectives. We must distinguish between the Great Society and the Poverty-less Society. The more is subsumed under the definition of "poverty," the more the Poverty-less Society simply *becomes* the Great Society. Every step we take toward an equation of the two goals takes us further toward elimination of the need for, and in fact the possibility of, a separate consideration of poverty as a distinct problem.

It is possible to pay exclusive attention to one or another antipoverty objective. Moreover, once such a commitment is made, all extraneous consequences must be excluded in order to secure the maximum impact from a given antipoverty budget. A familiar theorem in economics rules out the possibility of maximizing more than one objective at the same time. If the activities that promote each objective use some of the same scarce resources, and if the objectives are truly different, then one must be prepared to accept a reduced level of success for one objective in exchange for the other; it is impossible to get more of both. Two possible resolutions are: (1) to ignore one of the objectives or (2) to reformulate the problem by defining a new objective that is an explicit combination of the two objectives, that is, to admit that the original definition of the poverty problem was incorrect.

The concept of poverty developed below is restrictive, both in the sense that any specific concept must be restrictive and in the sense that it excludes from consideration sociological, political, psychological, and physical ills that are weakly or strongly associated with poverty. This does not indicate a presumption that these goals are unimportant. What it does indicate is the presumption that poverty is a specific ill in itself; that poor people, while they share many other problems with the nonpoor, are unique in having a relative shortage of goods and services at their disposal; and that, finally, poverty in the more restricted sense can be eliminated, is worth eliminating, both for its inherent injustice and for its fallout effects on related problems, and will be eliminated more promptly by policies that are aimed at a compact, rather than a diffuse, target.

I. THE NEOCLASSICAL MODEL OF ECONOMIC CHOICE

The concept developed takes from the basic model of economic choice the idea of separating preferences from constraints. Associating poverty with extremely limiting constraints, the definition incorporates a broader view of the economic constraint derived from Milton Friedman's theory of permanent income [2]. Consideration also is given to the problem of weighting and aggregating varying degrees of poverty and to the notion of a social welfare function.

A very simple analytic tool, the neoclassical model of economic choice, can provide a framework for analyzing the behavior of decision-making economic units. Its flexibility permits application to consuming units or producing units of varying levels of complexity. The consuming units with which we are immediately concerned are the individual and the family.

Stated most simply, the model postulates that there is a set of objects of choice that the decision-maker ranks according to his particular, and perhaps peculiar, preferences. Confronted with one or more considerations that limit his choice to a subset of these objects, the decision-maker will, according to the model, choose the highest-ranking alternative available in that subset. For example, a family may prefer a suburban bungalow to a high-rise apartment, which in turn is favored over a walk-up flat, and all three are regarded as better than remaining in (or returning to) a rural tar-paper shack. If it is limited by income or discrimination to either the flat or the shack, however, it will choose the former. This is, loosely speaking, the extent of the rationality assumption that is so often used as a club with which to beat economists. It is possible, of course, to make more restrictive assumptions and to get more substantial derivative propositions from the theory. But these are not necessary in general, nor are they needed for the development of the concept that follows.

In more specific terms, consider the set of choice objects to be possible rates of consumption of two categories of consumer goods and services: necessities and luxuries. (We may indulge in the abstraction that there are only two goods, measured in some convenient scale, and each good is perfectly divisible, so that amounts can be varied in a continuous manner.) The decision-making unit, which we may take to be an individual or a family, has a system of preferences among these objects that may be represented by an "indifference map" imposed on a two-dimensional space as in Figure 1. Each point in the positive quadrant corresponds to a unique combination of luxury and necessity consumption. The point A in Figure 1 corresponds to consumption of X units of necessities and Y units of luxuries per month. Each curved line consists of points that are considered equally good by the family. (There is such a line through every point—only a few representative ones are drawn.) Points to the northeast of any one curve are all preferred over points on or to the southwest of the same curve. In this manner, a system of indifference curves can describe completely a particular ranking; any pair of consumption levels or two-dimensional points on the diagram can be evaluated as better, worse, or equally good, compared to any other pair.

This system of preferences is regarded as a characteristic of a particular individual and may be quite different for some other individual. The preference ordering represents the tastes, values, and knowledge possessed by the individual; they will reflect his culture. As such, the preferences are not immutable, but, like culture, they are treated as stable enough to make worthwhile the abstraction that they remain constant for analytic purposes.

Given these preferences, now consider which combinations are available to the decision-maker. Assume that he has a fixed income flow to

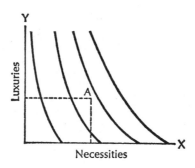

Figure 1

be spent and can purchase any amount of each good at prices that do not depend on the size of his purchase. We may now draw a straight line, PP′, that divides the space into a portion that he can afford and one that he cannot, as shown in Figure 2. The point P on the vertical axis is simply the number of luxury units that could be bought if the entire income were spent on luxuries; P′ is similarly derived from income and the price per unit of necessities. The model is now complete and indicates that a family with preferences as shown, faced with a budget limit and prices as drawn, would choose to consume necessities at rate A and luxuries at rate B.

The external and relatively objective factors that determine the available alternatives are usually regarded as subject to variation. For example, an increase in income would shift the constraint outward in a parallel manner and, as drawn, would lead to increased purchases of both commodities. A change in relative prices will rotate the constraint and thus alter the level of purchases. Usually an increase in price of one good, other things remaining constant, will result in a reduction of consumption of that good and an increase in the consumption of the other.

II. POVERTY AND AFFLUENCE AS DEGREES OF CONSTRAINT ON CHOICE

The above excursion into basic economic theory was made to lay a foundation for the concept of poverty. The distinction made between preferences and constraints provides a useful basis for limiting the

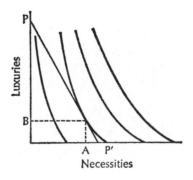

Figure 2

notion of poverty to the relatively objective constraint side of the problem. Poverty is, in this view, a property of the individual's situation, rather than a characteristic of the individual or of his pattern of behavior. Of course, overt behavior or ex post facto choices will reflect both preferences and constraints (both values or culture and situation), but poverty is associated solely with severe constriction of the choice set. Similarly, affluence corresponds to a much larger area of attainable alternatives. Indeed, poverty and affluence are, in this view, the names we give to the two ends of a scale measuring level of generalized command over real goods and services. Current income is an important part of this command over goods and services, but it is not, as will be argued below, the sole determinant.

There are two features of a definition based on the choice constraint that recommends it. First, it avoids imposing a norm on the tastes and values held by individual decision-makers. Instead of arguing that anyone who consumes less than X units of food or Y units of housing is poor, it would argue that anyone who has sufficient command over goods and services to achieve X and Y simultaneously must be at least as well off if he actually chooses some other combination.

It is, of course, a value judgment on the part of economists that the diversity of tastes and values reflected in different allocations of consumption at the same level of general command ought to be respected. Accordingly, that a particular family allocates a given budget in a way contrary to a typically middle-class outsider's notion of how he would do it or at variance with some statistical average of families at a comparable budget level should not be taken as evidence that the family is worse off or poorer.

The second salutary feature of this definition pertains to the elimination of troublesome questions about the level of satisfaction or happiness achieved by particular families from a given budget. The theory of choice requires only a ranking of alternatives; it does not require any measure of the magnitude or intensity of the distinctions made in rank, nor does it require any absolute measure of the pleasure derived from a particular allocation. Neither economics nor, as far as I know, social science in general can contrive a measure of satisfaction that would make one comfortable about asserting that Mr. A, with very aristocratic tastes and only two Picassos, does not feel more deprivation from want of a third than does Mr. B, who has not been able to buy shoes for the last three years. Lacking such a measure and possessing egalitarian tendencies, one is attracted to a definition of poverty that focuses on the means for pursuit of happiness rather than on happiness itself.

III.   GENERALIZED COMMAND OVER GOODS AND SERVICES

The prevailing practice of measuring the extent of poverty according to levels of money income can be construed as a choice of a constraint-oriented poverty concept, as recommended above, combined with a choice of current annual money income as the measure of command over goods and services. Probably everyone remotely connected with developing and working with these statistics has acknowledged the crudity of this measure. But if the argument in favor of a constraint-oriented measure is accepted, then it follows that improvement lies in adopting a more comprehensive measure of the constraint on household choice. The income measure is crude because of its incomplete coverage of sources of command over goods and services and its short time horizon—*not* because it is narrowly economic, lacking in humanity, or oblivious to subjective subtleties. The following paragraphs indicate how the measure can and should be broadened both on conceptual and empirical levels of analysis.

The economic literature contains a concept of income that comes very close to meeting the present need for a comprehensive measure of command over goods and services. Milton Friedman's permanent income concept has proved useful both in clarifying theoretical analysis of household behavior and in improving our ability to predict behavior. The value of the largest sustainable level of consumption is one, slightly circular, way of describing Friedman's more comprehensive concept. More precisely, it is the sum of income flows from property, from sale of labor services, and from transfers (unilateral "gifts"), from other persons, or from governmental units, whether received in money or in "real" form. These flows are evaluated at the normal rate they can be expected to maintain over the long run instead of at the current level. The reason for this is that current income may be higher or lower than normal because of temporary good fortune or misfortune. Friedman terms these deviations "transitory income," which, together with "permanent income," divides current income receipts into two additive components.

Expansion of the time horizon for purposes of measuring income broadens the concept substantially. As developed by Friedman, there are two bases for income via the market: human wealth and nonhuman wealth. The latter is relatively familiar owing to its similarity to *wealth* in common usage: real and financial property. Money income from this source is usually counted in current measures, although year-to-year variation in profits or dividends may exaggerate the dispersion of the income distribution. However, it is not common to consider the wealth itself, as distinct from the income it generates, as part of a household's command over goods and services. But, considering that households do accumulate wealth with the intent of decumulating it during retirement (or passing it on to succeeding generations), it would seem appropriate to convert net wealth (assets minus liabilities) into equivalent life annuities for purposes of measuring the capacity to sustain a level of consumption. This modification would primarily affect the aged or near-aged family units.

An important example arises from the directly consumed services of owner-occupied housing. The value of such services is, conceptually speaking, a form of income and is no less worthy of inclusion because the income does not accrue in money. The income will be appropriately accounted for if owner-occupied housing is included among the assets used in the net-wealth calculation discussed above. It is specifically singled out here because of the ubiquitousness of home ownership and because it is easily overlooked.

The notion of human wealth is a major improvement over current earnings as a measure of command over goods and services. The effective capacity to earn money income by selling labor services in the market or to produce directly consumed services in the home is the second component of permanent income. As compared with current earnings, it both takes into account a longer period of time and incorporates real income as well as money income. The longer period tends to substitute average rates of unemployment for intermittent full and zero levels of employment. It also offsets the quite low levels of current income usually enjoyed by those who are adding to their stock of capital by education or training.

In terms of this broader concept, an unemployed dishwasher would be counted as poorer than an unemployed plumber, even though both had the same zero level of current earnings. A black assembly-line worker who currently earns the same wage as the white worker at his side would be credited with a smaller long-run command over goods and services by being subject to a higher risk of future unemployment.

Another feature of the generalized measure of human wealth is its ability to include the home-produced and home-consumed services of the homemaker and other adult family members. The conventions of income taxation and national-income accounts do not give explicit recognition to this source of income. The anomaly has been pointed out with respect to the national-income accounts, but in the absence of any threat of drastic changes in human nesting patterns, it has not been regarded as an important weakness. When making interfamily comparisons, however, particularly at income levels in which nesting patterns frequently diverge from the ideal nuclear family, it is quite indefensible to ignore the direct contributions of adult family members to the services, or even goods, available to the family.

Finally, there are transfer payments among persons. These may be entirely voluntary, as within a family; or be covered by contract, as in the case of alimony; or arise out of public programs, such as social security. Persons are able to obtain command over goods and services in such ways without a current quid pro quo. Insofar as these claims are secure, either through law or through convention, there is no reason to treat them as different from income that accrues to human or nonhuman wealth.

There are, of course, substantial problems involved in measuring "permanent income." But if it is possible to obtain some general agreement on the suitability of the concept for analysis of poverty, there are many possibilities for improving on the measures now in use. Furthermore, if, as I believe, the generalized concept is relatively free of the many weaknesses criticized in the current money-income concept, then its adoption may make it possible for a wider range of analysts to work within a common conceptual framework.

IV. THE INDEX OF POVERTY

The preceding discussion has argued that a measure of poverty should be related to the individual's or family's "permanent" level of command over goods and services. There remains the problem of specifying standards of comparison that will permit evaluation of commensurate degrees of poverty for families of different size or composition, in different places, and at different times. The "poverty lines" now in use are intended to provide such standards in terms of annual money income. The Orshansky [3] thresholds vary according to family size, they have been adjusted for changes in the consumer price index for intertemporal comparisons, and they allow for differences between farm and nonfarm residence.

In the simplest terms, the poverty lines represent the level of income that divides the families of a particular size, place, and time into the poor and the nonpoor. Hence the set of poverty lines are intended to designate equivalent levels of deprivation. Similar thresholds could be obtained for the more comprehensive constraint measures presented above that could be used to divide the population into poor and nonpoor.

However, it has been argued above that poverty is not really a discrete condition. One does not immediately acquire or shed the afflictions we associate with the notion of poverty by crossing any particular income line. The constriction of choice becomes progressively more damaging in a continuous manner. As a first step, it would seem appropriate to maintain the graduation provided by a continuum, but to seek a scale along which differently situated families can be compared. For this purpose, a ratio of the measure of permanent income to the poverty threshold might be taken as a first approximation. Symbolically, let $\hat{Y}(N, L, t)$ denote the poverty threshold for a family of size N, in place L, at time t. Define a family's "welfare ratio" w as the ratio of its permanent income, Y, to the appropriate poverty threshold, that is,

$$w = Y/\hat{Y}(N, L, t).$$

This scale extends the notion of equivalence *at* the poverty thresholds to equivalence at any proportional distance *from* the poverty thresholds, for example, 15 percent below.

This welfare ratio will, of course, permit the same bifurcation into poor and nonpoor, the latter having ratios greater than one and the former less than one. But it also preserves the notion that those who are 5 percent above the threshold are not much better off than those who are 5 percent below. The welfare ratio also leads into consideration of more sophisticated ways of aggregating the detailed data into one-dimensional measures of the nation's poverty problem.

The "nose count" in poverty is one such measure that has little but its simplicity to recommend it. The "dollar gap," or the total amount by which the incomes of the poor fall short of the poverty lines, is a somewhat better measure because it counts a family that is at half the poverty line as five times as severe a problem as one that is at 90 percent of the same line. A further improvement would recognize that poverty becomes more severe at an increasing rate as successive decrements of income are considered; in other words, that poverty is reduced more by adding $500 to a family's command over goods and services if the family is at 50 percent of the poverty line than if it is at 75 percent.

A simple and mathematically tractable measure that has this property would be the logarithm of the welfare index. It is not, by any means, the only such scale, but it offers a definite improvement over the current practice. The logarithmic function,[1] as shown in Figure 3, takes on negative values for fractional welfare ratios (incomes below poverty) and positive values for ratios greater than one. For purposes of more aggregative measures of poverty, it would be appropriate to sum the

[1] Cf. [1, p. 68].

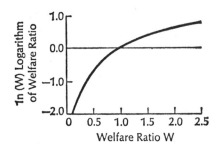

Figure 3

logarithms of welfare ratios, weighted by family size, over some part or all of the lower half of the distribution of families, that is,

$$P = \sum_{i \in L} N_i \log(W_i)$$

where L is the set of subscripts belonging to families with $W \leq W^* \leq$ median W, N_i is the ith family size, and W_i is the ith family's welfare ratio; $\log(X)$ denotes the logarithm of any (positive) number X. W^* is an essentially arbitrary threshold value comparable to the "poverty line."

If $W^* = 1$, then P cannot take on positive values. It would have a limiting value of zero if no one were below the poverty line. The more severe is poverty, according to this scale, the more negative is the value of P. For $W^* > 1$, P could take on positive values and could do so even though some families remained below the poverty line. However, in both cases, an objective of maximizing P would provide a tenable guide to policy formation.

It would be possible to use some old and honorable terminology to add further perspective to the measure proposed here. Without doing excessive violence to the ideas of the utilitarians, one could specify an overall utility function for society as the sum of *all* welfare ratios:

$$U = \sum_{\text{all } i} N_i \log(W_i).$$

This magnitude could be broken into two parts:

$$P = \sum_{i \in L} N_i \log(W_i)$$

where L is the set of subscripts for families with $W \leq 1$, and $\bar{L}$ is all the remaining subscripts,

$$A = \sum_{i \in \bar{L}} N_i \log(W_i)$$

$$U = P + A$$

Here P will be a negative number (unless there are no poor) and could be interpreted as the disutility suffered by society because of poverty. The sign of A will be positive and could be termed the affluence level of society, part of which is "wasted" as an offset to P in the calculation of total utility.

It should be explicitly noted that the interpretation discussed above incorporates a fairly radical form of egalitarian value bias. It assumes that, except for the adjustments introduced in defining W (family size, location, etc.), all persons have equal needs; and that, other things being equal, including total output of goods and services, society would attain its highest satisfaction from an absolutely equal distribution of incomes. No positive value is attached to dispersion of the income distribution even for the sheer delight of variety. Practically speaking, there is a relation between total output and income dispersion that would almost certainly prevent complete equality from being an optimal or even an attainable solution.

Regarding P as simply an objective function, it is useful to consider how it would tend to allocate effort among the various levels of income. The derivative of P with respect to the welfare ratio of a particular family is an indicator of the relative importance of increasing that family's welfare ratio. That derivative for the logarithmic function is:

$$\frac{dP}{dW} = \frac{N_i}{W_i}$$

for all families with $W_i < W^*$ ($= 0$ otherwise). Hence, for a family of four, at half of the poverty line, the derivative is $8 = 4 \div 0.5$. Compared to a family of four only 20 percent below the poverty line which would have a derivative of $5 = 4 \div 0.8$, it is seen to be 60 percent more important to raise the welfare ratio of the former. It would be preferable to promote an increase in welfare for the poorer family unless it were 60 percent more expensive to do so.

CONCLUDING REMARKS

It appears to many that calculations of the sort carried out above are symptomatic of an extreme insensitivity to human values. How can one justify the contention that if it costs too much—when "too much" is given a definite numerical value—it would be better to forsake the poorer family and help the less poor one? The simplest, and least invidious, answer is a pragmatic one. If the 8:5 ratio does not seem right, we can specify a function that will make it, say, 100:1. But at some point, with limited budgets for fighting poverty, choices of this sort have to be made. They cannot be made more sensibly by *refusing* to look at the distributional implications than by looking at them. An economist draws very little satisfaction from engaging in interpersonal comparisons that, according to his training, cannot be grounded in objective fact, but must be plainly labeled as value judgments. He cannot profess any expertise in making such judgments, but he can, and must, insist that such judgments be made explicit, both to promote democratic debate and to permit consistent analysis and choice of policy alternatives.

A poverty function of the sort displayed above should be carefully distinguished from an overall social welfare function. The former is at best appropriate for guiding the choices of an agency charged with eliminating poverty. For choices that have to be made at the presidential level, a much larger set of national objectives, inevitably conflicting at the margin, have to be balanced against one another. The poverty level should be one of these, but so should the affluence level, national security, mental health, and at least several others.

Finally, it should not be assumed that because the poverty index depends solely upon the level of command over goods and services, the optimal means of reducing poverty must be to increase that level as directly and as immediately as possible, for example, to hand out money or public jobs. There is nothing in the definition that prevents Head Start or even prenatal nutrition from being the most efficient means of reducing poverty in the sense of amount of poverty reduced *per dollar spent*. Some kinds of direct transfers would almost surely be among the least efficient.

REFERENCES

1. Dalton, H. 1954. *Principles of public finance,* 4th ed. London: Routledge & Kegan Paul.
2. Friedman, M. 1957. *A theory of the consumption function.* National Bureau of Economic Research. Princeton, N.J.: Princeton Univ. Press.
3. Orshansky, M. 1965. Counting the poor: another look at the poverty profile. *Social Security Bulletin,* January, pp. 3–29.

II

An Income–Net Worth Approach to Measuring Economic Welfare*

BURTON A. WEISBROD AND W. LEE HANSEN

INTRODUCTION

Economists and public policymakers alike have long been concerned with the relative and absolute economic welfare of various segments of the population. This interest reflects an underlying concern both about the equity of the existing distribution and about our ability to explain and forecast more effectively the behavior of producers and consumers.[1] But given the many possible dimensions of a comprehensive measure of economic welfare, the single-dimensional, money-income measure so commonly used leaves much to be desired.

The concern of this paper is with the development of an approach for measuring current economic welfare which is operationally feasible and broader in scope than the traditional money-income measure. The measure proposed is based on a combination of current income and current net worth (assets minus liabilities). These are made commensurable by converting net worth into an annuity value, which is added to current income. While this proposed measure stops well short of an "ideal" measure, we show that even this change leads to policy prescriptions rather different from those generated by the current income measure of economic welfare.

Reprinted by permission of the American Economic Association and the authors from *American Economic Review* 8 (December 1968): 1315–29.

* The authors wish to acknowledge the excellent research assistance of Martha Strayhorn, and the helpful comments on an earlier draft made by Robert J. Lampman and Hirschel Kasper. This research was supported by funds granted to the Institute for Research on Poverty, pursuant to the provisions of the Economic Opportunity Act of 1964.

[1] There is a considerable literature on the measurement and extent of inequality in the size distribution of income. For a review of some of this work as well as for useful bibliographic references, see Irving B. Kravis [5]; and T. Paul Schultz [12].

I. OUR PROPOSED MEASURE OF ECONOMIC WELFARE

The proposed measure rests on the assumption that current income and current net worth are both important determinants—although not the sole determinants—of the "economic position" of a consumer unit. A unit's economic well-being or economic position should be thought of as a function of the flow of services over which it has command. This flow depends importantly on the consumer unit's current income and also on the services it receives from its assets, net of liabilities.[2]

It is well known that the distribution of income and the distribution of net worth differ significantly.[3] Were it not for these differences—if the relative position of the various consumer units were more nearly identical in the two distributions—then it would be less important to attempt to integrate the two distributions. Such an integration would still be useful, however, if we wished to apply an absolute standard for determining the level of economic position, e.g., "affluence" or "poverty."

Although data on income and net worth are frequently available, the two types of information have not been combined, presumably because income is a flow while net worth is a stock. The procedure we set forth involves converting net worth into an income flow by recognizing that it is translatable mathematically into an annuity.[4]

For any given consumer unit—individual, family or household—we propose measuring its "economic position," Y^*, in time period t, as the sum of (1) its current annual income (the precise measure of income, which is net of yield on net worth, will be specified later), Y_t, and (2) the annual lifetime annuity value of its current net worth, expressed as $NW_t \cdot A_n$, where A_n is the value of an n year annuity whose present value is \$1.[5]

(1) $$Y_t^* \equiv Y_t + NW_t \cdot A_n.$$

---

[2] Of course, expected future income or "permanent" income is also relevant, particularly insofar as it may influence current access to capital markets. Although in our empirical work below we disregard expected future income, this variable certainly deserves further attention.

[3] See Dorothy S. Projector and Gertrude S. Weiss [11]; and Harold F. Lydall and J. B. Lansing [7].

[4] The authors used this approach in examining the relevance of assets to the definition of "poverty," in an unpublished memo (August 1964) while staff members for the Council of Economic Advisers. The approach has also been used by Janet Murray [9]. Also see Projector and Weiss [11] for a somewhat similar approach.

[5] $$\left(A_n = \frac{r}{1 - (1 + r)^{-n}} \right).$$

Y_t^* is, thus, the income obtainable in period t if the unit's net worth were converted so as to yield a lifetime flow.

The annuity value, $NW_t \cdot A_n$, is a function of the amount of net worth, NW_t, the life expectancy of the consumer unit, as denoted by n, and the rate of interest, r. Thus, for any given interest rate, the greater the net worth of the unit, and the shorter its life expectancy, the greater will be the annual annuity, and therefore the greater will be the difference between Y_t^* and Y_t. This suggests that the distribution of economic position by age will differ significantly depending on whether the combined income–net worth measure or the current income measure is used. In particular, since older people have higher ratios of net worth to current money income, as well as shorter life expectancies, their economic position will be most affected by the consideration of net worth.

In proposing our measure we are not implying that people generally *do* purchase annuities with any or all of their net worth nor that they necessarily *should* do so nor that then *can* do so. The problem of making income and net worth commensurable is conceptually independent of the practical possibilities for converting net worth into an annuity. For the fact is that, if our method of combining income and net worth is regarded as unsatisfactory—on the grounds that actual conversion is either difficult or undesirable—some other method is needed for combining them. It is hardly satisfactory to disregard net worth, and any measure of economic position which considers both necessarily implies some tradeoff between them.[6]

Before we turn to several applications of the income–net worth measure, it is useful to consider alternative periods over which net worth might be annuitized. At one extreme, net worth could be annuitized over an infinite period. Economic position would then be measured solely by current money income, since the annuity would consist entirely of interest, and that would be included in current money

[6] With regard to the practical aspects of conversion, there are some interesting issues which, however, are outside the bounds of this paper. For example, consider the net worth of older people, in the form of housing. They frequently prefer to continue occupying homes rather than relocating in smaller quarters more appropriate to their reduced family size; and although they may not be opposed to the idea of converting their homes into annuities by selling them and leasing them back, the market for such transactions seems quite undeveloped. We can only speculate as to why this sort of arrangement is so unusual. This market may have been simply overlooked by financial institutions. Alternatively, there may be no real demand for conversion of home equity into an annuity. In addition, it does seem that commercial annuities have paid very conservative rates of interest, and thus have been rather unattractive. Clearly, additional research into the operation of annuity markets is in order.

income. Thus, in effect,

$$(2) \qquad\qquad Y_t^* \equiv Y_t.$$

At the other extreme, economic position might be measured under the assumption that net worth is to be annuitized entirely during the current period;[7] this implies a measure of economic position:

$$(3) \qquad\qquad Y_t^* \equiv Y_t + NW_t,$$

where Y_t should be interpreted as net of the yield from net worth, since this yield would be lost if net worth were depleted in the current period. The alternative which we have used involves the assumption that net worth is to be annuitized over the expected lifetime of the consumer unit.[8] This decision, while arbitrary, is consistent with the spirit of much recent empirical research that suggests that saving (net worth accumulation) is in large part motivated by a desire to smooth out patterns of normal lifetime consumption and to build up reserves to take care of unanticipated needs arising from, for example, medical expenditures [4] [6].

A decision to annuitize all of a unit's net worth over its lifetime, or indeed over any shorter period, implies that no net worth will remain at the time of death of the unit. But if a portion of net worth should be regarded as being held in trust as an estate for the survivors or for others, then only the remaining portion of net worth should properly be annuitized.[9] In any case, a decision regarding the treatment of estates should be recognized as involving both a factual question of the extent to which people *do* save for estate purposes,[10] and a social value

---

[7] This case is discussed by Martin David [3].

[8] There are still other alternatives. One is to assume that net worth is annuitized over some arbitrarily specified time period, such as the maximum time period consistent with raising Y_t^* by some specified level. For an example of this approach, see Projector and Weiss [11].

[9] If an estate of size E is desired at the time of "expected" death n years hence, then with an interest rate r, the amount of net worth available for conversion to an annuity at time t will be

$$NW_t - \frac{E}{(1 + r)^n}.$$

If, alternatively, it is desired to guarantee an estate no smaller than size E regardless of when death occurs, then the amount of net worth available for conversion to an annuity will be smaller, namely, $NW_t - E$.

[10] The fact that intergenerational transfers are so frequently made via the estate route rather than by transfers before death may be less an indication of people's desires to pass on their wealth than it is a reflection of their inability to anticipate the time of their death.

judgement regarding the desirability of intergenerational wealth transfers (at death and at other times)—that is, whether people *ought* to save for estate purposes, and how much they ought to save [4]. These issues clearly deserve more attention.

In the empirical work that follows we shall arbitrarily base our calculations on the assumption of lifetime annuitization of net worth with no estate exclusion. The approach presented is general enough, however, to embrace alternative assumptions regarding the period of annuitization and size of estate, and, indeed, whether all components of net worth should be included. When the phrase "income–net worth" is used in the remainder of this paper, it refers to Y_t^* in expression 1 above, with net worth being annuitized over the consumer unit's expected lifetime.

II. APPLICATIONS AND IMPLICATIONS

Uses for the income–net worth measure of economic position are numerous, ranging from reassessment of the extent of economic inequality to use in predicting consumer behavior. In this section we focus, first, on the extent of economic inequality as indicated by the combined income–net worth measure of economic position for families, then touch upon the implications of the findings for government antipoverty policy and for the definition of tax progressivity and regressivity, and, finally, venture a comment on the usefulness of the measure for the prediction of consumer expenditure behavior.

The basic sources of data for our income–net worth estimates of economic position are the *Survey of Financial Characteristics of Consumers* (SFCC) and the *Current Population Survey* (CPS) for 1962. The SFCC provides data on families by age of head, income, and net worth;[11] the CPS provides data on family income by age of head, broken down into finer income classes. In view of the greater detail on income provided by the CPS data, and its larger sample size at the lower income levels, we chose to combine the SFCC data on net worth with the CPS data on income.

Briefly, the nature of the calculations employed to create the income–

[11] Net worth refers to all assets less all debts covered in the SFCC; the only important assets excluded were life insurance investments and equities in annuities and in retirement plans. Assets or wealth include the following: own home, automobile, business or profession (farm and nonfarm), liquid assets, investment assets, and miscellaneous assets. Debts include debt secured by own home, debt secured by investment assets, personal debt, and debt on life insurance policies. See Projector and Weiss [11].

net worth measure of economic position are as follows. From the SFCC the median value of total net worth for families by income size class was determined.[12] It was then assumed that the net worth for this income class in the SFCC data was equivalent to the net worth for the same income class from the CPS data. However, since the income data already include a return from income-yielding assets, this return had to be deducted from income before the annuity value of net worth was added; otherwise there would have been double counting of net worth.

We then determined the size of the lifetime annuity that total net worth could produce. In calculating the value of the annuity we used a 4 percent and a 10 percent interest rate, alternatively, to give a notion of the sensitivity of the results. In estimating joint life expectancy values— the other component of the annuity calculation—we assumed that family heads (males) were five years older than their wives, and that the full annuity would be received while both husband and wife were alive but that the surviving spouse would receive two-thirds of the annuity during the remainder of his or her life.[13]

It is clear that a number of simplifying assumptions have been made in our empirical work. Consequently, our estimates should be regarded as somewhat rough, their principal objective being to illustrate our approach.[14]

A. Extent of Economic Inequality

One important application of the income–net worth concept is to the measurement of economic position or of the extent of economic inequality. In this subsection we compare results obtained through use of the income–net worth measure with those obtained through use of the more conventional current money income measure.

If economic position is measured by current money income, then the distribution of economic position of United States families in 1962 is as indicated in Table 1, column 1. It shows, for example, that 20 percent of

[12] Median rather than mean net worth was used, in view of the highly skewed distribution of net worth holdings within income size classes. The net worth data in the SFCC—unlike the CPS income data—did not distinguish between families and unrelated individuals as we would have preferred, except for the under $3,000 income class.

[13] Here we follow the approach used by Murray [9].

[14] After this study was completed, the basic SFCC data tapes became available. We plan to use these data for additional applications of the income–net worth measure. Use of the basic data will eliminate the need for many of the assumptions made above and thus will provide a check of the adequacy of these estimates.

TABLE 1
Percentage Distribution of Families by Two Measures of Economic
Position, by Income, 1962

	Percentage distribution of families		
	(1) Current money income	Income–net worth	
Income size class		(2) 4 percent	(3) 10 percent
Under $3,000	20	18	17
3,000– 4,999	19	17	16
5,000– 7,499	27	25	24
7,500– 9,999	17	17	16
10,000–14,999	13	15	17
15,000–24,999	4	6	7
25,000 and over	1	2	3
Total	100	100	100
Median	$5,960	$6,480	$6,750

Source: Column 1—see [14, Table 3, p. 26]. Columns 2, 3—
based upon data from [14, Table 3, p. 26] and [11].

all families—9.3 million—were below $3,000, and 18 percent—8.3 million—were above $10,000.

If, however, economic position is measured by the more comprehensive income–net worth measure, the entire distribution is shifted upward and its shape is altered, as is shown in Table 1, columns 2 and 3. By this measure, the fraction of all families whose economic position is below $3,000 per year *falls* to 18 percent at a 4 percent rate of interest—a drop of nearly 1 million families—and to 17 percent at a 10 percent rate of interest—a drop of 1.4 million families. The fraction above $10,000 *rises* to 23 and 27 percent, respectively—increases of 2.2 to 4.2 million families. The median economic position, $5,960 per year by the current income measure, also rises—to $6,480 at a 4 percent rate and $6,750 at 10 percent.

The shift in the entire distribution is portrayed by the Lorenz curves in Figure 1.[15] They indicate that the degree of inequality is greater by the income–net worth measure than by the income measure alone. The greater inequality reflects the fact not only that net worth holdings are, on average, positive in all income classes specified, but also that, except

[15] The Gini coefficients are as follows: for the income measure, .37; for the income–net worth measure at a 4 percent interest rate, .42; and at a 10 percent interest rate, .47.

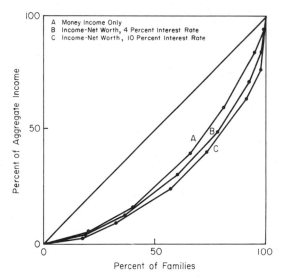

Figure 1. Lorenz curves: percentage share of income and income–net worth received by families, 1962. (Note: None of the Lorenz curves cross.)

for the lowest income class, the ratio of net worth to income rises with income, as shown in Table 2.[16]

The effect of considering net worth in addition to income varies considerably with the age of the group, as noted earlier. This is illustrated in Table 3, which shows that the ratio of net worth to income rises dramatically with age, while life expectancy obviously decreases with age. Lorenz curves in Figure 2 for the four major age groups reveal clearly how the distributions of money income and of income–net worth diverge with age.[17]

---

[16] The lowest-income class violates this generalization largely because it contains a higher proportion of aged—roughly one third—than does the next-higher income class—for which the fraction is about one-fifth (calculated from Current Population Report [14]). This fact is significant because the aged (65 years and older) have a higher average ratio of net worth to income than do younger families; see Table 4, *infra*.

[17] The Gini coefficients for the income measure and the income–net worth measure based on a 10 percent interest rate, are as follows:

Age of family head	Income	Income–net worth
Under age 35	.31	.34
35–54	.34	.43
55–64	.39	.50
65 and over	.45	.61

TABLE 2
Median Income and Median Net Worth of Families, by Income, 1962

Income size class	(1) Median income	(2) Median net worth	(3) Ratio (2)/(1)
Under $3,000	$ 1,780	$ 2,250	1.3
3,000– 4,999	4,040	2,330	.6
5,000– 7,499	6,170	5,560	.9
7,500– 9,999	8,650	11,290	1.3
10,000–14,999	12,500[a]	18,320	1.5
15,000–24,999	20,000[a]	37,020	1.8
25,000 and over	N.A.	455,900	N.A.

Source: Column 1—see [14, Table 3, p. 26]. Column 2—see [11, Table A, pp. 96–97].

N.A. = Not available.

[a] Estimated to be equal to the midpoints of the income class.

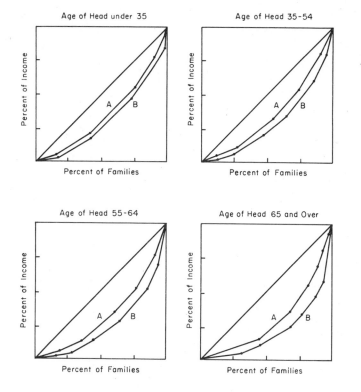

Figure 2. Lorenz curves: percentage shares of money income (A) and income net worth, at a 10 percent interest rate (B), received by families, by age of head, 1962.

TABLE 3
Median Income, Median Net Worth, and Life Expectancy of Families, by Age of
Family Head, 1962

Age of family head	(1) Median income	(2) Median net worth	(3) Ratio (2)/(1)	(4) Family life expectancy (years)[a]
Under 35	$5,585	$ 759	.14	49
35–54	6,918	7,664	1.11	34
55–64	6,219	13,210	2.12	21
65 and over	3,204	9,719	3.03	11
All	$5,956	$ 8,329	1.40	

*Source:*Column 1—see [14, Table 3, p. 26]. Column 2—see [11, Table A 1, pp. 96–97].
Column 4—based upon data from [15].

[a] "Family life expectancy" is weighted average of the life expectancies of husbands and
wives at the mean age of the family head and on the assumption that wives are five years
younger than their husbands. A weight of two-thirds is given to the additional years of life
expectancy of the wife; this results from the assumption that widows will receive an
annuity of two-thirds of the amount of the annuity previously received by the combined
husband and wife unit.

This section establishes that the distribution of economic position by
the proposed measure differs from that shown by current money income
because of differences among age groups in life expectancies and in the
relationship between income and net worth.[18] To further illustrate the
usefulness of the new measure we now examine the extreme low and
high ends of the distribution of economic position.

B. Implications for Measurement of "Poverty"
   and "Affluence"

What impact does our measure of economic position have on the
magnitude and age distribution of "poverty" in the United States? In
answering this question we shall define the poverty line for families as
$3,000 of current income, or, alternatively, as $3,000 of income–net

[18] Were we to use a more comprehensive measure of economic position that included
expected income as well as current income—as we have said earlier would be desirable—
the picture of the age distribution of economic position would be altered further. In
particular, since the incomes of younger people can be expected to rise, their economic
position will be improved in the future. For older persons, however, the opposite will more
likely be the case since, if anything, their expected income path is declining rather than
rising. We are planning to examine the possibilities of incorporating expected income into
our measure.

worth per family. (Many an ideal measure of welfare would include many other variables.) One especially important limitation to either of these measures is that they fail to distinguish among families of diverse size. Family size is important in looking at the amount and composition of poverty among age groups, since there is considerable variation in size by age of family head. As Orshansky has shown [10], the family size adjustment reduces the total number of poor *families*, though it leaves the total number of poor *people* unchanged. The reduction in the number of poor families is particularly great among those headed by persons over 65, since the average size of these families is relatively small. For simplicity, we have used the now-antiquated $3,000 poverty line. Our objective, in any case, is to emphasize not the absolute number of poor families but rather *changes* in that number and in the age composition when net worth is considered in addition to income.

The effect of using income–net worth rather than current income is shown in the top panel of Table 4. If current income is used alone to measure the extent of poverty, then—recognizing that no adjustment has been made for family size—the table shows that 47 percent of the aged are "poor." When net worth is annuitized at a 4 percent rate the percentage falls to 36, and to 32 at a 10 percent rate.[19] A glance up the columns shows, again, the decreasing effect of net worth as successively younger families are considered. Thus, the "poverty problem" appears to be much less a problem of the aged when net worth is taken into account than is the case when current income alone is the criterion. Moreover, apart from the distribution of the "poor," the total number of "poor" families falls, from 20 percent—9.3 million families—to 17 percent—8.0 million families—when net worth is considered (at a 10 percent interest rate).

If we now look at the age distribution of poor families, we find that whereas the aged poor constituted 34 percent of all poor families by the current income measure, they comprise only 28 percent of all poor

---

[19] A comparison of our results with those of Murray [9] can be made only for families aged 65 and over with annual money income less than $3,000—for only these aged families were examined in her study. By our income–net worth concept and at a 4 percent interest rate, the number of aged poor is reduced by 23 percent, i.e., from 47 to 36 percent. The Social Security study also used a 4 percent interest rate, but employed two income measures: income with prorated assets excluding home, and income with prorated assets including home. The first measure reduced the number of the aged poor by only 11 percent; from 54 to 48 percent. When homes were included among prorated assets, the number was reduced by over one-third, from 54 percent to 35 percent, i.e., a total reduction of 35 percent. Differences in the underlying data as well as use of assets rather than net worth would appear to account for the difference in her results and those presented here.

TABLE 4

Numbers and Percentages of Families with Incomes and Income–Net Worth of Less than $3,000 per Year, and of More than $10,000 per Year, by Age of Head, 1962

Age of family head	Less than $3,000 per year					
	Families with current money income below $3,000		Families with current income–net worth below $3,000, at			
			4 Percent interest rate		10 Percent interest rate	
	(1) Percent of all families in age group	(2) Number of families (millions)	(3) Percent of all families in age group	(4) Number of families (millions)	(5) Percent of all families in age group	(6) Number of families (millions)
Under 35	17	2.0	17	2.0	17	2.0
35–54	13	2.7	12	2.7	12	2.6
55–64	19	1.4	17	1.2	15	1.1
65 and over	47	3.2	36	2.4	32	2.2
All	20	9.3	18	8.4	17	8.0

More than $10,000 per year

Age of family head	Families with current money income over $10,000		4 Percent interest rate		10 Percent interest rate	
	(1) Percent of all families in age group	(2) Number of families (millions)	(3) Percent of all families in age group	(4) Number of families (millions)	(5) Percent of all families in age group	(6) Number of families (millions)
Under 35	9	1.1	10	1.2	11	1.3
35–54	24	5.1	29	6.1	34	7.2
55–64	22	1.6	30	2.2	36	2.6
65 and over	9	0.6	16	1.0	21	1.4
All	18	8.3	23	10.5	27	12.5

Families with current income— net worth above $10,000 (spanning columns 3–6)

Source: Same as Table 1.

TABLE 5

Median Income and Median Net Worth of Families with Incomes of Less than $3,000 per Year and of More than $10,000 per Year, by Age of Family Head, 1962

| Age of family head | Less than $3,000 per year | | |
	Median net worth (NW)	Median income (Y)	Ratio NW/Y
Under 35	$ 0	$ 1,782	0
35–54	385	1,760	.22
55–65	5,625	1,646	3.42
65 and over	6,667	1,844	3.62
All	$ 2,250	$ 1,788	1.26

| Age of family head | More than $10,000 per year | | |
	Median net worth	Median income	Ratio NW/Y
Under 35	$ 7,634	$12,969	.59
35–54	20,349	13,449	1.51
55–64	35,524	12,420	2.86
65 and over	45,800	14,084	3.25
All	$21,714	$13,454	1.61

Source: Same as Table 3.

families according to the income–net worth measure. In absolute numbers, their total drops from 3.2 million to 2.2 million families. Consequently, the relative as well as the absolute number of the "aged poor" is substantially reduced. Again, the rising ratio of net worth to income with age, shown in the top panel of Table 5, coupled with the falling life expectancy, is of critical importance.

The question of how poverty should be measured for purposes of governmental policy remains open; it is certainly not resolved by our brief foray into the issue.[20] Illuminating, nonetheless, is the fact that the proposed income–net worth measure of economic position—by accounting for net worth and life expectancy as well as income—portrays a smaller magnitude of poverty, and a rather different age composition of the poor.

It might be argued that the more conventional measures of poverty,

[20] For example, there is the issue of how prospective social insurance benefits, or more broadly the full range of public services, should be treated. But this topic has barely been opened up. We owe this point to Robert J. Lampman.

based on current income alone, have assumed *implicitly* some level of net worth holdings, or that they *ought* to have made such an assumption. If the income–net worth measure is viewed as useful, the question still remains as to what level of income–net worth should be regarded as a poverty line for purposes of measurement or eligibility for public programs.

It seems reasonable that the "official" measures of poverty adopted by the U.S. Office of Economic Opportunity, which consider current income and family size, could be extended to encompass net worth as well. Indeed, something very similar to this has already been implemented by the College Scholarship Service which, in determining the eligibility of college students for financial aid—from both private and public sources—relies upon family net worth data in addition to current income and family size. The 1966 Survey of Economic Opportunity (SEO) makes this approach applicable to a more general class of decisions regarding "poor" or "needy" people, for it will provide extensive data on the net worth of low-income families by family size.

Turning briefly from the poor to the "affluent," we see in the bottom panel of Table 5 what effect consideration of the annuity value of net worth has on the upper end of the distribution of economic position. Considering money income only, 18 percent of U.S. families, or 8.3 million families, were over the $10,000 mark; but this rises to 27 percent—12.5 million families—when net worth is annuitized at a 10 percent rate of interest. And, as with the low end of the distribution, the effect of considering net worth is markedly age-specific.

C. Implications for Defining Tax Progressivity and Regressivity

The income–net worth measure may be viewed as an alternative standard for viewing whether a given tax is "really" regressive, progressive, or proportional. We suggest that the ratio of taxes paid to current income may be a less useful standard for assessing vertical tax equity than is the ratio of taxes paid to income–net worth.

When net worth is considered in addition to income—in the manner we propose—the progressivity or regressivity of the tax system with respect to particular groupings of people will change in a systematic way. The essential reason for this is, as discussed above, that the ratio of income to income–net worth is not the same, either among income classes within age groups, or among age groups. Within any age group the use of the income–net worth base will show any tax, or the tax system as a whole, to be less progressive or more regressive, as the case may be, than if the conventional income base is used. This results from the fact that the ratio of net worth to income rises with respect to income. Similarly, the use of the income–net worth base will show any given tax to fall less heavily upon aged people than upon younger people. This results from the rising ratio of net worth to income with respect to age, and from the decline of life expectancy with respect to age. Both of these factors are captured in the proposed income–net worth measure but not in the current income base.

These illustrations can be generalized as follows. The net effect of the (1) rising ratio of net worth to income over the life cycle, (2) decreasing life expectancy over the life cycle, and (3) rise and then decline of income over the life cycle, will determine the precise dimensions of shifts in progressivity or regressivity by the income–net worth measure relative to that indicated by the use of current income alone. It is clear, however, that the picture of how our tax burdens are related to "ability to pay" is very different when our more comprehensive measure of "ability" is used. This suggests the desirability of undertaking studies of effective tax rates based not on current income but on ability-to-pay—as measured by income–net worth—for various taxes and for the tax system as a whole.[21]

D. Consumption Behavior Estimation

The approach presented in this paper for measuring economic position may be applied fruitfully to the prediction of consumer behavior. Indeed, *any* measure of economic position would seem to imply a theory of behavior, and vice versa. Thus, if economic position can be viewed as a function of annuitized net worth as well as of current income, then we might expect consumer expenditure levels also to depend on these factors.

Consider, for example, the relationship between the level of consumer expenditures in a given time period, and the level of permanent income, or alternatively, the level of windfall income in that period. Employing our income–net worth approach we suggest that the MPC out of permanent income should be higher, in general, than the MPC out of windfall income—and that the difference should narrow with age.

The reasoning is as follows: an increment of windfall income may be viewed as, in effect, a lump sum transfer of net worth (simply assets in

---

[21] The relevance of net assets to the "regressivity" of the sales tax has been discussed by Harold M. Somers in a statement prepared for the Joint Economic Committee [13].

this case). As such, its effect on current consumption expenditures would tend to be determined not by the size of the capital transfer but by its annual lifetime annuity value. Given the size of the capital transfer and the interest rate, the annuity value will depend on the life expectancy of the recipient, and, hence, will vary directly with the recipient's age. In all but the limiting case in which life expectancy does not extend beyond the current period, the annuity value will be less than the capital value. Thus, even if the recipient's MPC with respect to *annuity* income were unity, the observed MPC with respect to the *capital* value would be less than unity, and would be smaller the younger is the recipient.

It is interesting to note that this testable prediction is similar to that arrived at by Modigliani–Brumberg–Ando [8], [1]. While they started with the objective of predicting consumption behavior, their work implies a measure of economic position—namely, that economic position at a point in time is the sum of net worth plus the present value of expected income, divided by the length of expected life. We on the other hand started with the objective of measuring economic position, but some of the implications of the measure for consumption patterns became apparent as our work progressed. It is to be hoped that in the future closer rapport will develop between researchers concerned with measures of economic welfare and those concerned with the theory of economic behavior.

CONCLUSIONS

The income–net worth measure proposed here, while incomplete as a measure of economic welfare and imperfectly measured in this paper, has a number of useful attributes, the major one being that of merging two disparate but obviously related measures of economic position into a unified measure. The most striking result is its impact on the economic position of the aged, who by this measure appear to be considerably "better-off" than is shown by the current income measure. This results from the interaction of income, net worth holdings, and life expectancy. In addition to questions about the distribution of economic position, the income–net worth measure may be useful as a basis for redefining tax progressivity and regressivity, and as an explanatory variable in consumption behavior studies. Finally, it seems apparent that the measurement of economic welfare and the prediction of economic behavior are really two sides of the same coin, and that more explicit recognition of this fact would enrich the work in both areas.

50

REFERENCES

1. Ando, A., and Modigliani, F. 1963. The "life cycle" hypothesis of saving: aggregate implications and tests. *American Economic Review* 53:55–84.
2. Bridges, B., Jr. 1967. Net worth of the aged. *Research and Statistics Note,* no. 14. Washington, D.C.: Department of Health, Education, and Welfare.
3. David, M. 1959. Welfare income and budget needs. *Review of Economics and Statistics* 41:393–99.
4. Guthrie, H. W. 1963. Intergeneration transfers of wealth and the theory of saving. *Journal of Business* 36:97–108.
5. Kravis, I. B. 1962. *The structure of income: some quantitative essays.* Philadelphia: University of Pennsylvania.
6. Lansing, J. B., and Sonquist, J. 1967. "A cohort analysis of changes in the distribution of wealth." Paper presented at Conference on Income and Wealth. Mimeographed.
7. Lydall, H. F., and Lansing, J. B. 1959. A comparison of the distribution of personal income and wealth in the United States and Great Britain. *American Economic Review* 49:43–67.
8. Modigliani, F., and Brumberg, R. E. 1954. Utility analysis and the consumption function: an interpretation of cross-section data. In *Post-Keynesian economics,* ed. K. K. Kurihara, pp. 388–436. New Brunswick: Rutgers Univ. Press.
9. Murray, J. 1964. Potential income from assets: findings of the 1963 survey of the aged. *Social Security Bulletin,* December, pp. 3–11.
10. Orshansky, M. 1965. Counting the poor: another look at the poverty profile. *Social Security Bulletin,* January, pp. 3–29.
11. Projector, D. S., and Weiss, G. S. *Survey of financial characteristics of consumers.* Washington, D.C.: Federal Reserve System, Board of Governors.
12. Schultz, T. P. 1965. *The distribution of personal income.* Washington, D.C.: U.S. Congress, Joint Economic Committee.
13. U.S. Congress, Joint Economic Committee. 1966. *Tax changes for shortrun stabilization.* Hearings before Subcommittee on Fiscal Policy, 89th Cong. 2d. sess. Statement prepared by H. M. Somers, pp. 100–106.
14. U.S. Department of Commerce, Bureau of the Census. 1963. *Current Population Reports,* series P-60, no. 41.
15. U.S. Public Health Service. 1964. *Vital statistics of the United States.* Vol. 2, part A, "Mortality."

III

Earnings Capacity, Economic Status, and Poverty

IRWIN GARFINKEL AND ROBERT HAVEMAN

INTRODUCTION

Whether or not a household is counted among the poor depends upon its annual money income. As a measure of economic status, however, annual money income has serious limitations. In this paper an alternative indicator of economic status, called earnings capacity, is developed. Earnings capacity is designed to measure the ability of a living unit to generate an income stream if it were to use its physical and human capital at capacity. Using this measure, the composition of the poverty population is estimated and compared to the composition of the poverty population according to the official definition. In addition, the socioeconomic and demographic determinants of poverty as measured by earnings capacity and by annual money income are compared and contrasted.

The problem of accurately measuring the economic status of family units and individuals is of long standing in both poverty research and analyses of horizontal and vertical inequality. The standard indicator of economic status—annual family money income—is the basis both for the official definition of poverty in the United States and for nearly all studies of economic inequality. Yet, the limitations of the money income measure as an indicator both of the command over goods and services and of relative economic status are often noted. Annual money income fails to incorporate the value of human and nonhuman capital into the measure of economic status; it neglects the benefits of in-kind public

Reprinted by permission of the *Journal of Human Resources*. Copyright 1977 by the Regents of the University of Wisconsin System.

transfers and public services and the tax costs required to finance them; it does not account for intrafamily flows of income and services or for differences in leisure time; and, for many units, it is dominated, in any given year, by transitory influences. In short, annual money income is a seriously inadequate indicator of the potential real consumption of a living unit, yet it is the indicator most widely used.

An alternative indicator of economic status is suggested here, and empirically estimated for the national population. This indicator—earnings capacity—is designed to measure the ability of a living unit to generate an income stream if it were to use its physical and human capital at capacity. Using this measure, the composition of the poverty population is estimated and compared to the composition of the poverty population according to the official definition. Because of the characteristics of the concept, the poverty population defined by earnings capacity will be relatively more heavily populated by those with low permanent income than will the poverty population based on the intertemporally unstable concept of annual money income.[1] Moreover, living units will not be included in the poverty population simply because of relatively strong preferences for leisure as opposed to money income.

I. ESTIMATION OF EARNINGS CAPACITY

Earnings capacity reflects the ability of a family—given its current endowment of physical and human capital—to generate a net income flow if it uses that endowment at capacity. In this study an estimate of family earnings capacity is developed for each of 50,000 families interviewed in the 1971 Current Population Survey (CPS).[2]

[1] Such transitory fluctuations can substantially influence a family's ranking in the money income distribution. See James Morgan et al. [9]. By eliminating the effects of income instability, the earnings capacity concept is akin to, though not identical with, the present value of expected lifetime consumption. Earnings capacity takes as given the stock of human and physical capital at a point in time and estimates the return accruing to capacity use of these assets. Conceptually, earnings capacity is more closely related to Gary S. Becker's [1] notion of "full income."

[2] The March 1971 CPS was "aged" to allow for demographic changes, economic growth, and inflation through 1973. In addition, the 6.0 percent unemployment rate of 1970 was adjusted to 4.9 percent by randomly assigning unemployment and duration of unemployment to groups identified by age, sex, occupation, and unemployment experience using the RIM model developed by the Urban Institute. See Nelson McClung, John Moeller, and Eduardo Siguel [7]. This data base was chosen because of its combination of extensive background characteristics of husband and spouse and large number of observations. This latter characteristic is essential for developing reliable estimates of the composition of the poverty population by narrowly defined socioeconomic groups.

In order to derive an indicator of a family's relative economic status that reflects neither the family's tastes for income nor temporary fluctuations in income, we first develop estimates of the annual earnings capacity of each family head (EC_H) and spouse (EC_S). Capacity for each individual is taken to be at least 50 weeks of full-time work. The earnings capacities of the head and spouse are imputed on the basis of their present socioeconomic characteristics from four regression equations in which annual earned income is the dependent variable. Separate regression equations are estimated for black and white men and for black and white women. Through coefficients estimated in these regressions, average full-time, full-year earnings of men and women with different sets of demographic characteristics are estimated. The independent variables in each race–sex equation include age, years of schooling, marital status, and location.[3] Only those individuals with positive earnings are included in the sample used to fit the earnings equations.

Reliance on a human capital framework leads to a number of a priori expectations regarding the size and direction of the relationship between the independent variables and earnings. Consistent with that framework, earnings in the early and middle adult years are expected to increase with age due to job experience and on-the-job training. In the later adult years, earnings are expected to decrease as skills become obsolete and physical and mental capacities deteriorate. Earnings are also expected to increase with the education and training as measured by years of schooling. The use of separate equations for race and sex groups presumes the existence of labor market discrimination. For individuals with otherwise identical characteristics, earnings are expected to be

---

[3] These variables are consistent with those conventionally employed in empirical studies based on the human capital approach to analyzing wage or earnings differences. While effort was made to include only exogenous or permanent individual characteristics as explanatory variables, some of the independent variables clearly contain an element of choice. For example, while earnings depend positively upon the productivity associated with education, the amount of education an individual ultimately attains may also depend upon his expected earnings. Similar elements of choice affect the marital status and location variables. An ideal procedure would be to specify a complete structural model containing a series of equations in which each dependent variable is a function of factors which are clearly exogenous to it. Such a model could then be estimated as a series of simultaneous equations by two-stage least squares techniques. The limitations of data used in this study make this procedure impossible; in effect, the approach chosen yields structural estimates that represent the conditional expectation of the log of earnings given the individual's socioeconomic condition, which is assumed to be fixed in the short run. For a more complete discussion of the specification of wage and earnings models based on human capital theory, see Jacob Mincer [8] and Alan S. Blinder [3].

smaller for blacks than for whites, and for women than for men. Similarly, differences in earnings reflect both regional cost of living differentials and real differences in productivity not captured by our other variables. Married men are expected to earn more than single men with otherwise identical characteristics on the presumption that the incidence of physical and mental disabilities is higher among single than among married men.[4] While the incidence of mental and physical disabilities is higher among single than married women as well, this difference will likely be swamped by differences in work experience among single and married women and among women with and without children. Because earnings are expected to be positively related to experience and on-the-job training, it is anticipated that women in marital and parental status categories with a smaller probability of recent work experience (e.g., married women with children) will have lower earnings than those in categories with a greater probability of recent work experience (e.g., single women without children).

Previous studies have shown that the effect of several of these variables on earnings varies with age. Hence, the regression equations are specified to permit these interactions. To capture the relationship between wage rates or productivity and intermittent (e.g., seasonal) or part-time work, the regressions also include a set of dummy variables for weeks worked and for whether or not the individual normally worked part or full time during the weeks worked.[5]

Although experimentation was undertaken with both a linear and a log-linear model, only the estimates derived from the log-linear model are reported. First, contrasts between current income and earnings capacity measures of economic status are quite insensitive to the functional form used in the development of the estimates of earnings capacity. Second, there are a number of a priori reasons for preferring the log-linear model. The most important consideration is the required nonnegativity of predicted earnings from a log-linear model. In addition, it is likely that the variance in earnings is smaller the smaller is the level of human capital. The linear model neither requires nonnegative predicted values nor positively relates the variance in earned income to the

---

[4] In addition, married men typically have more dependents than single men and, hence, face larger family needs which must be covered by money income. In principle, this factor reflects individual choice and is not properly included in the regression. Because of data limitations however, it cannot be separated from the more permanent characteristics associated with marital status and excluded from the regression.

[5] This specification presumes that deviation from full-time, full-year work is attributable to choice. As described below, it is this choice which is suppressed in the estimation of earning capacity.

level of human capital. Finally, by standard measures, the log-linear model appears to yield a somewhat better fit.

The estimated earnings functions are presented in Table A-1 (pp. 72–73). The R^2 in the regressions range from .52 for white males to .63 for black females.

Two further adjustments are made to the estimates of EC_H and EC_S before they are aggregated into an estimate of family earnings capacity. The procedure described above leads to estimates of individual capacity in which all individuals with the same age, sex, race, years of schooling, location, and marital and work status are assigned an earnings capacity equal to the mean of the cell within which they are included. In other words, all within-cell variance is artificially suppressed by this technique. To the extent that this within-cell variance is attributable to unobserved human capital differences or to chance, such suppression is inappropriate for our purposes. Assigning of the cell mean would exaggerate the probability that individuals with certain characteristics— for example black southern female head with little education—will be poor.

To avoid this problem, individual observations within a cell are distributed randomly about the mean of that cell. This distribution is accomplished through a random number generator technique which incorporates the assumption that the distribution of observations within cells is normal, with a standard deviation equal to the standard deviation of the regression equation.[6] From this procedure, the mean value of earnings capacity for each cell is retained, but a normal distribution of observations within cells is achieved.

Second, some individuals do not work full time for the full year because of either health disabilities or insufficient aggregate demand. In order to take account of such exogenous limitations on economic capacity, the earnings capacity estimates of the head and spouse are multiplied by the fraction: $(50 - W_{SU})/50$, where $W_{SU} = $ weeks sick or unemployed.

Adjusting for illness and unemployment builds some temporary reductions in income into the earnings capacity measure for an individual family. While many reported disabilities are permanent, some reflect temporary illness. However, because of limitations in our data, it is

---

[6] The random number generator routine RANNB generates a sequence of pseudo-random numbers with a normal (Gaussian) distribution with mean 0 and variance 1 by the method of Box and Muller [3]. For a description of computation procedures, see Random Number Routines Reference Manual 1110, Academic Computing Center, the University of Wisconsin, Madison.

impossible to separate reductions in employment due to permanent disabilities from those due to temporary disabilities. Moreover, while all unemployment and nonpermanent illness may represent a temporary reduction in a particular individual's earnings capacity, from the perspective of the overall economy both are permanent phenomena. Viewed in this way, neither differences in unemployment nor in health status reflect taste differences, and it is the elimination of such differences which our measure of economic status is designed to accomplish.[7]

By summing the randomized adjusted estimates of EC_H and EC_S within a household, we obtain a measure of family gross earnings capacity. For three reasons, however, this measure of earnings capacity does not fully reflect a family's economic position. First, it does not include any measure of returns to assets. Second, it does not include income from transfer programs in which an individual's rights are vested. Finally, it does not take account of the costs of working.

In order to account for returns to assets and intrafamily cash transfers, we add to our measure of family gross earnings capacity the following: income from interest, dividends, rents, alimony, and miscellaneous sources other than government transfers (Y_1).

Because income from interest, dividends, and rents is a measure (albeit a crude one) of a family's ability to generate income from its

---

[7] Three problems with this adjustment procedure are worth noting. First, to the extent that differences in unemployment and health status are taste related, our adjustment will understate the difference between earnings capacity and current income that is due to taste. Second, at least some of the time that individuals spend unemployed is attributable not to the absence of a job but to the absence of a job that the unemployed individual deems suitable. For this reason, the adjusted capacity measure will yield an underestimate of earnings capacity for some individuals. Third, there are individuals who, having been unemployed for long periods, are no longer in the labor force and other individuals who are ill or disabled but are neither seeking nor holding employment whose estimated earnings capacity is not subject to this adjustment. The earnings capacity of these individuals will be overstated relative to that of individuals with identical characteristics who are labor force participants. It follows that the earnings capacity of groups having a high incidence of nonparticipation in the labor force will be biased upward relative to groups with a low incidence of nonparticipation. However, the extent of this bias is small. We found that the proportion of earnings capacity poor who had no earners in the family changed only slightly if we did not adjust the estimates of capacity for unemployment and illness. While adjustments for nonparticipants in the labor force could have been imputed on the basis of adjustments estimated for participants of like characteristics, this approach was not followed for two reasons. First, the absence of a close relationship between demographic characteristics of labor force participants and illness, disability, and unemployment would cause the adjustment for nonparticipants to be little more than random assignment. Second, and more important, expected illness, disability, and unemployment are themselves determinants of the labor force participation choice, hence destroying the basis of imputation based on like characteristics.

assets, such income should be counted in ascertaining the family's economic status.[8] In adding actual income flows to human capital earnings capacity, it is implicitly assumed that a family's nonhuman capital assets are being used at capacity. On the other hand, because income from transfer programs does not constitute a measure of the family's ability to generate income, such transfer payments are excluded from our earnings capacity measures.[9] Thus, our measure of a family's gross earnings capacity is equal to:

$$(1) \qquad GEC = EC_H \frac{50 - W_{SU}}{50} + EC_S \frac{50 - W_{SU}}{50} + Y_1.$$

GEC, then, measures family economic status as a flow of gross income, and reflects explicit judgments regarding the definitions of capacity work effort, capacity use of physical assets, and property rights in certain transfer benefits. It makes no allowance for the fact that attainment of this capacity may entail real costs which vary among families. While some of these costs are associated with the type of work undertaken in attaining capacity and would therefore be reflected in the wage rate, others are occasioned by obstacles to employment due to circumstances of family structure or location, in combination with socially established standards for avoiding these obstacles. Because economic status viewed from the perspective of the individual family

[8] Some assets, such as home equity, have no reported monetary return. Hence, this measure underestimates the earnings capacity of families receiving services from owner-occupied housing. See Burton W. Weisbrod and W. Lee Hansen [12].

[9] In an earlier version of this paper (Institute for Research on Poverty Discussion Paper #299) as well as related work (see [5]), we mistakenly asserted that Social Security payments and government and private pensions were included in our measures of earnings capacity. There are at least two good reasons for including these transfers. First, Social Security payments and pensions may be viewed as a substitute for savings. Second, they can be viewed as a flow of income from an asset. (This latter is also the rationale for including alimony.) Including these transfers in our measures of earnings capacity, however, would only increase the contrasts between earnings capacity and current income that we identify in the text. For example, below we show that if poverty is defined in terms of earnings capacity rather than current income, a greater proportion of the poor live in families with workers and with nonaged heads. Had we included Social Security payments and pensions in our measure of earnings capacity, the incomes of people living in families with aged heads who do not work would increase, thereby increasing further the proportion of the earnings capacity poor who live in households headed by nonaged workers. Thus, even though we would prefer to have presented estimates of earnings capacity that included Social Security payments and pensions, we do not because: (1) doing so would have required a substantial amount of reprogramming work and (2) our qualitative results would not change.

depends on the magnitude of these latter costs, an alternative measure of family economic status can be obtained by subtracting them from *GEC*.

Clearly, the largest component of these costs, and the component which varies most among families, is that due to children in the home requiring care. The contribution of such children to family economic status is a complex matter. In most cases, the presence of children conveys utility to the parents and an ideal measure of economic welfare would reflect this value. In an ideal framework, the net benefit of children would equal the gross flow of satisfaction which they convey less the costs required for their care. To the extent that the presence of children conveys no utility, only the subtraction of required child care costs is necessary. Even though our gross measure of economic status (*GEC*) does not reflect the value of children, we adjust its value for each family by subtracting an estimate of the cost of a minimally acceptable level of child care. The justification for this procedure rests on the following considerations. First, not all children are wanted, particularly at the lower end of the distribution. Moreover, if economic welfare is viewed from the perspective of the children, our procedure of simulating the returns from market work of mothers implies a loss to them which is not accounted for in the *GEC* measure. Finally, the adjustment does reflect the cost of overcoming the socially established obstacle to attaining full earnings capacity when there are children in the home. Consequently, in addition to the *GEC* measure, we calculate a net earnings capacity measure (*NEC*) for each family which is defined as follows:[10]

$$(2) \qquad \begin{aligned} NEC = GEC &- (\$1,510 \text{ per child aged 5 years or younger} \\ &+ \$376 \text{ per child aged 6–14 years}). \end{aligned}$$

Despite these adjustments, our estimates of earnings capacity are likely to deviate from the pure earnings capacity concept for several

---

[10] Data on minimally acceptable child care costs are 1968 estimates adjusted for inflation. The 1968 estimates are from B. Bernstein and P. Giacchino [2], as reported by Michael Krashinsky [6]. It can be argued that this adjustment is too high for families who can secure child care services by relying on relatives, older children in the family, or friends, and that observed child care expenses vary positively with *GEC*. With respect to the first point, it is reasonable to expect that the real costs to a family of securing child care services by exploiting relatives or friends are in excess of out-of-pocket expenses, and are more likely to approximate the dollar values which we use. On the second point, we note that our estimates are designed to reflect costs of meeting socially imposed standards for overcoming this obstacle to attaining earnings capacity, rather than actual family choices; hence, the use of costs required to meet a level of care which is officially designated as "minimally acceptable."

reasons. First, the estimating procedure fails to capture all of the determinants of earned income (for example, motivation, IQ, detailed physical characteristics, conditions of labor demand, and chance). Second, estimation of the capacity return from physical assets is incomplete. Third, only a portion (albeit the largest portion) of the required expenses for achieving capacity work effort are deducted from *GEC*. While these deficiencies may lead to a nontrivial misestimation of pure earnings capacity for any individual or family, *NEC* is likely to be a good estimate of the true net earnings capacity for the demographically homogeneous groups which we identify. Moreover, it is more independent of relative preferences for leisure than is money income, and it is largely free from the transitory exogenous impacts which affect annual money income.

II. COMPARISON TO CURRENT INCOME MEASURE

By placing the *GEC, NEC*, and current income (*CY*) measures of economic status over the 1973 poverty line for a family, three "welfare ratios" are obtained for each family unit.[11] Employing these welfare ratios, we can determine and compare the composition of families in *GEC, NEC*, and *CY* poverty.

According to the official definition of poverty, an individual is poor if he lives in a family in which the *CY* welfare ratio is less than unity. In 1973, about 11 percent of the total U.S. population were poor by this conventional definition. If this percentage figure is accepted as a bench mark, an equivalent number of individuals in families with the lowest *GEC* and *NEC* welfare ratios can be isolated and the composition of the groups compared. If earnings capacity is superior to current income as an indicator of economic status, we gain more accurate information about the characteristics of the poor by examining the composition of families with low earnings capacity welfare ratios than by examining the composition of families that are designated poor by the official statistics.

In Table 1, data on the composition of *GEC, NEC*, and *CY* poor *individuals* are presented, as well as data on the composition of *CY* poor

---

[11] The 1973 poverty lines for urban families are officially designated as follows: family size 1, $2,475; family size 2, $3,095; family size 3, $3,720; and so on. In addition to variation by family size, the poverty line is somewhat lower for rural families. For a discussion of the poverty threshold concept, see Molly Orshansky [11]. The concept and use of the welfare ratio were originated by James N. Morgan, Martin H. David, Wilbur J. Cohen, and Harvey E. Brazer [10].

TABLE 1
Percentage Distribution of Earnings Capacity and Current Income Poor Individuals and
Current Income Poor Households, by Selected Socioeconomic Characteristics,
Total Population, 1973

	NEC indi-viduals	*GEC* indi-viduals	Current income	
Characteristics			Indi-viduals	House-holds
Race of head				
White	59.96	60.90	67.70	76.37
Black	38.34	37.28	30.82	22.56
Other	1.70	1.81	1.33	1.33
Sex of head				
Male	49.88	40.57	45.60	45.95
Female	50.12	59.43	54.40	54.05
Age of head				
16–21	2.38	2.35	4.69	6.75
22–30	21.53	14.35	17.07	13.60
31–40	29.47	21.76	22.62	12.06
41–50	19.93	20.01	17.37	11.27
51–60	10.92	14.68	12.66	12.46
61–64	2.80	4.45	4.70	6.61
65+	12.96	22.41	20.87	37.26
Family size				
1	6.25	13.99	19.29	48.67
2	6.26	11.40	14.64	18.47
3–4	22.94	23.30	22.06	16.04
5–6	28.35	23.51	20.54	9.57
7–8	21.16	17.10	15.25	5.23
9+	15.24	10.17	8.22	2.02
Education of head				
0–8	46.71	51.23	48.94	49.53
9–12	47.76	42.37	41.65	38.19
13–16	5.23	5.46	8.36	10.81
17+	.31	.44	1.06	1.47
Occupation of head				
Professional	3.60	3.96	3.44	5.27
Farmer	2.95	2.65	12.84	11.13
Manager	5.12	4.97	8.15	8.14
Clerical	9.53	12.77	5.13	8.36
Sales	2.59	2.87	2.96	3.81
Craftsman	13.70	11.33	9.60	7.96
Operative	26.57	24.26	16.97	13.47
Private household	5.13	6.50	8.66	6.46
Service	15.68	18.00	17.34	15.55
Farm laborer	5.21	4.84	6.53	7.93
Laborer	9.90	7.84	9.33	10.96

(continued)

TABLE 1 (Continued)

| Characteristics | NEC indi-viduals | GEC indi-viduals | Current income | |
			Indi-viduals	House-holds
Region				
Northeast	17.41	18.44	15.72	18.29
North Central	21.49	21.12	22.61	24.57
South	46.44	46.12	46.24	40.78
West	14.66	14.20	15.42	16.36
Urban–rural				
Town	15.92	16.63	13.99	15.12
Rural	34.47	35.07	40.58	34.25
Suburb	15.84	15.10	14.44	16.73
Central city	33.77	33.20	30.99	33.90
Number of earners				
0	27.28	33.70	42.18	54.94
1	52.63	50.33	45.02	37.69
2	20.09	15.97	12.81	7.37
Weeks worked by head				
0	28.34	35.27	43.65	55.91
1–13	7.43	8.00	9.58	9.7
14–26	7.68	7.84	7.99	7.69
27–39	7.82	7.58	6.58	4.95
40–47	6.40	5.42	4.58	3.00
48–49	2.87	1.90	1.70	1.12
50–52	39.45	34.00	25.92	17.63
Full or part time				
Full time	83.44	79.86	73.44	65.84
Part time	16.56	20.14	26.56	34.16

households.[12] This table includes all individuals in the population. Two measures of earnings capacity are used—*NEC* and *GEC*—so that the effect of the child care deduction on poverty composition can be readily isolated.

[12] Although households are the typical units of measurement in analyses of the composition of the poor, this analysis focuses on individuals. Households are of interest not in themselves but only because they are aggregates of individuals. Clearly, if all households were of equal size, the household and the individual would be interchangeable units of measurement. However, if all individuals are to be treated equally, a household with 10 poor individuals in it must be of more concern than a household with but 1 poor individual. Similarly, eliminating poverty in a household with 10 individuals is more of an accomplishment than eliminating poverty in a household with a single individual. As Table 1 indicates, data on the composition of the poor in terms of households present a quite different—and perhaps misleading—picture compared to that presented by data on poor individuals.

Examining the composition of *CY* poor households and *CY* poor individuals, it is seen that the household measure seriously overstates the proportion of the poor who live in small households and, as a consequence, the proportion of the poor who are aged and who live in families with no earners. Although the differences are somewhat less dramatic, the proportions of *CY* poor individuals who are black and who live in the South are also understated when poverty is measured in terms of households.

Differences between the composition of *CY* poor individuals and the composition of earnings capacity (*EC*) poor individuals are equally striking. Moreover, they reinforce the compositional differences we found in moving from current income poverty measured by households to that measured by individuals.

Perhaps the most striking difference in composition between *EC* and *CY* poverty is in work status. While only 26 percent of the *CY* poor live in households in which the head worked 50–52 weeks, 40 percent of the *NEC* poor live in such households. This work status difference is easily explained. *CY* is closely related to how many workers there are in a household and to how much each of them works. *EC* is not directly related to either of these variables.[13] It should also be noted that the proportion of poor individuals who live in families with workers is higher among the *NEC* poor than among the *GEC* poor. This is largely due to the child care adjustment, which reduces the *NEC* of the nonaged population relative to that of the aged population. The former are much more likely to have children; the latter are much less likely to live in households with workers.

A second striking difference between the compositions of the *CY* poor and the *EC* poor is in racial composition. Whereas 31 percent of *CY* poor individuals are black, about 38 percent of the *EC* poor are black.[14] The *CY* measure of economic status understates the low economic status of blacks relative to whites. This result is, in large part, due to the higher labor force participation rate and more hours worked of black spouses.

The differences by sex of head are not nearly so dramatic; in fact, the difference in composition between the two *EC* measures (*GEC* and *NEC*) is larger than the difference between either of them and the composition of the *CY* poor. The proportion of individuals in families headed by males increases in moving from *GEC* to *NEC*, largely because intact (male-headed) families have more children on average than do single-parent families.

[13] It will be recalled, however, that the estimation of *GEC* and *NEC* are adjusted for reported unemployment.

[14] Blacks form only about 11 percent of the total population.

More striking is the effect of the child care deduction on the age composition of poor individuals. While 21 percent of the *CY* poor and 22 percent of the *GEC* poor live in households whose heads are aged 65 or older, only 13 percent of the *NEC* poor live in such households. Taking *NEC* as the preferred measure of economic status, the standard poverty measure appears to overstate the number of older people in the poverty population. On the other hand, it should be noted that since unhealthy aged individuals are much less likely than younger individuals to give health as the reason for not working, the estimates of *GEC* and *NEC* for the aged may be somewhat biased upward.

Even without the child care deduction, the difference in family size composition between the *EC* and the *CY* poor is notable. There are far fewer single *EC* poor persons and more with large families. Whereas almost 20 percent of *CY* poor individuals (48 percent of *CY* poor households) live alone, only 14 percent of the *GEC* poor and 6 percent of the *NEC* poor live alone. Indeed, over 15 percent of the *NEC* poor live in families with nine or more children (10 percent without the child care adjustment), while only 8 percent of the *CY* poor live in such large families. As we suggest below, however, part of this difference is attributable to the differential treatment of earners beyond the head and spouse in these two measures.

Another interesting difference is between the proportions of the *EC* and the *CY* poor who are farmers: 13 percent of the *CY* poor, but only 3 percent of the *EC* poor. This difference suggests that most farmers who are poor by the *CY* measure have sufficient human capital to do better economically if they were willing to leave their farms. Our measure of human capital, however, is imperfect. In particular, the earnings of individuals if they were to switch occupations and locations late in life may not be accurately measured. Because of this, the *EC* of at least some older farmers may be overstated. In any case, the small proportion of the *EC* poor who are farmers is offset by the larger proportion who are operatives (26 percent versus 17 percent of the *CY* poor), craftsmen (14 percent versus 10 percent), and clerical workers (10 percent versus 5 percent).

Some other differences are worth noting. The figures in Table 1 also indicate that a greater proportion of the *EC* poor than of the *CY* poor have fewer than 12 years of schooling, a greater proportion live in the South, and a somewhat greater proportion live in the central cities of larger SMSAs and in small towns.

To summarize, if our estimate of *EC* is a superior indicator of economic status, the use of a *CY* measure of economic status *understates* the proportion of the poor who are black, who have low levels of education, who live in very large families, who live in households with one or more full-time workers, who are younger than age 65 and older than age 22, who do not live alone, and who are not farmers. Moreover, analyzing the composition of CY poverty using households rather than individuals exacerbates these biases.[15]

III.   DEMOGRAPHIC CHARACTERISTICS AND POVERTY STATUS

While the comparisons in Table 1 are helpful in discerning how the composition of the poor population changes in moving from a CY definition of economic status to a definition based on EC, they can lead to faulty inferences regarding those variables that are the most important determinants of poverty status under each definition. For example, to observe that both families with low education and those in low-status, low-skill occupations are heavily represented in the poverty population gives no indication of the independent contribution of either education or occupation to poverty status. These independent effects can be captured only by answering the question, "How does the probability of being in poverty change in moving from, say, one level of educational

---

[15] These estimates of EC are generated by the randomization procedure described in note 6. Similar estimates were made of the composition of the poor using a second random number generation process and using the expected value for a family rather than the expected value plus or minus a random shock. This was done to determine the extent to which observed differences between the EC and CY poverty compositions are due to the randomization process.

The results of this exercise indicated that the differences in composition between the two randomized EC estimates are negligible. Some small differences existed between the composition of the poor estimated from random and nonrandom procedures. In general, the randomization procedure tended to reduce the difference between the EC and the CY poor in terms of race, years of schooling, region, and family size.

Also, estimates were made of the composition of *nonaged* poor individuals by the EC and CY indicators of economic status. Eleven percent of the total population, but only 9.9 percent of the population aged 64 or younger, live in families calssified as poor by the standard definition. In general, the compositional differences between EC and CY poverty observed in the total population are also present in the nonaged population. The primary differences occur in the proportion of individuals living in female-headed families (50 percent for NEC and 44 percent for CY, relative to 50 percent and 54 percent for the total population), in families with one or two workers (70 percent for NEC and 68 percent for CY, relative to 73 percent and 58 percent for the total population), and in families headed by blacks (41 percent for NEC and 34 percent for CY, relative to 38 percent and 31 percent for the total population).

attainment to another, holding constant other family characteristics related to poverty status?''

Through the use of multiple regression analysis, estimates of the independent contributions of various socioeconomic characteristics to the probability of poverty status can be obtained. By specifying a regression equation with a 0–1 dependent variable representing the poverty–nonpoverty status of individual families and with family characteristics as independent variables, the relationship to the probability of poverty status of changes in any one family characteristic—holding other characteristics constant—can be obtained.

In Table 2, regressions of this form are presented for both the *CY* and *NEC* poverty definitions for the total population. Several interesting contrasts between the two regressions are observable. First, as suggested above, the relationship of work status to poverty status is much weaker under the *EC* than under the *CY* measure of economic status. Moreover, female-head status—while an important determinant of poverty status for both definitions—has a much more powerful effect under the *EC* definition than it does under the *CY* definition. This is not surprising, given the fact that female-headed families typically have but a single adult who contributes to total family earnings capacity. On the basis of this alone, one would expect to find a substantially higher proportion of female-headed families in *EC* poverty than in *CY* poverty. But as indicated in Table 1, the proportion of female heads is approximately the same for the *CY* and *EC* definitions. A large number of female-headed families with children are counted as *CY* poor because the family head does not work. In contrast, such families form a high proportion of the *EC* poor, not because they do not work but because, relative to the rest of the population, they would earn so little even if they worked at capacity.

Perhaps one of the most striking findings is the effect of age— particularly old age—on the probability of being poor according to the two definitions. The pattern of the age coefficients in the *NEC* regression can be explained primarily by an underlying age–wage rate profile that is common in the human capital literature. An opposite result is present in the current income regression, which shows that the probability of *CY* poverty decreases with age—particularly after age 65. This result is due to old age insurance and disability insurance payments; an aged nonworker is less likely to be poor than a nonaged nonworker. Also, the large positive value on family size 1 to some extent offsets the negative value on old age in the current income definition.

While the effect of family size is large for both poverty definitions, it

TABLE 2
**Effect of Family Characteristics on the Probability of Poverty Status, by *NEC* and
CY Poverty Definitions**

Demographic characteristics	CY		NEC	
	Coefficient	*t*-value	Coefficient	*t*-value
Race				
White	—	—	—	—
Black	11.0	25.5	13.95	33.2
Other	4.01	3.34	1.84	1.6
Sex				
Male	—	—	—	—
Female	12.79	29.17	30.42	71.2
Age				
16–21	13.94	13.95	10.96	11.3
22–25	3.91	6.59	12.15	21.1
25–35	2.97	8.3	7.82	22.6
35–45	—	—	—	—
45–55	−1.44	3.96	.2	.6
55–64	−2.97	4.82	2.64	5.7
65+	−11.81	20.3	1.74	3.1
Education				
0–8	9.5	21.6	10.33	24.2
9–12	2.72	7.6	3.44	9.9
13–16	—	—	—	—
17+	−.45	.8	−.46	.8
Family size				
1	5.57	9.3	−19.71	33.7
2	−2.3	5.3	−8.06	19.0
3	−1.89	4.5	−4.21	10.4
4	—	—	—	—
5	1.4	3.4	3.44	8.7
6	2.82	5.98	7.48	16.3
7	8.99	15.5	13.98	24.7
8	10.04	13.4	21.91	30.0
9+	6.6	9.65	26.61	40.0
Region				
Northeast	−.93	2.7	−.26	.8
North Central	—	—	—	—
South	3.76	11.6	3.66	11.5
West	.25	.67	.82	2. 2
Urban–rural				
Town	1.6	3.8	2.54	6.4
Rural	3.31	9.8	2.26	6.9
Central city	.26	.8	.19	.6
Suburb	—	—	—	—

(continued)

TABLE 2 (Continued)

Demographic characteristics	CY		NEC	
	Coefficient	t-value	Coefficient	t-value
Weeks worked (head)				
0	—	—	—	—
1–13	10.57	10.3	8.21	8.23
14–26	−2.73	.3	2.51	2.6
27–39	−9.93	10.6	.52	.6
40– 47	−12.58	13.3	−5.34	5.8
48– 49	−15.33	14.26	−5.21	4.9
50+	−16.16	20.2	−7.23	9.3
Weeks worked (spouse)				
0	—	—	—	—
1–13	−.44	.8	−1.38	2.5
14–26	−2.88	4.8	−1.65	2.8
27–39	−3.29	5.1	−2.77	4.4
40– 47	−2.81	3.6	−2.56	3.4
48– 49	−2.94	2.6	−3.28	3.0
50+	−2.2	4.8	−3.13	6.98
Occupation				
Farmer	20.39	24.2	−.86	1.1
Manager	2.68	5.2	1.13	2.2
Professional	—	—	—	—
Clerical	−4.38	6.8	−.18	.3
Sales	.81	1.2	1.18	1.8
Craftsman	−1.53	2.9	.01	.024
Operative	−2.16	3.9	1.34	2.5
Private household	15.57	10.0	11.95	7.8
Service	1.06	1.6	1.3	2.1
Farm laborer	20.29	16.4	9.18	7.6
Laborer	2.24	3.1	.58	.8
Full or part time (head)				
Full time	−9.15	14.8	.58	.97
Part time	—	—	—	—
Full or part time (spouse)				
Full time	−2.9	6.9	.97	2.38
Part time	—	—	—	—
Constant	21.72	31.4	−.40	.6
R^2	.276		.3155	
F	368.9		445.4	

is more powerful for large families under the *EC* definition. The stronger effect of family size on the probability of *EC* relative to *CY* poverty is, in part, attributable to the differential treatment by these two measures of earners beyond the head and spouse in a family. While the numerator of the *CY* welfare ratio for a family includes the contribution of such workers to family income, the numerator of the *EC* ratio does not include their contribution to earnings capacity. Because the probability that such earners will be present in a family is related to its size, the incidence of large families in *EC* poverty will be upward biased relative to the incidence of such families in *CY* poverty. To test the potential importance of this bias, we ran another *CY* poverty regression with a variable for earnings of family members other than the head and spouse. The coefficient was negative and highly significant. More important its presence increased the coefficients of the family size 7, 8, and 9 variables to 11,16, and 10 respectively. From these results we conclude that some but not all of the differential effects of family size on *CY* and *EC* poverty status is attributable to the differential treatment of earners in addition to the head and spouse.[16]

Finally, the impact of occupation on poverty status in the two definitions should also be noted. Consistent with the results in Table 1, those in Table 2 indicate that being a farmer, a farm laborer, and to a lesser extent, a household worker—holding other characteristics constant—substantially increases the incidence of *CY* poverty relative to *EC* poverty.

IV. FAMILY TYPES AND POVERTY STATUS

The data in Table 2 can be readily adapted to provide an estimate of the probability of *CY* and *EC* poverty status for various family types. In Table 3 several types of family units are characterized and the probability of each family type being in *CY* and *EC* poverty is indicated. These probability estimates suggest some similarities and some substantial differences between the *EC* and *CY* poverty definitions in terms of which sorts of families are classified as poor.

Members of female-headed black families, large southern rural families, and migrant worker families have the highest probabilities of being

---

[16] We are grateful to a referee of an earlier version of this paper for pointing out this bias.

TABLE 3
The Probability of Poverty Classification of Several Family Types, by Earnings Capacity and
Current Income Definitions

Family characterization	NEC	Current income
1. Black female head with children—"AFDC stereotype"[a]	70.94	72.1
2. Large southern rural family[b]	42.18	46.89
3. Migrant worker family[c]	50.54	49.75
4. Single, youth—"independent student"[d]	.15	41.46
5. Middle-aged midwestern farm family[e]	1.53	20.93
6. Elderly couple[f]	3.81	15.08
7. Large male-headed low-education family—"working poor family"[g]	21.08	9.3

[a] The characteristics are: black, female head, age 35–45, education 9–12, family size 5, Northeast, central city, head worked 1–13 weeks part time, no spouse, private household.

[b] The characteristics are: black, male head, age 35–45, education 0–8, family size 8, South, rural, head worked 40–47 weeks full time, spouse a nonworker, farm worker.

[c] The characteristics are: black, male head, age 35–45, education 0–8, family size 7, West, rural head worked 27–39 weeks full time, spouse worked 14–26 weeks full time, farm laborer.

[d] The characteristics are: white, male head, age 16–21, education 12–16, family size 1, Northeast, central city, head worked 1–13 weeks full time, no spouse, laborer.

[e] The characteristics are: white, male head, age 45–55, education 9–12, family size 6, North Central, rural, head worked 50+ weeks full time, spouse worked 48–49 weeks part time, farmer.

[f] The characteristics are: white, male head, age 65+, education < 8, family size 2, North Central, central city, head worked 0 weeks, spouse nonworker, craftsman.

[g] The characteristics are: white, male head, age 35–45, education 9–12, family size 8, South, central city, head worked 50–52 weeks full time, spouse worked 14–26 weeks full time, laborer.

poor by both definitions—about .71, .45, and .50, respectively. More-over, the probabilities of members of each of these family types being poor are very similar for the two definitions. The similar probabilities for female heads are consistent with the previous observation that female headship per se has a bigger effect on *EC* poverty status than on *CY* poverty status that just about offsets the small effect of work status on *EC* poverty status. Similarly, the greater effects on *EC* poverty status of educational attainment and family size tend to offset the smaller effects of being a farm worker for members of the large southern rural and the migrant worker families.

Perhaps even more interesting than these similarities, however, are the differences between the *EC* and *CY* measures in the probabilities of being poor for members of the other four family types. The most striking difference is in the probabilities of a single young student being poor by the two definitions. Whereas the probability is approximately .40 that such a person will be poor by the *CY* measure, it is virtually zero by the *EC* measure. Low income for members of this group is clearly a temporary phenomenon. Moreover, it reflects a voluntary choice to postpone consumption now in order to enhance future consumption. Hence, the *EC* measure seems to reflect the generally accepted judgment that the low income of these individuals is not nearly as pressing a social problem as the low incomes of other members of society.

The case of the middle-aged midwestern farm family is similar in some respects to that of the student. First, the probability that members of this family type will be poor in earnings capacity is much lower—.02 versus .21—than the probability that they will be income poor. Second, the relatively low income of some members of this group is attributable, at least in part, to their preference for farm life vis-à-vis town or city life. That is, many members of this group have estimated earnings capacities that exceed their actual incomes. How many of them could actually earn more if they left the farm now and searched for jobs in towns or cities is less clear. Even though our estimates of earnings capacity do not take account of the effect of particular kinds of previous job experience on current earnings abilities, it seems clear that at least a portion of the observed current income poverty of farmers is voluntary.

As with the middle-aged farm family type, there is also some ambiguity in accounting for the different probabilities of being poor for the elderly couple type. On the one hand, the lower probability of the elderly being counted among the *EC* poor than among the *CY* poor—.04 versus .15—is certainly attributable, at least in part, to the greater consumption of leisure by the aged than by the rest of the population. On the other hand, as noted above, the estimates of earnings capacity do not adequately reflect health disabilities among those over age 65 and do not reflect at all labor market discrimination against the aged.

While the probability of being counted among the *EC* poor is much lower than the probability of being counted among the *CY* poor for the student, farm family, and elderly couple types, it is much higher—.21 versus .09—for the working poor type. The reason is quite clear. Whereas *CY* depends directly on how much heads and spouses actually work, *EC* does not. Thus, while a strong attachment to the labor force reduces the probability of being poor in *CY* terms to a very low level, the probability of being among the *EC* poor depends on the relative ability to generate income. Many working poor families not classified among the *CY* poor earn more than other families because they more fully utilize their earnings capacity.

CONCLUSION

In this paper, we have compared and contrasted the composition of the *EC* poor with that of the *CY* poor. To the extent that our estimate of *EC* is a superior indicator of economic status, use of the *CY* measure of economic status *understates* the proportion of the poorest 11 percent of the total population who are black, who live in very large families, and who live in households with strong attachments to the labor market. Similarly, the *CY* measure *overstates* the proportion who are farmers, who are old or very young, who live alone, and who live in families with no workers. Analyzing the composition of *CY* poverty on a household rather than an individual basis exacerbates these under- and overstatements. These differences in composition between the *EC* and *CY* poor hold for both the nonaged population and the total population.

In addition, the socioeconomic and demographic determinants of *EC* and *CY* poverty were examined. Not surprisingly, the effect of work status on poverty status was found to be much weaker for the *EC* than for the *CY* measure. Similarly, holding work status constant, female headship and old age per se were found to be much stronger determinants of *EC* poverty than of *CY* poverty. Finally, when the determinants regression was used to predict the probability that members of certain stereotypical families would be poor, we found not only that AFDC female-headed families, large southern rural families, and migrant worker families had high probabilities of being poor by both measures of economic status, but also that for these stereotypical families the probabilities were virtually insensitive to the measure of economic status. In contrast, the probability of being counted among the *CY* poor is much higher than the probability of being counted among the *EC* poor for farm families, elderly couples, and particularly for independent students. Significantly, precisely the opposite is true for the working poor type family—compared to the *EC* definition, the standard poverty definition seriously understates the probability that such families will be poor.

TABLE A-1
Earnings Functions for Black and White Males and Females

Independent variables	Males		Females	
	White coefficient (t-value)	Black coefficient (t-value)	White coefficient (t-value)	Black coefficient (t-value)
Years of schooling	.0212 (3.0)	−.0088 (−.4)	−.0106 (−.7)	−.0229 (−.7)
Years of schooling^2	.0007 (3.2)	.0017 (2.8)	.0033 (6.5)	.0047 (4.3)
Age	.0711 (33.3)	.0525 (7.1)	.0479 (13.3)	.0234 (2.2)
Age^2	−.0008 (−42.6)	−.0007 (−10.0)	−.0006 (−18.1)	−.0004 (−4.0)
Age − years of schooling	.0005 (5.6)	.0004 (1.5)	.0001 (.5)	.0004 (.8)
Weeks worked				
1–13	−1.9636(−85.8)	−2.0173(−31.1)	−2.2937(−111.8)	−2.0924(−39.4)
14–26	−.8201(−44.2)	−.8324(−17.1)	−.9790(−48.0)	−.8835(−16.4)
27–39	−.4103(−27.2)	−.3742(−8.5)	−.4851(−22.6)	−.4215(−7.8)
40–47	−.2067(−13.9)	−.2563(−5.9)	−.2395(−9.8)	−.2097(−3.4)
48–49	−.1434(−7.1)	−.0970(−1.6)	+.1446(−4.0)	−.0124(−.1)
50–52	—			

Full- or part-time work
during week

Full-time	—	—	—	—
Part-time	−.9105 (−51.0)	−.9827 (−21.2)	−.9162 (−61.3)	−.8767 (−22.4)
Location				
Northeast	−.0149 (−1.6)	−.0197 (−.5)	.1292 (7.5)	.1154 (2.2)
North Central	—	—	—	—
South	−.1120 (−12.2)	−.2362 (−7.5)	−.0416 (−2.5)	−.2017 (−4.4)
West	−.0541 (−5.3)	.0132 (.3)	−.0299 (1.6)	−.0316 (−.5)
SMSA suburb	.1542 (18.7)	.2664 (7.1)	.1790 (11.7)	.2647 (4.9)
SMSA central city	.0685 (8.0)	.1609 (5.7)	.1883 (12.2)	.2133 (5.2)
Nonurban	—	—	—	—
Marital status				
Not married—no children			.1243 (6.1)	−.0113 (−.2)
Not married—with children			.0524 (2.1)	−.0378 (−.9)
Married—no children			.1261 (7.8)	−.0030 (−.1)
Constant	7.2901 (96.8)	7.6699 (32.5)	7.1515 (49.0)	7.5754 (20.3)
R^2	.5252	.6068	.6026	.6337
F	1813.7819	266.8581	1498.4130	247.2347

73

REFERENCES

1. Becker, G. S. 1965. A theory of the allocation of time. *Economic Journal* 75:493–517.
2. Bernstein, B., and Giacchino, P. 1971. Costs of day care: implications for public policy. *City Almanac*. August.
3. Blinder, A. S. 1974. *Towards an economic theory of income distribution*. Cambridge: MIT Press.
4. Box, G. E. P., and Muller, M. E. 1958. A note on the generation of random normal deviates. *Annals of Mathematical Statistics* 28:610–11.
5. Garfinkel, I., and Haveman, R. 1974. Earnings capacity and the target efficiency of alternative transfer programs. *American Economic Review* 64:196–204.
6. Krashinsky, M. 1973. Day care and welfare. U.S. Congress, Joint Economic Committee. *Studies in Public Welfare*. Washington, D.C.: Government Printing Office.
7. McClung, N., Moeller, J., and Siguel, E. 1971. *Transfer income program evaluation*. Working Paper 950-3. Washington, D.C.: Urban Institute.
8. Mincer, J. 1974. *Education, experience, and earnings*. New York: National Bureau of Economic Research.
9. Morgan, J., ed. 1974. *Five thousand American families—patterns of economic progress*. Vols. 1 and 2. Ann Arbor: University of Michigan, Institute for Social Research.
10. Morgan, J., David, M., Cohen, W., and Brazer, H. 1962. *Income and welfare in the United States*. New York: McGraw-Hill.
11. Orshansky, M. 1965. Counting the poor: another look at the poverty population. *Social Security Bulletin* 28, No. 1:3–29.
12. Weisbrod, B., and Hansen, W. L. 1968. An income–net worth approach to measuring economic welfare. *American Economic Review* 58:1315–29.

IV

Aspects of the Variability
of Family Income

THAD W. MIRER

INTRODUCTION

Even a cursory examination of families' incomes shows how greatly they vary from one time to another. Part of this variation can be attributed to fluctuations in the economy or to changes in families' real income-earning capacities, but much of it appears to be due to chance occurrences at the individual level. For some investigative purposes this apparent random variability can be ignored, but for many it should not be.

This paper brings together some evidence and arguments relating to the phenomenon of income variability. The study examines the distributional incidence, explores some effects on attitudes, and notes some methodological implications of this variability.

Year-to-year changes in the income status of individuals were analyzed by Friedman and Kuznets [5] and were important in Friedman's [4] study of the consumption function. The flourishing literature on the permanent income theory of consumption has led to ingenious techniques for abstracting from, or ignoring, transitory income.

Students of the distribution of income have sometimes noted the variability of family incomes over time. Using a panel of Wisconsin taxpayers, David [3] examined the relative income status of individuals, and measured the variation of income among individuals in occupation–

Reprinted by permission of the Institute for Social Research and author from *Five Thousand American Families—Patterns of Economic Progress*, vol. 2, ed. J. Morgan, pp. 201-12. Ann Arbor: Survey Research Center, 1974.

age groups as well as the variability of individuals' incomes over time. Recently, other researchers have looked directly at this phenomenon. Kohen, Parnes, and Shea [8] used panel data for two and three years to calculate "relative instability coefficients" for individual men in different age groups, and examined the instability characterizing various subgroups; in addition, they tried to isolate the sources of the instability. Benus [2] used five-year reports from the Panel Study of Income Dynamics, and analyzed income instability and factors associated with it.

A problem with these studies is that they tend to lump together all changes of income in a single measure of instability. For purposes of distributional analysis, it may be useful to consider separately three types of income change: (1) change due to fluctuations in the economy and inflation, (2) change due to real growth in family income-earning capacity, and (3) change due to a host of economic phenomena of a chance or ephemeral nature—illness, unusual overtime, or job shifting, to name a few. The analysis of "income variability" in this study relates only to the effects of the third group of factors.

I. ANALYSIS

A. A Measure of Income Variability

To abstract from income change of the first type, consider a relatively short sequence of time periods characterized by steady-state growth conditions on the aggregate level. Let the ith family's income be determined as

$$(1) \qquad\qquad y_i(t) = x_i \cdot (1 + g_i)^t \cdot e^{u_i}$$

where
  $y_i(t)$ is the income received in period t,
  x_i is a never-observed income base,
  g_i is a real rate of growth,
  u_i is a random variable with mean zero.

The family's income is composed of two components: $x_i \cdot (1 + g_i)^t$, the family's permanent income,[1] which is growing at rate g_i; and e^{u_i}, a

---

[1] In this interpretation, a family's permanent income may be continuously changing. No substantive or semantic problems are created by this interpretation, and it is fully consistent with Friedman's [4] seminal discussion.

multiplicative transitory component which depends on the random term u_i.

The real growth rate, g_i, may vary among families because of life-cycle reasons: families' earnings tend to grow rapidly in early years, and then grow more slowly with increasing age—even decreasing before retirement. In addition, among families of the same age, growth rates will vary according to occupational and human capital investment patterns.

A comparison of the income variability of different families reduces to a comparison of the probability distributions of the random determinant, u_i. If each u_i were assumed to be normally distributed, then the standard deviation σ_{u_i} would completely characterize each distribution. This standard deviation is adopted as the measure of each family's income variability in this study.[2] If the standard deviations, σ_u, for two families are equal, they are said to be subject to the same "variability." Of course, being subject to the same variability does not necessarily mean being equally well off; this is a matter to be considered below.

In an unchanging steady-state macroeconomic environment, chance variations in income are reasonably viewed as multiplicative rather than additive, especially for purposes of comparison among families. For example, one week of unemployment decreases the actual incomes of all workers affected in proportion to their permanent incomes.

This simple model will be used to examine the effects of income variability in a panel sample of the United States population for the years 1967–1969, which were years of full employment and fairly steady growth. After deflating income items by changes in the Consumer Price Index, and restricting the analysis to these years, the working presumption is made that the data reflect family income experiences in a steady growth economy. Taking natural logarithms of equation (1),

(2) $$\log y_i(t) = \log x_i + t \cdot \log(1 + g_i) + u_i$$

or

(2′) $$\log y_i = \alpha_i + \beta_i \cdot t + u_i.$$

Fitting this trend line to the data separately for each family provides estimates of the three dimensions of income: $\hat{\alpha}_i$ is permanent income

---

[2] For distributions other than the normal, σ_u does not fully describe what one would want to mean by variability; indeed, for some distributions the standard deviation does not exist. These problems are not too pressing, however, for the empirical sections of this paper.

level (when $t = 0$), $\hat{\beta}_i$ is a measure of the income trend ($\beta_i \simeq g_i$ for small g_i), and $\hat{\sigma}_{u_i}$ is the measure of income variability.

The data used are the first three years of the Panel Study of Income Dynamics. To focus on units with relatively continuous income-earning capacity, those families in which the head or the head's spouse changed over the course of the sample period are excluded. The primary income concept used here is pretax total money income, which includes all family members' labor earnings, transfer payments, and income from capital. Capital gains and losses are not included.

Equation (2') is fitted separately for each family, using ordinary least squares with three income observations (1967–1969).[3] The resulting estimates are subject to considerable error but nonetheless provide useful measures. These estimates of permanent income level (for the middle year, 1968), trend, and variability are then added to the basic data set containing three years' observations on approximately 3,700 stable families.

B. The Incidence of Income Variability

The measure of variability developed above is useful for comparing the relative uncertainty attached to the income anticipations of different families. Families whose random determinants have the same probability distribution face equal prospects of having their observed incomes be any particular proportion of their permanent incomes. Families whose random determinants have a higher variability face greater chances of having their actual incomes be much greater or much less than their permanent incomes.

Income variability may reasonably be regarded as a burden to families—the greater the variability, the greater the burden. On theoretical grounds, the common behavioral assumption that people are averse to risk suggests that most families would prefer to have their incomes come in a steady flow, rather than with some random variation around the same flow. On practical grounds, having a variable source of income

---

[3] For each family, estimated permanent income for 1968 is the midpoint of the fitted line and is equal to the geometric mean of the three income observations. The measure of income variability, $\hat{\sigma}_u$, is taken to be the root mean square error around the least-squares line. More efficient estimates of σ_u could be obtained if one knew the actual rate of growth of families' incomes. Holbrook and Stafford [6] attempted this in a consumption study using extraneous information on the growth of class incomes. Of course, this is not "knowing" the growth rates, and such an ad hoc procedure has unknown effects.

makes it more difficult to plan long-term family finances and to contract
debt obligations; this is especially so for families with low permanent
incomes.

How is the burden of variability distributed among income receivers?
One approach to this question is to relate income variability to permanent income level. For this analysis, families were grouped into income
classes, and the mean variability measure for each class was computed.
This procedure was repeated for three definitions of income: (1) total
family income, (2) the sum of the head's and the spouse's labor income,
and (3) the head's labor income. Table 1 shows these results.

On the average, the measure of variability of total family income
decreases as the level of permanent income increases up to $15,000 or
so; above this level, the measure of variability increases with income
(for more broadly-defined income classes). In assessing these results, it
should not be forgotten that there is wide variation among families in
each income class.

When the sum of the head's and the spouse's labor income is

TABLE 1
Income Level Incidence of Variability

Permanent income class	Variability		
	Total family income	Head and spouse labor income	Head's labor income
$ 0–999	.186	.407	.378
$1,000–1,999	.167	.221	.214
$2,000–2,999	.139	.172	.173
$3,000–3,999	.130	.127	.121
$4,000–4,999	.117	.101	.091
$5,000–5,999	.108	.089	.081
$6,000–6,999	.093	.086	.078
$7,000–7,999	.077	.069	.062
$8,000–8,999	.083	.069	.059
$9,000–9,999	.074	.063	.055
$10,000–10,999	.064	.063	.051
$11,000–11,999	.074	.056	.060
$12,000–12,999	.066	.054	.049
$13,000–13,999	.061	.059	.058
$14,000–14,999	.072	.068	.069
$15,000–19,999	.064	.059	.074
$20,000–25,000	.084	.073	.069
Above $25,000	.095	.056	.059

examined, the measure of variability first decreases then remains level—
or wobbles a bit—as permanent income increases. When only the head's
labor income is examined, the pattern of variability is similar to that for
combined labor income of head and spouse, but the variability is nearly
always smaller in magnitude—especially for families with incomes below
$10,000. This finding suggests that the spouse's job-holding behavior is
not predominantly an offset to current diminutions in the head's income.
Rather, it seems that the spouse's jobholding is independent of the
head's, or possibly that it serves as an offset but with some lag.

When either labor income variability pattern is compared to that for
total family income, the patterns are found to cross. For low-income
levels, total family income is less variable than total labor income; for
these families, transfer payments (including unemployment insurance)
help to dampen the variability of income. For high-income families
(above $20,000), total income is more variable than labor income; in this
range, property income, which is highly variable, accounts for the
difference.

The reported results were also analyzed for three subgroups of the
sample: families with heads aged 25–44, 45–64, and 65 and over. This
was done in order to see if the pattern was caused by differences in
variability relating to age or life-cycle status.[4] The patterns reported for
the entire sample also held for each of the subgroups for incomes up to
$15,000 or $20,000. Above this level, sample size does not permit useful
disaggregation.

The welfare implications of the relation between variability and level
of permanent income are interesting to consider. Measures of the
distribution of permanent income are recognized to be useful indicators
of the distribution of welfare. But, if income variability leads to a
welfare loss, and if this burden is distributed as indicated in Table 1,
then the distribution of welfare is even more inequitable than one would
have determined simply from looking at the distribution of income
levels.[5]

---

[4] The mean variability in the two older groups are about equal, while that for the
youngest groups was somewhat smaller. For the families with heads aged 18–24, which are
not analyzed here as a special subgroup, the mean variability was higher than for other age
groups.

[5] In this comparison, "inequitable" means that low-income families are relatively worse
off. Given the U-shaped incidence of the variability of total income, the Lorenz curve of
the utilities derived from permanent income anticipations would cross that derived from
the level-plus-variability anticipations. The relative inequality in these two states is
ambiguous, if one measures inequality by the Gini coefficient.

C. Attitudinal Effects of Income Variability

Behavioralists have given considerable attention to the direct effects of attitudes on economic behavior. One may expect, however, that the experience of income variability has important feedback effects on persons' attitudes regarding their economic affairs.

We investigate these effects on three indexes of attitudes: (1) sense of personal efficacy, which is intended to identify the respondent's satisfaction with himself and confidence about his future, (2) trust (or hostility), which is operationalized by the respondent's self-assessment of trust in others, tendency to get angry easily, and sensitivity to what others think, and (3) aspiration, which includes both personality measures and future employment plans. High scores indicate that the respondent (usually the family head) has positive feelings of personal efficacy, trusts other people and the economic environment, and has strong ambitions to improve his economic situation.

As an exploratory analysis of one part of what must be a very complex behavioral system, respondents' attitudes as expressed in 1970 are related in linear regressions to three important dimensions of their families' previous income experience: level (permanent income in 1968), trend, and variability. The results are reported in Table 2, for families with permanent incomes less than $25,000.

Level and variability have statistically significant effects on most of the attitude measures, but the regression results hardly stand as a model of attitude formation. The causal direction, of course, is particularly difficult to prove. Yet, it seems quite reasonable that persons' income experiences do shape the way they approach income-earning activities, and the evidence supports this. In particular, variability seems to be a psychological burden as well as an economic one.

High levels of permanent income are associated with increased feelings of efficacy and trust, but decreased ambition. A higher trend (rate of growth of income) has the same effects as a high permanent income level—increased feelings of efficacy and trust, and decreased ambition. On the other hand, the higher the degree of income variability (uncertainty), the lower the sense of efficacy and trust and the higher ambition. Evidently, experiencing variability makes people feel alienated, but it also makes them try harder.

When these regressions are repeated for the three life-cycle subgroups noted above, the results conform closely to the overall behavior. Variability was negatively but insignificantly related to efficacy, while positively and significantly related to trust and ambition for all cases

TABLE 2
Attitudinal Regressions

	Dependent variable		
	Efficacy	Trust	Ambition
Constant	2.670*	1.901*	2.807*
	(.059)	(.044)	(.057)
Permanent income	.104*	.058*	−.024*
	(.006)	(.004)	(.006)
Trend	.247*	.136	−.138
	(.109)	(.081)	(.107)
Variability	−.135	−.517*	.978*
	(.233)	(.173)	(.228)
R^2	.09	.06	.01

Note: Parentheses contain standard errors. An asterisk (*) indicates an estimated coefficient which is significantly different from zero, using a 0.05 significance test. The variable means are:

Efficacy   = 3.4

Trust   = 2.3

Ambition   = 2.7

Permanent Income = 7.29 ($ thousand)

Trend   = .063

Variability   = .10

except one, in which significance was lacking for the oldest group. The sign and significance patterns were similar to the overall relations for permanent income level and trend.

D. Implications of Income Variability for Distributional Analysis

If a random component model such as equation (1) describes the essence of the short-run determination of family income in a steady state, then investigators of changes in the distribution of income must be aware of certain methodological implications. For example, an appreciation of the various causes of income change, including random variability, is necessary for the analysis of the dimensions of the poverty problem and for the evaluation of various solutions.

In comparing the poverty populations in 1965 and 1966, Terrence

Kelly [7] found that 35 percent of persons who were poor in 1965 were not poor in 1966. Reportedly, this finding was interpreted by policymakers to mean that the poor can work themselves out of poverty, and therefore that there is little need for special antipoverty programs.[6] However, this much gross flow past the poverty line can be predicted to be due simply to random fluctuations, with no real change in families' income-earning capacities. This suggests that it remains a reasonable task for the nation to increase the permanent incomes of poor families, by special programs or by other means.

To see how a prediction of gross flows across the poverty line can be made from the random component model, consider a comparison of incomes for families in "before" and "after" periods t_b and t_a, letting all $g_i = 0$ and assuming that each u_i is normally distributed and not autocorrelated. In addition, assume that permanent income (x_i) is lognormally distributed in the population and that each family is subject to the same variability. In the two periods, each family's incomes are determined according to

$$\text{(4)} \qquad \log y_i{}^b = \log x_i + u_i{}^b$$

$$\text{(4')} \qquad \log y_i{}^a = \log x_i + u_i{}^a$$

with $\sigma_u{}^2 \equiv \sigma_{u^b}^2 = \sigma_{u^a}^2$ being equal for all i. In the population,

$$\text{(5)} \qquad \text{Var}(\log y) \equiv \text{Var}(\log y^b) = \text{Var}(\log y^a) = \text{Var}(\log x) + \sigma_u{}^2.$$

In period b, $\log y^b$ has a normal distribution among families, and likewise for $\log y^a$. Therefore, $\log y^b$ and $\log y^a$ have a bivariate normal distribution with positive covariance, and

$$\text{(6)} \qquad \rho(\log y^b, \log y^a) = \frac{\text{Var}(\log x)}{\text{Var}(\log y)} .$$

Two parameters need to be determined to make the prediction: the correlation coefficient (ρ) between log values of successive years' incomes, and the relative poverty line. Friedman [4] cites studies indicating that ρ is likely to range between .8 and .9; here, .85 is taken as a reasonable value for this parameter. In 1965, 13.9 percent of all families and 17.3 percent of all persons were poor; for convenience, the poverty line is taken to be that income which defines 15.9 percent of the population as poor.

From tabulations of the bivariate normal distribution [11], the proba-

---

[6] This interpretation is not Kelly's—his own view of the need for antipoverty programs is just the opposite.

bility of escaping poverty in period t_a after having been in poverty in period t_b is found to be .335—nearly the same as actually occurred in 1966, according to Kelly. The point to be made is not that the simple model used here fully accounts for the observed facts, but that much of the movement into and out of poverty is due to transitory forces rather than permanent changes in families' income-earning capacities.

A related observed phenomenon is predictable from the simple income variability model: when the inequality of the distribution of income is calculated on the basis of multiyear total income for families, it is found to be less unequally distributed than any one year's income.[7] Income variability also presents special problems to investigators wishing to analyze year-to-year changes in the distribution of income.[8]

II. SUMMARY

(1) Using the standard deviation of the random determinant of income as a measure of instability, we find that families with the lowest income have the greatest instability.

(2) The variability in head's income is smaller than the variability in the income of the head and wife, suggesting that income of the wife does not offset transitory changes in the husband's income.

(3) The variability of total income is less than that of labor income for low-income families while the reverse is true for those with high incomes.

(4) Although a full model of attitude formation has not been developed, we do find that both high levels of income and high growth rates are associated with increased feelings of efficacy and trust but with decreased ambition. On the other hand, greater variability may lead to a lower sense of efficacy and trust but greater ambition. Instability seems to be a psychological burden as well as an economic one.

(5) Random variability rather than permanent income changes can account for a great deal of movement into and out of poverty.

The causes of income variability have largely been ignored here; at least from the macroeconomist's point of view, the phenomenon is largely random. However, if variability does lead to a net loss in social welfare, public policy might be implemented to alleviate or shift part of this loss. Unemployment insurance is one existing response to the

---

[7] See J. Benus [1].
[8] See T. Mirer [9].

problem. Further action to help reduce friction in labor markets and to improve job information may yield benefits that would justify its costs.

REFERENCES

1. Benus, J. 1973. Dimensions of inequality. Working paper, Survey Research Center, University of Michigan.
2. Benus, J. 1974. Income instability. In *Five Thousand American Families—Patterns of Economic Progress*, vol. 1, ed. J. Morgan. Ann Arbor: University of Michigan, Institute for Social Research.
3. David, M. 1971. Lifetime income variability and income profiles. *Proceedings of the Annual Meeting of the American Statistical Association*, pp. 285–92.
4. Friedman, M. 1957. *A theory of the consumption function*. National Bureau of Economic Research. Princeton, N.J.: Princeton Univ. Press.
5. ———, and Kuznets, S. 1945. *Income from independent professional practice*. New York: National Bureau of Economic Research.
6. Holbrook, R. and Stafford, F. 1971. The propensity to consume separate types of income: a generalized permanent income hypothesis. *Econometrica*, 39: 1–21.
7. Kelly, T. 1970. Factors affecting poverty: a gross flow analysis. In *Technical studies*. President's Commission on Income Maintenance Programs. Washington, D.C.: U.S. Government Printing Office.
8. Kohen, A.; Parnes, H.; and Shea, J. 1975. Income instability among young and middle-aged men. In *The personal distribution of income and wealth*, ed. J. Smith. New York: National Bureau of Economic Research.
9. Mirer, T. 1973. The distributional impact of the 1970 recession. *Review of Economics and Statistics* 55: 214–24.
10. Morgan, J., et al. 1970. *A panel study of income dynamics: study design, procedures, available data (1968–1970 interviewing years)*. Ann Arbor: University of Michigan, Survey Research Center, Institute for Social Research.
11. Pearson, K., ed. 1931. *Tables for statisticians and biometricians, Part II*. London: University College, Biometric Laboratory.

V

The Economic Welfare
of the Aged
and Income Security Programs*

MARILYN MOON

INTRODUCTION

This paper develops a comprehensive measure of economic status for aged families. The measure attempts to capture yearly potential consumption for each aged family, consistent with a life cycle hypothesis of saving. Several important nonincome sources of economic welfare are incorporated into the resource constraint. The empirical estimates, based on the 1967 Survey of Economic Opportunity, include the distributions of aged families by current income and by the expanded measure of economic status. Both the absolute level of economic welfare and the rankings within the distribution of families are substantially different from those obtained by a current income distribution. Subsequently, the target efficiencies of eleven transfer and tax expenditure programs available to aged families are examined. Comparisons are made both among the programs and between the current income and economic welfare distributions.

Reprinted by permission of the International Association for Research in Income and Wealth and the author from *Review of Income and Wealth*, series 22, no. 3 (September 1976).

* This research was supported by funds granted to the Institute for Research on Poverty at the University of Wisconsin—Madison pursuant to the provisions of the Economic Opportunity Act of 1964, and by the Social Security Administration (contract no. PMB-74-272). The opinions expressed are those of the author, who wishes to acknowledge the many helpful comments of Glen Cain, Martin David, J. Douglas Gomery, Robert Haveman, Robert Lampman, and Eugene Smolensky.

Current money income is an inadequate measure of economic status, particularly for such population groups as the aged. For example, in-kind transfers to the aged total more than 10 percent of the size of their current money income. Net worth holdings spread over an average aged family's remaining expected lifetime would add as much as 30 percent to its current money income each year.[1] Both the absolute amount of resources and the rankings of families by economic well-being are likely to vary when a more comprehensive measure is used. Such changes can be very important for evaluating the effectiveness of government programs in terms of direct benefits to various target groups. This paper examines several nonmoney components of economic welfare in both a theoretical and an empirical framework, computes the distributional ranking of aged families arising from such a measure, and subsequently examines the target effectiveness of eleven federal programs directed at the aged.

Heretofore, studies of the distribution of economic welfare have been infrequent and incomplete. In general, research in this area has concentrated on measuring only one new component of economic welfare. For example, studies by Peter Steiner and Robert Dorfman [16], and by Burton A. Weisbrod and W. Lee Hansen [26] attempt to incorporate net worth into the definition of economic welfare. Steiner and Dorfman, concentrating on aged families, use a measure of "total receipts"— current money income plus any dissaving during the year. In contrast, Weisbrod and Hansen estimate potential consumption by converting net worth into a constant yearly annuity flow and adding this flow to current income. Another study, by Ismail Sirageldin [14], adds to current income an estimate of the value of time spent in both leisure and nonmarket productive activities.

The two most important studies on the measurement of economic status do, however, introduce several additional components. James Morgan et al. [9] discuss a number of additional aspects of economic welfare, including such nonmoney components as benefits from residing with relatives, imputed rent to homeowners, and home production. Their measure also decreases a family's measured welfare by its federal income tax liability, and adjusts for family size and composition. The second study, by Michael Taussig [18], represents the most recent and comprehensive attempt at extending the measure of economic welfare. Taussig's study brings together a number of components, including

---

[1] See, for example, U.S. President [24]; and U.S. Department of Health, Education, and Welfare, Social Security Administration [23].

those analyzed by others. He uses the net worth approach of Weisbrod and Hansen and values leisure time with a method similar to that of Sirageldin. Taussig incorporates into his measure regional differences in the cost of living, adjustments for family size, federal income, and payroll tax payments, and a method of accounting for unusual earnings fluctuations. However, since Taussig does not concentrate on the aged, he fails to capture some of the components important to this group.

I. THE MEASURE OF ECONOMIC WELFARE

A theoretical discussion of the measure of economic welfare can best begin with a standard utility function framework.[2] Resources that extend the budget constraint of a family increase its potential consumption, subject to preferences expressed through the family's utility function. Although this study examines economic welfare at only one point in time, the utility maximization problem nonetheless is consistent with a permanent-income hypothesis such as that proposed by Albert Ando, Franco Modigliani, and Richard Brumberg [1].

The Ando–Modigliani–Brumberg life cycle hypothesis asserts that utility is a function of consumption in both current and future time periods. The utility function is then maximized subject to the resources available to an individual over time. The present value of total lifetime resources (V_o) is defined by the following formula:

$$V_o = A_o + Y_o + \sum_{t=1}^{N} \frac{EY_t}{(1 + r)^t} ,$$

where

$\quad A_o$ = stock of assets at beginning of current period,

$\quad Y_o$ = current nonproperty income,

EY_t = expected nonproperty income in period t,

$\quad N$ = years of life expectancy for individual,

$\quad r$ = the rate of return on assets.

[2] A caveat about economic welfare should be made. The ideal measure of economic welfare for a family is the level of satisfaction attained as measured by its utility function. However, even if such measures were attainable, the limitations of standard consumer theory would prevent comparisons of the magnitude of one family's preferences with any other family's preferences. Neither ordinal nor cardinal rankings can be obtained. In this sense, then, economic welfare may never be truly measurable. This should not, however, be viewed as a counsel of despair. Comparisons among families by current money income are often used in distributional studies as crude approximations of economic welfare. The measure developed here can certainly improve upon a money-income ranking of individuals.

Consumption in any given time period is proportional to the present value of the total resource flow accruing to an individual over the remaining years of his life. The exact proportion of consumption in each period depends upon the age of the person, the rate of return on assets, and the form of the utility function. Consumption is expressed as

$$C_t = \gamma_t V_t,$$

where
   C_t = consumption in period t,
   γ_t = the proportionality factor for period t.

It is assumed here that as a result of the lifetime utility function, γ_t dictates an equal share of lifetime resources in each period t. Moreover, if in any time period t current nonproperty income (Y_t) is viewed as exogenous, then only assets and expected future nonproperty income can be altered to yield the appropriate level of C_t. For any one year, expectations about future nonproperty income will be reflected in the amount of assets consumed—through saving or dissaving. Consequently, the level of potential consumption (C_t), consistent with the life cycle model, can be divided into two parts:

$$C_t = Y_t + S_t,$$

where
   S_t = the portion of net worth allocated to consumption during the period.

Y_t is current nonproperty income as defined above and is assumed to be exogenous for any period t. S_t is the share of net worth that ensures that current consumption is consistent with the lifetime utility function. The determinants of S_t can be expressed as follows:

$$S_t = f(A_t, \gamma_t, EY_t, r, N).$$

EY_t influences S_t through its size and stability over time in comparison to the size of Y_t. For example, if future expected income equaled Y_t in all subsequent periods (and since consumption has already been assumed to be equal across all periods), then S_t would also be the same for all t and depend only on the size of assets and the values for life expectancy (N) and the interest rate (r). Thus, S_t could be viewed as a constant annuity. However, if EY_t were expected to decrease over time, then to maintain consumption at a constant level, S_t would have to increase. In this case, S_t would correspond to a variable annuity formulation such that the current share of assets consumed would be small relative to the share consumed in later periods.[3]

Since information about future expectations and past experience is limited, the measure proposed here may not fully capture C_t, but it should yield a reasonable approximation. Moreover, although the life cycle hypothesis was originally formulated only for current nonproperty income and net worth, this research expands the scope of the resources included. Resources that either directly provide goods or through some other means allow an individual command over goods and services can appropriately be viewed as increasing potential consumption over time. These components of economic welfare are treated in the same manner as nonproperty income, incorporating both current and expected future benefits into the resource constraint. For example, government-provided commodities, leisure time, and nonmarket-produced goods all enhance the level of utility enjoyed by a family. Thus, the measure of economic welfare (W_t) expressed here includes these and other nonincome sources:

$$W_t = \hat{C}_t = \hat{Y}_t + S_t,$$

$$\hat{Y}_t = R_t + O_t + G_t + I_t + L_t,$$

where
$\hat{C}_t$ = "expanded" current potential consumption;
$\hat{Y}_t$ = all current net inflows of resources available for consumption (except property income);
R_t = earned income;
O_t = "other" income: remainder not captured in earnings, property income, or cash transfers;
G_t = contribution of government expenditures net of taxes;
I_t = intrafamily transfers;
L_t = value of nonmarket productive activities and leisure time.

R_t and O_t appear to be the only aspects of current income included in the measure. However, G_t contains cash government transfers from current money income. Property income is not included here since it is captured in S_t of the preceding equation.

The portion of net worth assumed to be available for consumption during any time period (S_t) depends upon the size of total net worth, the

---

[3] Although the issues are not addressed here, S_t could also be negative, indicating income greater than consumption. Such a formulation might be appropriate for younger families, but S_t is implicitly assumed to be positive or zero for aged families.

expected change in the size of $\hat{Y}_t$ over time, the expected rate of return on assets, and the form of the lifetime utility function that dictates consumption over time. The more that changes over time in the separate components of $\hat{Y}_t$ offset one another, the more stable S_t becomes. Where the utility function dictates equal consumption over time and $\hat{Y}_t$ is expected to remain constant—for example, for a retired family with a fixed level of resources—S_t will also be constant over time.

II. THE EMPIRICAL ESTIMATE OF ECONOMIC WELFARE

The empirical measure of economic welfare provides somewhat less comprehensive coverage than the theoretical measure discussed above. In particular, the value of nonmarket productive activities and leisure time have been excluded. Also, several portions of G_t—direct government expenditures and some in-kind transfers and taxes—are not incorporated into the measure. To facilitate comparisons among families, the measure adjusts the level of economic welfare by family size.[4] Thus, the estimated measure of economic welfare (W_t^*) for an aged family appears as follows:

$$W_t^* = \lambda(S_t + Y_t^*),$$

$$Y_t^* = R_t + O_t + G_t^c + G_t^{k*} - T_t^* + I_t,$$

where

λ = adjustment by family size;
Y_t^* = estimated current resources for family;
G_t^c = government cash transfers;
G_t^{k*} = estimated government in-kind transfers: Medicare, Medicaid, and public housing;
T_t^* = estimated tax liability from federal income, payroll, and property taxes.

In addition, the value of Y_t^* is assumed to remain stable over time so that S_t can be expressed in a constant annuity form.[5] Following a brief discussion of the data source and the adjustment for family composition,

---

[4] The adjustment also includes a differentiation between farm and nonfarm residence.

[5] This is not an unreasonable assumption for the majority of aged families, in which all members have retired from the labor force. Pensions and other fixed transfer payments are likely to make up the bulk of current resources. Moreover, to the extent that various government transfer programs provide earnings replacement upon retirement, the sharp drop in private sources of economic welfare can be mitigated.

the following sections present the estimation procedures for each of the components.

A. The Survey of Economic Opportunity

This analysis uses a subsample of the 1967 Survey of Economic Opportunity (SEO) comprised of all families with at least one aged person. The sample includes more than 7,000 persons aged sixty-five and over in 6,300 families. Weights have been assigned to each family to yield population estimates. The survey contains information on asset and income sources as well as on a wide range of demographic variables. Therefore, the annuitized values of net worth and intrafamily transfers are estimated from the data at hand. An earlier version of the SEO containing information about public housing is matched to the 1967 survey in order to identify housing beneficiaries. For the other in-kind public transfers, separate data sources supplement the SEO.

B. Standardizing the Distributions

In order to compare families of varying size, the estimated level of economic welfare for each family is multiplied by a weighting factor. This procedure standardizes the welfare level for each family to a level comparable to the welfare of an aged couple. The weight is obtained by dividing $1,970, the 1966 poverty threshold for an aged couple, by each family's appropriate poverty threshold. For example, an aged individual's level of welfare, multiplied by a weight of 1.25, yields a level comparable to the economic welfare of an aged couple. With this adjustment, only one distribution is necessary to summarize the economic welfare of aged families of any size.

C. Net Worth

Dissaving from net worth can play an important role in raising the level of well-being of an aged family. The constant annuity formula for converting the stock of wealth to a yearly flow is consistent with a life cycle hypothesis for saving, given that other current resources are stable over time and that the family desires a constant yearly consumption pattern. Thus, the estimate for S_t uses a constant annuity formula with a 4 percent interest rate and an average life expectancy figure based on the age and sex of each aged family member and spouse.

Net worth is defined as all assets minus all debts reported by each family. Where the SEO has missing or unusable net worth information, a value is imputed for each family from a linear regression model. This model predicts net worth from socioeconomic variables of those families whose records are intact. For those living in larger extended family groups, net worth is assumed to "belong" to the nuclear family that contains the household head.[6] If the head is under age sixty-five and not the spouse of an aged person, the aged family is assumed to have no net worth.[7]

A downward adjustment in the value of home equity included in net worth reflects the problem of rationing the flow of housing services over one's lifetime so as to exhaust the full measure of value. The adjustment assumes that a private individual could contract now to sell his home in exchange for a current annuity, with the purchaser assuming control of the house upon the aged person's death. Thus, at any point in time the family would receive both the current flow of housing services and some portion of the discounted value of services that will remain after the death of the last family member.

This reduction in the value of the home is estimated from a formula based on the life expectancy of family members. The estimate approximates the difference between the value of the home to the family if it were able to consume all housing services and the smaller resulting value if it were to purchase an annuity with those housing assets expected to remain after the death of the family members. The greater the life expectancy of family members, the smaller the necessary reduction in value. This reduced value of home equity is then included in the net worth computations.[8]

D.   Cash Components

The first three components of $Y_t{}^*$ are portions of money income—earnings, government cash transfers, and "other" income. Since these components come directly from SEO data on income, they pose no substantial estimation problems. However, for those families who reside in extended family groups, some division of these components is necessary. Earnings are listed separately for each member; also, those

---

[6] An extended family is assumed to exist when there are one or more persons between the ages of 18 and 64 in the household who are not the spouses of aged persons. Aged relatives living together are considered one family unit and not an extended group regardless of their relationship.

[7] Although this is a rather arbitrary assumption, its effect will later be reduced with the estimation of intrafamily transfers, which will result in the sharing of net worth and other resources among members of the extended family.

[8] A more detailed specification of this adjustment is available from the author.

portions of cash transfers and private pensions that are retirement-oriented are assumed to accrue to the aged subfamily. The remaining portions of "other" income and unemployment insurance, workmen's compensation, and public assistance are allocated among the subunits in proportion to the size of each nuclear family within the extended unit.

E. In-Kind Transfers

The in-kind programs included in this research are the important medical transfers, Medicare and Medicaid, and public housing. Other transfers were excluded because of difficulties in identifying recipients. However, in 1967 these other transfers were small in size and would not significantly alter the final distribution of economic welfare. For the in-kind transfers included, expenditures are used as the measure of benefits, rather than using the cash value that a recipient would accept in place of the in-kind transfer. Hence, benefits identified here represent an upper bound [15].

Medicare is treated as a health insurance program for persons over age sixty-five.[9] Per capita benefits are, therefore, the amount of the insurance premium subsidized by the government, allocated among all persons *eligible* to receive payments. In this study, the eligible population consists of all persons over age sixty-five, although in actuality about 4 percent of the aged are not covered by either Part A or Part B of the Medicare program. Consequently, the insurance benefit for Medicare is calculated by dividing payments plus administrative costs of the program by the number of eligible persons. From this "gross" insurance benefit, the premium required for enrollment in Part B is subtracted. Although Medicare is a national program, Martin S. Feldstein [5] has found that real benefits vary widely across states. Hence, the value of the subsidized insurance for any aged beneficiary should be computed for the state in which he resides. Since the SEO data preclude a statewide breakdown, regional insurance values are imputed instead.[10]

---

[9] By assuming that all the aged benefit from the insurance nature of Medicare, the problem of overestimating the well-offness of those in ill health is avoided. That is, if benefits were allocated according to actual payments received, the more medical bills incurred by an individual, the better off that individual would appear to be. Certainly most persons consider themselves less well-off when they are ill, and since some of the medical costs must still be borne by the individuals, their needs rise even though their Medicare benefits increase. Thus, an aged person who is ill is likely to be less well-off than his healthy counterpart. This is particularly important since no adjustment to well-offness is made because of ill health.

[10] The benefits average $183 and range from $141 to $247. Derived from Stuart [17].

Medicaid is also estimated as an insurance program in which benefits accrue to all eligible persons. Under the general Medicaid heading, there are actually two programs for providing health care, each with different eligibility requirements. Consequently, benefits are estimated separately for those who receive Medicaid through participation in public assistance programs and for those considered "medically indigent." In 1967, the latter was the more restricted program, with only twenty-three states participating compared to thirty-seven for the public assistance portion.[11] In addition, benefits varied substantially among the states.

To obtain the insurance value for the first portion of Medicaid, payments for medical services for the group plus administrative costs of the program are divided among the Old Age Assistance (OAA) recipients. This calculation is done for each of the four census regions, since state data are unavailable. For the second group, income and asset limits used for determining medical indigence are averaged by census region. The eligible population in each region is subsequently defined as any family having income and assets under the limits and not receiving public assistance. Again, benefit payments plus administrative costs in each census region are divided by the eligible population. Thus, eight sets of per capita Medicaid insurance premiums are estimated for the two programs and four census regions.[12]

Two separate steps are necessary to obtain information about public housing benefits. First, recipients are identified by matching data from the 1966 SEO, which contains information on public housing, to the 1967 survey. The second step involves the more difficult problem of valuing the housing subsidy. One appropriate method is to measure the differences between the market value of the rental units and the rent actually paid. This research uses the methods of Eugene Smolensky and J. Douglas Gomery [21] to obtain an estimate for market value based on the 1967 statutory provisions for public housing. Units may rent for no more than 80 percent of market value and must cost tenants no more

---

[11] See O'Connor [12]. However, the lack of a Medicaid program should not be interpreted as indicating a complete lack of medical programs for the aged in a particular state. The 1960 Kerr-Mills provisions for Medical Assistance for the Aged (MAA) allowed generous federal matching grants to states to provide for medically needy aged persons. In addition, many states provided some care through public assistance programs. The programs were certainly more limited than Medicaid, but for the aged they were sometimes important sources for medical care. Where appropriate, benefits from these programs have been included.

[12] Average benefits to public assistance recipients were $309.18, while average per capita benefits to the medically needy were $209.65. Derived from U.S. Department of Health, Education, and Welfare [22].

than 20 percent of their income. These figures establish a proxy for the market rent of public housing units equal to 25 percent of the appropriate income limit for region of residence and family size. The housing subsidy for a family is therefore equal to the difference between this market value and the rent actually paid. Regional estimates capture differences among local housing authorities.

F. Taxes

An exhaustive study of tax incidence for the aged is beyond the scope of this research. Consequently, only three taxes are examined: the federal personal income tax, the Social Security payroll tax, and the residential property tax.

The incidence of the income tax is assumed to fall directly on those who are taxed. Moreover, several simplifying assumptions aid in imputing tax liabilities for each family. First, assume that all aged families file separately (even if they reside in extended family groups) and take full advantage of available tax expenditures. Aside from the tax expenditures that will subsequently be examined, not all provisions are specifically included in computing tax liabilities. In general, this study uses the simplifying assumptions of Robert E. Hall [7] and Taussig [18]. Taxable income includes earned income, dividends, interest and rental income, and the "other" income category. From taxable income, a $600 personal exemption for each family member is deducted. In addition, the standard deduction is computed as $200 plus $100 for each family member, or 15 percent of taxable income, whichever is higher. Calculations by Taussig indicate that this 15 percent figure is a better approximation of standard and itemized deductions for all income classes than the actual statutory provisions.[13] For aged families, additional calculations are necessary to include the effects of available tax expenditures. One of the three major tax expenditures—the exclusion of government transfer income—has implicitly been incorporated into the initial calculations. The remaining two are the retirement income tax credit and the extra $600 personal exemption allowed all persons over age sixty-five.

The incidence of the employer's contribution to the payroll tax for Social Security is a controversial topic.[14] While the argument has not been finally settled, this research attributes only the 4.2 percent em-

---

[13] Although there is a legal limit of $1,000 on the standard deduction, the 15 percent reduction evidently captures other provisions in the tax laws that limit the liability of persons at higher income levels.

[14] See, for example, Brittain [3] [4], and Feldstein [6].

ployee contribution on the first $6,600 of earnings (or 6.15 percent for self-employed workers in 1966) as a cost to the worker. The limited importance of this tax for the aged reduces the significance of the issue in this study.

Finally, estimates of the property tax represent only that portion assessed against residential property and ignore taxes on commercial property. Although the residential portion represents only about one-half of the revenue from the property tax, its incidence can more readily be computed. From previous studies there seems to be a consensus that taxes on residences are shifted only to the extent that the occupant bears the burden. That is, if an individual rents his home, he, rather than the owner, pays the tax.[15] Therefore, in this research we assume that the burden of the property tax falls on the occupant of the house regardless of whether that person is the owner or the renter. The actual burden of the tax is estimated separately for each census region. For homeowners, a percentage of the value of the home, ranging from .8 to 2.2 percent, is assessed. Taxes for renters are estimated as a percentage of rental payments.[16] While these estimates fail to pick up the higher burden of property taxes found in some metropolitan areas, the regional break-downs provide some meaningful property tax variations.

G.   Intrafamily Transfers

Nearly 30 percent of all aged families live with relatives in extended family units, often for economic reasons [10]. Although the potential importance of such living arrangements is undeniable, the lack of guidelines for allocating potential welfare gains or losses to the aged from such living arrangements has hampered work in this area. The estimation procedure used here attempts to compute a conservative value for such transfers.

Because intrafamily transfers depend upon the economic positions of both the younger and older subunits relative to their needs, estimation of the value of such transfers uses the welfare measure derived thus far for each family. Two assumptions dictate the form of the transfer equation. First, it is assumed that the highest priority of the extended family is to ensure all its members a subsistence level of consumption. For those extended families whose total welfare is less than or equal to a

---

[15] An exception is the portion of the tax that is charged against the land. This would not be shifted to the renter, but since this portion is usually less than 10 percent of the tax, it will be ignored [11].

[16] Derived from U.S. Bureau of the Census [19] and U.S. Congress, Joint Economic Committee [20].

subsistence standard (poverty threshold), this assumption indicates that the welfare ratios are equalized. Everyone in the extended family shares equally the burden of too few resources. Second, for families with resources greater than subsistence, transfers to the "needy" subfamily are assumed to rise as the level of total economic welfare rises, but somewhat less than proportionally. For example, an elderly person residing with relatives would benefit from their higher levels of economic welfare, but it seems unlikely that the family would ensure the aged relative a proportional share of all its resources. Thus, when total family welfare is high enough to allow each nuclear family a welfare ratio greater than one, the needy subfamily is still subsidized and assured a welfare ratio greater than or equal to one, but its welfare ratio remains less than that of the "donor" subfamily.

In the estimation procedure, the "donor" is always the nuclear family with the higher welfare ratio. The higher the total extended family's welfare ratio and the higher the welfare ratio of the recipient nuclear family, the greater the allowed differences between the welfare ratios. To achieve this, the equation for equalizing the welfare ratios uses a weighting function, δ:

$$I_{12} = \delta \left(\frac{p_2(W)}{p_1 + p_2} - W_2 \right),$$

where

$$\delta = \begin{cases} 1 & \text{when } W - p_1 - p_2 \leq 0, \\ \dfrac{f_1 - f_2}{f_1 + f_2} & \text{when } W - p_1 - p_2 > 0; \end{cases}$$

I_{12} = intrafamily transfer from subfamily 1 to subfamily 2;
W = total level of economic welfare for extended family;
W_i = that portion of the welfare (in dollars) attributable to subfamily i;
p_i = the poverty threshold for subfamily i;
$f_i = W_i/p_i$, the welfare ratio.

The final effect of intrafamily transfers is to increase or decrease the level of welfare for an aged family, depending upon whether the family is the recipient or the donor of the imputed transfer. The allocation procedure used here is a purely judgmental and synthetic relationship. However, it is consistent with the small amount of information available on such transfers [2]. Aged persons tend to live with relatives for economic reasons, preferring otherwise to remain independent [9]. Thus, it seems reasonable to assume some sharing of resources, particularly among those who have very little. Moreover, the fraction δ tends to fall rapidly as *W* increases, resulting in a conservative estimate of the transfer among families.

III. THE DISTRIBUTION OF ECONOMIC WELFARE

This section compares the distribution of economic welfare to the distribution of money income. Before the distributions are presented, Table 1 illustrates the relative size of the various components estimated here.[17] The small size of earnings relative to both cash transfers and the net worth annuity is particularly interesting. In addition, the size of transfers often thought to be oriented exclusively at low-income groups, such as public assistance, public housing, and Medicaid, is small in comparison to the size of other government transfers. While intrafamily transfers overall tend to be offsetting, the absolute value of these resource flows is substantial. In general, the nonmoney-income components of economic welfare are very important to the aged.

Table 2 presents the changes in the distribution as additional components are added. The intermediate distribution in column 1 includes only the cash-income components and the annuity value for net worth. A comparison with current money income clearly illustrates the effect of the annuity calculation.[18] The number of families with total resources under $2,000 drops by fifteen percentage points with the substitution of the annuity for interest income, while the median dollar value rises by more than $1,000. The addition of in-kind transfers also has a substantial effect on the distribution, largely as a result of the assumption that all aged families receive Medicare benefits. Again, the number of families with resources below $2,000 drops substantially, and the median rises by

[17] However, these figures do not necessarily correspond to the appropriate national aggregates. The totals computed here are based on the size of each component after its conversion into "equivalent" dollars as described earlier. Moreover, the definition of aged families differs in two respects from the norm, thus affecting the distribution of income. In order to be consistent with the measure of economic welfare, income of aged families living with relatives is computed separately for the aged subunit. Also, most studies count as aged only those families where the head is over age sixty-five. The definition used here includes any family where head *or* spouse is sixty-five or over.

[18] It is important to note from the outset that order does matter in assessing the distributional consequences of a particular component. That is, the annuitized value of net worth appears to have a different effect on the distribution depending upon whether or not cash transfers are already included. Therefore, while a reasonable ordering for the inclusion of these components has been attempted, care should be taken in the interpretation of marginal changes in the distribution.

TABLE 1
The Components of Economic Welfare

Component of economic welfare	Size (in thousands of dollars)	Average per aged family	Percentage of families receiving	Average per recipient family
Money income components				
Earnings	$16,372,026	$1,210.00	32.68	$3,700.30
Other income	2,747,659	203.07	16.87	1,279.58
Cash transfers				
Social Security	14,866,341	1,098.72	81.13	1,354.27
Public assistance	1,091,108	80.64	10.30	782.91
Government pensions	2,925,992	216.25	10.58	2,043.95
Veterans' benefits	1,491,749	110.25	9.38	1,175.37
Unemployment and Workmen's Compensation	132,068	9.76	2.80	348.57
Annuity	34,638,336	2,560.00	81.62	3,125.00
In-kind transfers	5,168,689	382.00	100.00	382.00
Medicare	3,599,140	266.00	100.00	266.00
Medicaid	1,503,926	111.15	31.90	348.43
Public housing	65,623	4.85	1.28	378.91
Taxes				
Income	2,045,421	151.17	19.23	786.12
Social Security	538,653	39.81	30.50	130.52
Property	1,825,143	134.89	78.05	172.71
Intrafamily transfers				
Positive	3,457,880	255.56	15.28	1,672.49
Negative	4,040,778	298.64	12.56	2,377.72

Note: Size figures do not necessarily correspond to national aggregates. See note 17.

almost $400. The inclusion of tax liabilities has little effect on those families at the bottom of the distribution. However, the median falls as families at higher levels incur the tax liabilities. Intrafamily transfers reduce both tails of the distribution and raise the median slightly. About 4 percent fewer families have resources below $2,000 as a result of these intrafamily transfers.

Substituting the final measure of economic welfare (column 4) for money income obviously moves a large number of families above the $2,000 line. However, it is more significant that even with all the increased opportunities to move up, almost 14 percent of the aged families remain below $2,000. It is important to note that although the Orshansky poverty threshold measure of $1,970 for an aged couple is designed for use with a current income measure of economic status, the

TABLE 2
Distributions for Current Income and the Intermediate and Final Measures of Economic Welfare

Income or welfare class	(1) $Y_t^e + O_t + G_t^c + S_t$	(2) Column 1 $+ G_t^{k*}$	(3) Column 2 $- T_t^*$	(4) Column 3 $+ I_t$	(5) Current money income
$-500--1	.07%	.03%	.03%	.03%	.13%
0	1.30	0	0	0	1.92
1–499	2.20	.61	6.1	.17	3.19
500–999	6.31	3.44	3.52	1.65	8.73
1,000–1,499	7.45	5.68	5.74	3.91	13.37
1,500–1,999	7.88	7.46	7.82	7.82	12.92
2,000–2,499	7.65	8.17	8.56	8.76	11.30
2,500–2,999	7.24	8.10	8.55	8.96	8.91
3,000–3,999	12.59	15.26	15.86	17.72	13.13
4,000–4,999	11.31	11.86	12.00	13.53	7.35
5,000–5,999	8.16	9.25	9.30	9.57	5.43
6,000–7,999	10.06	11.17	11.09	11.93	5.60
8,000–9,999	5.47	5.80	5.58	5.58	2.95
10,000–14,999	5.97	7.59	6.26	5.85	3.13
15,000+	5.35	5.56	5.06	4.50	1.93
Under $2,000	25.21	17.22	17.72	13.59	40.36
Under $2,500	32.86	25.39	26.28	22.35	51.66
Median	$3,743	$4,105	$3,956	$4,072	$2,427
Gini coefficient	.482	.442	.432	.398	.458

inclusion of these additional nonmoney resources still cannot raise all aged families over this bench mark.

Comparisons of the final distribution of economic welfare and money income are displayed graphically in Figure 1. Overall, the economic welfare measure lies to the right of current income, while the shapes of the distributions also differ somewhat. Moreover, as summary statistics in Table 2 for these two measures indicate, economic welfare is more equally distributed than is current income. The Gini coefficient for income is .458; that for economic welfare is only .398.[19] While including the annuity value for net worth creates more inequality, the other

[19] The Gini coefficient estimates the area between the line of equality and the Lorenz curve as a proportion of the total area under the line of equality. A decrease in the coefficient indicates an increase in the equality of a distribution.

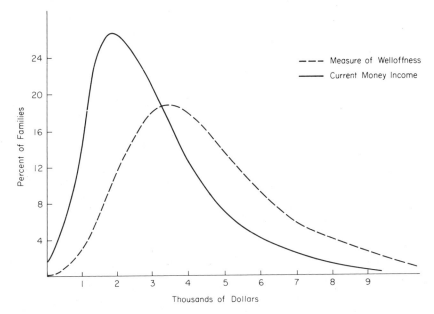

Figure 1. Relative frequency distributions.

nonincome components—taxes, in-kind transfers, and intrafamily transfers—all increase the equality of the distribution.

Table 3 indicates differences in the ranking of families within the
distribution depending upon whether current income or the economic
welfare measure is used. Both distributions are divided into deciles.
Each row of the table indicates where families in each decile of income
rank when measured by economic welfare. Families do not benefit
uniformly from the additional resources included in the economic
welfare measure. For example, only about three-fourths of the bottom
40 percent of families as measured by current income are in the bottom
four deciles of the economic welfare measure. Even those families in the
lowest 10 percent of the distribution of current income change position
substantially when ranked by economic welfare; 59 percent move to
higher decile rankings. Moreover, above this first percentile a number of
aged families fall in rank when the expanded measure is used. Thus, the
measure of economic welfare derived here affects not only the measured
level of resources available to a family, but also the equality of the
distribution and the ranking of families within the distribution.

TABLE 3
Comparison of Decile Rankings of Aged Families by Current Income and Economic Welfare

Distribution of current income by deciles	Economic welfare										Total
	1	2	3	4	5	6	7	8	9	10	
1	4.1%	1.9%	1.3%	.5%	.6%	.4%	.3%	.3%	.4%	.2%	10.0%
2	3.4	2.4	1.2	1.0	.6	.6	.5	.2	.1	.1	10.1
3	1.0	3.2	1.8	1.6	.9	.7	.3	.4	.1	.1	10.1
4	.3	1.6	3.1	1.7	1.1	.9	.4	.5	.1	.2	9.9
5	.4	.4	1.8	2.6	1.9	1.2	.7	.5	.4	.1	10.0
6	.2	—a	.5	1.7	2.3	2.1	1.4	1.1	.5	.2	10.0
7	.3	.3	.1	.6	1.9	2.3	2.2	1.2	.7	.3	9.9
8	.2	.1	.2	.1	.5	1.6	2.8	2.3	1.7	.6	10.1
9	0	.1	.1	.1	.1	.2	1.1	3.0	3.2	2.1	10.0
10	—a	0	—a	.1	.1	—a	.2	.5	2.9	6.2	10.0
Total	9.9b	10.0	10.1	10.0	10.0	10.0	9.9	10.0	10.1	10.1	

a Less than .05 percent.
b Where rows and columns do not total 10 percent, it is as a result of rounding errors.

IV. THE IMPACT OF GOVERNMENT PROGRAMS
ON THE AGED

Government transfer programs constitute fully 34 percent of the total measured economic welfare of the aged. This section examines the effects of each of these major tax expenditure and transfer programs on both current money income and the measure of economic welfare. The specific cash transfer programs included are Social Security and Railroad Retirement, government employee and military retirement programs, Veterans' Disability pensions and compensation, and public assistance. In-kind transfers include Medicare, Medicaid, and public housing. Finally, benefits from tax expenditures that are targeted directly at the aged—the double personal exemptions, exclusion of Social Security and other transfer income, and the retirement income tax credit—are also examined.[20]

The marginal contribution of each government program is obtained by "subtracting" the program from the measure of economic welfare. The difference between the resulting distribution and total economic welfare indicates the contribution of the program to each welfare class.[21] A similar procedure is used for examining the effect of each cash transfer on current income. Since tax expenditures and in-kind transfers are not included in current money income, no adjustments are made when computing the distributional effects of these programs. Comparisons with the economic welfare measure indicate how the distributional effects differ depending upon the measure used. Since for nearly every family dollars of welfare are higher than dollars of income, comparisons are based on a fixed percentage of families at the bottom of each distribution.

Several measures of "target efficiency" are used for evaluating the

[20] Tax expenditures provide benefits to aged families through a reduction in the income tax liability they face. The benefit from each tax expenditure is calculated as the difference between a family's tax liability and the liability that would exist without the particular tax expenditure. For example, to compute the incidence of the double personal exemption, tax liabilities are recalculated for each family without subtracting the additional $600 for each member over age sixty-five. This amount should be greater than or equal to the tax liability computed with the exemption. When the latter is subtracted from the former, a positive (or zero) benefit will result.

[21] Actually the process is somewhat more complicated. Since intrafamily transfers are assumed to vary by the relative size of each family's resources, these transfers are recomputed for each new distribution when a transfer or tax expenditure is subtracted. When the aged family benefits more from a program than the younger members of the extended family, the marginal changes to the distribution of welfare will be somewhat offset.

effectiveness of a program in aiding families at the bottom of each distribution. Target efficiency as defined by Weisbrod [25] refers to the "degree to which the actual redistribution coincides with the desired redistribution." The target groups used here are defined by various percentages of families at the bottom of each distribution. For example, in both Table 4 and Table 5, the first column indicates the percentage of total benefits from a transfer program received by the lowest 15 percent of families.

Any comparison of transfers must proceed with caution. The programs vary widely by size and distributional goals. As a consequence, while comparisons among the programs are of interest, no one statistic can offer conclusive evidence about their ultimate value to the aged. For example, one program might be very target efficient, but, because of its size, benefit only a small number of people. Moreover, since any one program may have multiple goals, it is difficult to rank the transfers in any meaningful way. This section compares these programs only for their effectiveness in providing benefits to those at the bottom of each distribution.

The most striking result in a comparison of Table 4 with Table 5 is the similarity in both the rankings of the transfers and the actual target efficiency measures. These findings might imply that the ranking of recipient families did not change between the two distributions. Such an explanation would seem to be valid for public assistance, for example, where benefits are both income and asset conditioned. However, Table 3 shows that substantial numbers of families do shift by decile ranking between the two distributions, making this explanation less likely for programs such as Medicare, unemployment compensation, and government pensions. Another plausible explanation is that for those families in the middle range of the income distribution whose rankings do change, benefits may be randomly distributed. One notable exception to the similarities in target efficiencies is the much higher 15 percent figure for public housing when the economic welfare measure is used. It is also interesting that while the target efficiencies of the three tax expenditures are very low, they are consistently higher for the economic welfare distribution.

Within each table, the rankings of the transfers based on target efficiency remain remarkably stable for all the measures. As would be expected, public assistance and public housing are quite target efficient. Although the Medicaid program is ranked as third- or fourth-most target efficient, its percentage efficiency is substantially lower than the figures for public assistance. Moreover, benefits are less than proportional for the Medicare program in every instance, and Social Security comes very

TABLE 4
Target Efficiency Measures by Distribution of Economic Welfare

Government program	Percentage of benefits from each program to aged families					
	Lowest 15 percent of distribution	(Rank)	Lowest 30 percent of distribution	(Rank)	Lowest 40 percent of distribution	(Rank)
Cash transfers						
Social Security	15.69%	6	30.75%	6	40.33%	5
Public assistance	67.51	1	88.71	1	93.57	1
Government pensions	16.71	5	31.65	5	39.37	6
Veterans' benefits	30.24	4	46.13	4	58.40	4
Unemployment and Workmen's Compensation	9.52	8	19.98	8	28.11	8
In-kind transfers						
Medicare	12.63	7	26.59	7	36.64	7
Medicaid	33.21	3	63.65	3	77.54	3
Public housing	61.85	2	83.97	2	91.36	2
Tax expenditures						
Double exemption	1.91	9	3.61	9	7.09	9
Exclusion of transfers	1.62	10	2.65	10	6.85	10
Retirement credit	.35	11	.85	11	1.72	11

TABLE 5
Target Efficiency Measures by Distribution of Current Income

Government program	Percentage of benefits from each program to aged families							
	Lowest 15 percent of distribution	(Rank)	Lowest 30 percent of distribution	(Rank)	Lowest 40 percent of distribution	(Rank)
Cash transfers						
Social Security	14.41%	6	30.82%	6	41.40%	6
Public assistance	70.50	1	91.68	1	94.54	1
Government pensions	25.63	5	41.69	5	49.12	5
Veterans' benefits	29.27	3	46.07	4	56.71	4
Unemployment and Workmen's Compensation	11.04	8	23.52	8	27.60	8
In-kind transfers						
Medicare	13.20	7	26.73	7	36.56	7
Medicaid	29.14	4	56.60	3	73.54	3
Public housing	33.15	2	63.37	2	76.24	2
Tax expenditures						
Double exemption	trace	9	.13	9	.30	9
Exclusion of transfers	0	10	.02	10	.11	10
Retirement credit	0	11	0	11	0	11

close to being distributionally "neutral." While neither of these two programs is aimed specifically at low-income aged families, it is nonetheless important to note that they do not in any way favor the poor. The combined effect of Unemployment Insurance and Workmen's Compensation is particularly target inefficient. Finally, although the tax expenditure programs could a priori be expected to provide few benefits to aged families at the bottom of the distributions, in no case do they target substantial benefits to even the lower *half* of either distribution.

CONCLUSION

This paper has attempted to derive a theoretical measure of economic welfare for the aged in the form of a resource constraint defining a family's yearly potential consumption. From this definition, an empirical measure of economic welfare has been developed and applied to a large sample population, yielding the distributional rankings of those aged families.

The development of a broad measure of the economic welfare of the aged provides a valuable framework for a study of the distributional impacts of government transfer and tax expenditure programs. The results from this research are compared with a current money income measure. Consequently, this work represents a first step toward a better evaluation of government policy toward the aged.

REFERENCES

1. Ando, A., and Modigliani, F. 1963. The "life cycle" hypothesis of saving: aggregate implications and tests. *American Economic Review* 53: 55–84.
2. Baerwaldt, N., and Morgan, J. 1971. Trends in inter-family transfers. Working Paper, Survey Research Center, University of Michigan.
3. Brittain, J. 1971. The incidence of Social Security payroll taxes. *American Economic Review* 61: 110–25.
4. ———. 1972. The incidence of the Social Security payroll tax: reply. *American Economic Review* 62: 739–42.
5. Feldstein, M. S. 1971. An econometric model of the Medicare system. *Quarterly Journal of Economics* 85: 1–20.
6. ———. 1972. The incidence of the Social Security payroll tax: comment. *American Economic Review* 62: 735–38.
7. Hall, R. E. 1973. Wages, income, and hours of work in the U.S. labor force. In *Income maintenance and labor supply*, ed. G. G. Cain and H. W. Watts, pp. 102–62. Chicago: Markham.
8. Moon, M. L. 1974. The economic welfare of the aged: a measure of economic status

and an analysis of federal programs. Ph.D. dissertation, University of Wisconsin–Madison.

9. Morgan, J.; David, M.; Cohen, W.; and Brazer, H. 1962. *Income and welfare in the United States*. New York: McGraw-Hill.

10. Murray, J. 1971. Living arrangements of people aged 65 and older: findings from 1968 Survey of the Aged. *Social Security Bulletin,* September, pp. 3–14.

11. Netzer, D. 1966. *The economics of the property tax*. Washington D.C.: The Brookings Institution.

12. O'Connor, J. 1971. The redistributive effects of Title XIX of the Social Security Act: a statistical study for 1968. Ph.D. dissertation, Notre Dame University.

13. Orshansky, M. 1968. The shape of poverty in 1966. *Social Security Bulletin,* March, pp. 3–31.

14. Sirageldin, I. 1969. *Non-market components of national income*. Ann Arbor: University of Michigan, Survey Research Center.

15. Smolensky, E.; Stiefel, L.; Schmundt, M.; and Plotnick, R. 1974. Adding in-kind transfers to the personal income and outlay account: implications for the size distribution of income. Discussion Paper no. 199–74. Institute for Research on Poverty, University of Wisconsin–Madison.

16. Steiner, P., and Dorfman, R. 1957. *The economic status of the aged*. Berkeley: Univ. of California Press.

17. Stuart, B. 1971. *Health care and income*. Research Paper no. 5. Ann Arbor: State of Michigan, Department of Social Services.

18. Taussig, M. 1973. *Alternative measures of the distribution of economic welfare*. Princeton, N.J.: Princeton University, Industrial Relations Section.

19. U.S. Bureau of the Census. 1964. *Property taxation in 1962*. State and Local Government Special Studies, no. 47. Washington, D.C.: U.S. Government Printing Office.

20. U.S. Congress. Joint Economic Committee. 1968. *Impact of the Property Tax: Its Economic Implications for Urban Problems*. By D. Netzer. Washington, D.C.: U.S. Government Printing Office.

21. ———. 1973. Efficiency and equity effects in the benefits from the federal housing program in 1965. By E. Smolensky and J. D. Gomery. Benefit Cost Analyses of Federal Programs. Washington D.C.: U.S. Government Printing Office.

22. U.S. Department of Health, Education, and Welfare. 1971. *Recipients and amounts of medical vendor payments under public assistance programs, January–June, 1967*. NCSS Report B-3. Washington D.C.: U.S. Government Printing Office.

23. U.S. Department of Health, Education, and Welfare. Social Security Administration. 1967. *The aged population of the United States—the 1963 Social Security Survey of the Aged*. By L. Epstein and J. Murray. Washington D.C.: U.S. Government Printing Office.

24. U.S. President. 1972. *Special analyses of the budget for fiscal year 1973*. Washington D.C.: U.S. Government Printing Office.

25. Weisbrod, B. A. 1970. Collective action and the distribution of income: a conceptual approach. In *Public expenditures and policy analysis,* ed. R. Haveman and J. Margolis, pp. 117–41. Chicago: Markham.

26. Weisbrod, B. A., and Hansen, W. L. 1968. An income–net worth approach to measuring economic welfare. *American Economic Review* 58: 1315–29.

VI

Transfer Approaches to Distribution Policy*

ROBERT J. LAMPMAN

INTRODUCTION

There are two ways to alter the pattern of economic inequality among persons. One is to modify the distribution of factor income by changing the underlying distribution of factors or the prices or employment of those factors. The second is to modify the process by which factor income is redistributed away from its recipients. This paper is about the second way. We ask how the distribution to factor owners is and can be modified as income moves from its market origins to its disposition on goods and services. At the outset, we sketch an accounting framework within which to envision this process whereby "producer incomes" are transformed into "user incomes." In later sections, we review some current proposals for additional transfers to the poor.

I. THE PROCESS OF REDISTRIBUTION

The redistributive process involves receipts and payments of both a money and a nonmoney character. It occurs via private as well as public institutions, including the employer, the government agency, the private

Reprinted by permission of the American Economic Association and the author from *Papers and Proceedings of the American Economic Association* (May 1970): 270–79.

* The research reported here was supported by funds granted to the Institute for Research on Poverty at the University of Wisconsin by the Office of Economic Opportunity, pursuant to the provisions of the Economic Opportunity Act of 1964. The author was assisted in the preparation of this paper by Benton P. Gillingham. Earlier writings by the author on this topic include [9] [10] and [11].

TABLE 1

Public and Private Transfers and Distributional Allocations Received and Paid by All Households and by Pretransfer Poor Households, 1967

		(1) All households (billions of dollars)	Pretransfer poor families	
			(2) Percentage of column 1	(3) Billions of dollars
1.	Preredistribution income (factor income net of 2 and employer-financed part of 9)	644	3	19.3
2.	Increase in factor income due to direct subsidy	1	10	0.1
3.	Reduction in market price due to direct consumer subsidy	1	10	0.1
4.	Benefits of social welfare expenditures under public programs	100	40	40.1
	a. Social insurance	37	55	16.5
	b. Public aid	9	93	8.4
	c. Veterans	7	46	3.2
	d. Other welfare services and public housing	3	50	1.5
	e. Health	8	50	4.0
	f. Education	36	18	6.5
5.	Total of 2–4	102	39	40.3
6.	Taxes, user charges, fees, and public prices used to finance 5	102	9	9.2
7.	Public transfers and distributional allocations net of 6	0	—	31.1
8.	Income after public transfer and distributional allocation (1 + 7)	644	8	50.8
9.	Privately insured benefits related to health and income maintenance	17	5	0.9
10.	Direct interfamily gifts	10	50	5.0
11.	Gifts via philanthropic institutions	3	33	1.0
12.	Total of 9–11	30	23	6.9
13.	Family and employer payments for insurance, gifts by family	30	5	1.5
14.	Private transfers and distributional allocations less 13	0	—	5.4
15.	Income after public and private transfer and distributional allocation (1 + 7 + 14)	644	9	55.8

(continued)

TABLE 1 (Continued)

		(1) All households (billions of dollars)	Pretransfer poor families	
			(2) Percentage of column 1	(3) Billions of dollars
16.	Benefits of general government activity	100	8–9[a]	8–9[a]
17.	Taxes to pay for 16	100	7	7
18.	Benefits of 16 less taxes of 17	0	—	1–2
19.	Postredistribution income (1 + 7 + 14 + 18)	644	9	56.8–57.8
20.	Allocations other than 4 or 16 through government having no redistributive impact[b]	—	—	—
21.	Allocations through private sector other than 12 having no redistributive impact			

[a] Distributed so as not to alter distribution of income. Note pretransfer poor have 8 percent of item 8 and 9 percent of item 15.

[b] Omitted on grounds that these are like private nonredistributional allocations.

insurance carrier, the private philanthrophic agency, and the family. Two types of redistributional transaction are involved; namely, transfer and what we may call distributive allocation. Table 1 (see list of items and column 1; ignore columns 2 and 3 for the moment) sketches out the elements of and offers rough estimates of the amounts involved in this process which may be said to start with subsidy to factor incomes. It continues with public subsidies to consumers, money transfers, and distributive allocations, and with private gifts, transfers, and distributive allocations. Our accounting includes the payments for pure public goods, but, in effect, excludes the benefits of those goods on the grounds that such benefits are indivisible and hence not redistributive. It also excludes those merit-want goods which are produced in the public sector but are purchased on a user-charge or benefits-received basis and hence, like most private purchases, have no important redistributive effect.

As seen in Table 1, the items which intervene between preredistribution income and postredistribution income all have a positive and a negative side. Receipts by one family are canceled out by payments made by others. Hence, items 7, 14, and 18 will be zero in value for the nation as a whole. However, an individual family may have either a positive or negative balance in any one of these items and may gain or lose in the conversion from pre- to postredistribution income. The ranking of families and the overall inequality may be markedly different in the two distributions.

There is interest in the intermediate income concepts shown in the table. For example, one might want to know how the preredistribution income is altered by the public policies reflected in items 5 and 6, and therefore look to item 8. Or, one might want to investigate the effect of private activities as indicated by items 14 and 15.

There are several conceptual issues that surround this accounting scheme. One has to do with the inclusion of nonmoney items. Can we say that the purchase by a public agency of health care for a citizen is not only an allocation but also a "distributive allocation" or "transfer-in-kind"? Does it constitute an addition to "income" for the recipient rather than (or as well as) an investment in his future productivity? My answer to these questions is yes, but I must admit that drawing the line between what is and what is not an in-kind transfer to persons is hard. The line has to do with the distinction between merit wants and social wants, which, as Musgrave puts it, turns on whether the want can be satisfied for one person exclusively. It has to do with Ida C. Merriam's definition of "social welfare expenditures" as those that are directly concerned with income security, and the health, education, and welfare of individuals and families, but exclusive of community-wide utilities and services—such as water and sewer works, urban transportation, or public recreational facilities [14, p. iii].

Another conceptual issue is: should private and social insurance for health care and income maintenance be included? Is the purchase of insurance something that should be accounted for as a simple allocation, like the purchase of postage stamps or automobiles and hence excluded from Table 1? In one view, the benefit is realized at the time pure insurance (disregarding cash values) is purchased. One buys protection against risk and gets his money's worth even though he never has a claim. Transfer or subsidy might be said to arise only if premiums are not correctly adjusted to variations in risk or to size of potential benefits. However, insurance is distinguishable from family saving, which we include here only if it is transferred from one family to another by gift. The insurance intermediary, whether it be a private company or a government agency, does something a family cannot do in pooling risk and thereby converting factor income into payments that respond to stated contingencies rather than to accumulated contributions. Moreover, insurance benefits often flow to persons quite remote from the purchasers, who may be employers or general revenue taxpayers. For these reasons, insurance benefits and contributions paid in the year are included in the accounting of distributive allocations of that year.

II. BENEFITS AND LOSSES FROM REDISTRIBUTION

Having resolved the issue of what is being redistributed and how, we turn now to the matter of who receives how much benefit and who loses how much, from redistribution. One may rank families by total monthly income and measure how the share of income received by income-bracket groups changes as we move from one concept of income to another. Thus, Gillespie [5, see Table 2] moves from factor income (roughly the same as item 1 in Table 1) to a postredistributional income which takes no account of private transfers and distributional allocations (this is approximately the same as the sum of items 1, 7, and 18). Note that he finds that the share going to those with money incomes under $3,000 is converted from 5 percent to 8 percent in the redistributive process.

A similar pattern of change is documented by Morgan, David, Cohen, and Brazer [15, see Table 3], who reranked families each time they changed income concept. They show that the degree of inequality is reduced one-fifth of the way to zero by moving from gross factor income (about the same as item 1 in Table 1) to gross disposable income (similar to item 19). They also portray a significant shift of another one-tenth of the way to zero inequality, which is associated with a reranking of families by welfare ratio; that is, adjusting for family size. A welfare ratio of unity means that a family is at the poverty line. Similarly, they show that the inequality we measure is partly a function of whether we count families "doubled-up" in one household as one or two families. Apparently relatives tend to group together in such a way as to reduce inequality below what we would observe if each adult unit were separately accounted for. It is, of course, a key matter in the study of income redistribution to know how separate factor incomes are combined into a family unit income and how persons who do not receive factor income relate themselves to others who do.

Table 4 shows the finding of Morgan and his colleagues that what they call "net transfer," which takes account of only some of the items listed in Table 1—namely, nonfamily transfers plus public school benefits, less income and property taxes (note that they find the latter to be nonredistributive) and nonfamily contributions—amounted in 1959 to 26 percent of the gross disposable income of families below the poverty line.

TABLE 2

Distribution of Families and Income, before and after Fiscal Incidence of Federal, State, and Local Government Taxes and Expenditures, by Money Income, 1960 (in percentages)

Item	Family money income brackets							
	Under $2,000	$2,000– 2,999	$3,000– 3,999	$4,000– 4,999	$5,000– 7,499	$7,500– 9,999	$10,000 and over	Total
1. Families	14	9	9	11	28	15	14	100
2. "Broad income"	2	3	4	7	27	19	39	100
3. "Adjusted broad income"	3	5	5	7	26	20	33	100

Source: W. Irwin Gillespie [5]. Line 1 from Table 11; lines 2 and 3 from Table 13.

TABLE 3
Lorenz Coefficients of Inequality for Various Units of Analysis and Measures of Income, 1959

	Families	Adult units
Gross factor income	.419	
Less: Imputed rent of homeowners		
Less: Home production		
Plus: Regular money transfers		
= Money income	.385	
Less: Federal income taxes		
= Disposable money income	.355	
Plus: Imputed rent of homeowners		
Plus: Home production		
Plus: Nonmoney and irregular transfers including food and housing provided by relatives		
= Gross disposable income	.346	
Divided by budget standard		
= Welfare ratio	.309	.346

Source: Morgan, David, Cohen, and Brazer [15]. Derived from Table 20-2, p. 315.

By making use of the findings presented in the Morgan book and in the studies by Gillespie, Orshansky, McClung, Lurie, Bridges, and others, and by reference to some preliminary findings from the Survey of Economic Opportunity, we are able to put together rough estimates of the amount of redistribution to the pretransfer poor[1] done in 1967. These estimates are reported in the right-hand columns of Table 1. They show that the whole array of public and private givings and takings raised the share of pretransfer poor families from 3 percent of preredistribution income to 9 percent of postredistribution income (see items 1 and 19). This was accomplished by public transfers (positive and negative) and distributional allocations, which raised the share from 3 to 8 percent (item 8); by private transfers and allocations, which raised it to 9 percent (item 15); and by taxes for pure public goods, which raised it by less than 1 percent, so the share remains at about 9 percent (item 19). This gain in share was accomplished by an offsetting decline in share of income on the part of the pretransfer nonpoor families.

Instead of showing how income distribution is modified by redistributive institutions with respect to those in income brackets or welfare-ratio groupings (of which poor–nonpoor is a variant) one could show income redistribution with respect to age, sex, color, region, occupation, family

[1] This means those who have money incomes below the Social Security Administration poverty guidelines before the receipt of money transfers.

TABLE 4

Specific Transfers as Percentage of Gross Disposable Income of Adult Units and Families Classified by Welfare Ratio, 1969

	Welfare ratio					
Transfer items	.0– 0.8	0.9– 1.2	1.3– 1.6	1.7– 2.2	2.3 and over	All units
ᴬ Adult units						
Nonfamily transfers	26	12	9	6	5	8
Income tax	−1	−5	−9	−11	−19	−12
Nonfamily contributions	−4	−4	−4	−4	−7	−5
ᴮ Families						
Property tax	−2	−2	−2	−2	−2	−2
Public school benefits	13	7	4	3	1	4
Net transfer	26	7	−2	−7	−18	−6

Source: Morgan, David, Cohen, and Brazer [15]. Panel A derived from Table 16-23. Panel B derived from Tables 19-5 and 19-13.

size, home ownership status, health status, labor force status, educational level, or other characteristics of income recipients. Another method of presentation is to show how a particular item, say the income tax, alters distribution among successive groupings of the population. This is the method advocated recently by the Treasury Department.[2]

Table 1 suggests the range of approaches for redistributing income to any of the above-listed groupings. These include subsidies at the factor income level and in consumer markets, public and private transfers, and distributional allocations, and, on the other side of the ledger, taxes, insurance premiums, and gifts.

It is important to know that most of these methods have been increasing in quantitative importance over the years. (Solomon Fabricant discusses reasons for this trend in [4].) Social welfare expenditures under public programs (item 4 in Table 1) have been rising 10 percent or more per year and now amount to 14 percent of gross national product. The increase in the national redistributional effort as indicated by this rise is not having a maximum impact on the number of people counted in poverty nor on the size of the poverty income gap, since many of the greatest rises have been in such nonmoney items as schooling and health care.

However, the cash benefits in this series (see the right-hand section of Table 5) have been rising in step with the total and added up to almost

[2] See Joseph W. Barr [1, especially supplementary statement on "Tax expenditure: government expenditures made through the income tax system"].

TABLE 5
Social Welfare Expenditures under Public Programs (Total, and Cash Benefits under Public Income Maintenance Programs), for Selected Years, 1940–1968

Year	Total (in billions of dollars)	Cash benefits under public income maintenance programs (in billions of dollars)					
		Total	Retirement, Disability, and Survivors	Unemployment	Temporary disability	Workmen's compensation	Public Assistance
1940	8.8	4.2	0.8	0.5	—	0.2	1.0
1950	23.5	8.7	4.3	1.5	0.1	0.4	2.4
1960	52.3	25.9	8.2	3.0	0.4	0.9	3.3
1963	66.8	32.4	24.1	2.9	0.4	1.1	3.6
1967	99.7	42.6	33.4	2.4	0.5	1.4	4.9
1968	112.0	48.2	38.0	2.4	0.5	1.6	5.7
1969	126.8						

Source: Column 1, Merriam and Skolnik [14]. For 1969, Research and Statistics Note, Office of Research and Statistics, SSA, November 12, 1969. All other columns, *Social Security Bulletin* (September 1969), p. 33, Table M-1.

$50 billion in 1968. Since the latter are the only public expenditures, other than "direct subsidies to increase factor incomes" which immediately enter into total money income, and since the poverty line is stated in terms of preincome tax total money income adjusted for family size, they would seem to have unique relevance out of all the items listed in Table 1 to the question of poverty reduction. It does seem ironic that cash benefits went up from under $25 billion in 1959 to $43 billion in 1967, while the poverty–income gap fell only from $13.7 billion to $9.7 billion.

Thirty-two percent of all households received a cash transfer in 1965; yet only about 8 percent of all households were kept out of or taken out of poverty status thereby (see Table 6). We do not have a good series on the number of pretransfer poor, but it does appear that transfers have been taking gradually increasing numbers of households to posttransfer incomes above the poverty line. We found, using 1961 Bureau of Labor Statistics' Consumer Expenditure Survey data, that transfers took 4.7 million households out of poverty in that year [9]. This is the same number counted by Mollie Orshansky [16] (see Table 6) for government transfers only, for 1965. Irene Lurie found that transfers took 6.1 million households out of poverty in 1966 [12], and we confirm that number by an independent computation of Survey of Economic Opportunity data.

The increases in money transfers have been largely directed at the pretransfer nonpoor. Of course, the number of people counted as poor has declined dramatically—from 23 percent of the population in 1959 to 12 percent in 1968—but that is apparently due primarily to rising wage rates and improved employment opportunities for low-income people.

TABLE 6

Percentage of Households Receiving Selected Transfers and Number of Households Who Would Be Counted Poor but for Transfer, 1965

Transfer item	Percentage of families receiving	Number (in millions of families) who would be counted poor but for transfer payments, out of a total of 60.4 million households
Any payment	32.3	4.7
Social security	21.5	3.6
Public assistance	4.8	.4
Other	11.2	1.1

Source: Mollie Orshansky [16, pp. 26–30].

The unemployment rate fell from a postwar high of 6.8 percent in 1959 to below 4 percent in 1966 and has stayed there since that time.

Nothing said above is meant to minimize the importance of money transfers in reducing poverty. Money transfers, public and private, added substantially to the incomes of the poor in 1967 (see Table 7). We estimate that about half of the total of $59.1 billion of such transfers went to the pretransfer poor. They cut the pretransfer poverty–income gap almost in half,[3] and provided over half of the income of the posttransfer poor.

However, money transfers tend to do more for the better-off poor than for the poorest poor. They also tend to favor small families as opposed to larger families among the poor.[4] This insight into the bias of the existing set of transfer payments has led many people to advocate new kinds of transfers aimed at children in intact families or "the working poor."

III. DISCUSSION OF NEW TRANSFER PLANS

The question is persistent, why, in a rich country, having a large and rapidly growing redistributive system, can we not make some adjustment that will simply eliminate the poverty that remains? The dimensions of the problem seem small—only about 23 million people are poor and their poverty–income gap of under $10 billion is only 1 percent of gross national product. The most direct way to eliminate poverty would be to introduce a negative income tax with guarantees at the poverty lines. If all other income were subject to a special offset tax of 50 percent up to break-even points equal to twice the poverty lines for each family size, this would cost $27 billion in benefits and income tax forgiveness over and above what we are now spending on transfers [17, p. 18]. These net benefits would go to some 88 million people, leaving the upper 120 million to pay the $27 billion on top of the taxes they are now paying.[5] Worry about subjecting working people to a 50 percent marginal tax rate—and note that we are talking not about a few

---

[3] Note that no accounting is made for the possibility that transfers may have induced a reduction in the pretransfer income of some households.

[4] To be fair about this we need to mention that public school benefits and the income tax exemption system modify this bias in money transfers [9, pp. 143 ff.].

[5] It is interesting to recall Harry G. Johnson's 1964 comments on a transfer of this amount. He said that it "may well be politically unacceptable; but it is really small potatoes as war finance goes, if war on poverty is really what has been declared" [7, p. 545].

TABLE 7
Distribution of Pretransfer Income, Money Transfer Benefits, and Posttransfer Money Income, by Household Poverty Status, 1967[a]

	Total population (billions of dollars)	Pretransfer poor		Posttransfer poor (billions of dollars)
		Percentage of total	Billions of dollars	
Pretransfer money income	520	3	15.6	7.8
2. Increase in factor income due to subsidy	1.0	10	0.1	—
4. Benefits under social welfare expenditure programs (money only)	42.6	57	24.3	8.1
a. Social insurance	33.2	53	17.7	4.4
b. Public aid	4.9	93	4.5	3.0
c. Veterans	4.5	46	2.1	0.7
9. Private insurance (money only)	10.0	5	0.5	0.2
10. Direct interfamily gifts (money only)	6.0	33	2.0	1.0
11. Gifts via philanthropic institutions (money only)	0.5	33	0.1	0.1
Subtotal of 2, 4, 9, 10, 11	59.1	46	27.0	9.4
Posttransfer money income (pretransfer money income plus subtotal above)	579.1	7	42.6	17.2
Distribution of households (percentage)	100	25		15

[a] Item numbers correspond to items in Table 1.

categorical poor but about 40 percent of the population—leads some to advocate lowering the offset tax rate to, say, 33$^{1}/_{3}$ percent, thereby raising the break-even points to three times the poverty lines, and placing the whole tax load, which would then be expanded to cover about $50 billion of net new transfers to the lower two-thirds of the population, on the upper one-third. That amount would require a near doubling of the money transfer now being done by all public and private sources. In any event, what may look at the outset like an easy problem takes on greater scope as one surveys the alternatives. Certainly, it is a major disservice to rational discourse to suggest, as many have done, that the United States could eliminate poverty if we were only willing to transfer an additional $10 billion to the poor. There is no way to get that $10 billion into the hands of the poor without spending far more than that.

Realization of this—and some sense of the gradualness of change—has prompted many to offer less radical departures. Perhaps the least radical would modify existing programs. The transfer program now paying out the most cash to the poor is Old Age, Survivors, and Disability Insurance. This could be—and likely will be—expanded, but each extra dollar in benefits tends to yield only 10 to 20 cents for the poor; these benefits do not reach the noncategorical poor; and the payroll tax puts a heavy burden on the working poor. The second largest source of public transfer funds for the poor is the categorical public assistance programs dominated by Aid to Families with Dependent Children (AFDC). We could improve the status of many of the categorical poor by setting a federal floor under the benefits, now determined by the several states. This would cost relatively little, but it would not reach many of the poor—most of the poor are not in the categories—and would exacerbate the inequity between the working poor at low earned incomes and the categorical poor at relatively high benefit levels. The only way, via transfers, to remedy that inequity is to drop the age-old principle that receipt of transfers and employability must be mutually exclusive. And one way to broach the contrary principle is to pay benefits to all children. Since most of the nonwelfare poor are in families with children, a child allowance, which is a common type of transfer in other nations, would seem to have time and place utility for the United States.

There are numerous varieties of child allowance plans, but, like all transfers, they take from some and give to others, most obviously transferring income from households without children to those with children. They also tend to alter the distribution of income among families with and without children. Benefits can be conditioned in various ways and can be financed, at least in part, by offsetting reductions in existing ways of changing disposable income such as cash transfers and the exemptions for children in the income tax. In order to see how plans differ from one another it is useful to do, as Dorothy S. Projector [18] has done, a calculation of how disposable income would change for the average family in each income bracket. Table 8 shows some of her calculations for 1967 for four plans; namely, two suggested by Vadakin [20], one by Brazer [3], and the Family Assistance Plan (FAP) recommended by President Nixon in the fall of 1969 and introduced by Congressman John Byrnes as H.R. 14173. We have added parallel calculations for 1966 for the plan recommended in November by the Presidential Commission on Income Maintenance Programs (the Heineman Commission) [17], even though their plan would pay benefits to unrelated individuals and families with and without children and hence is not a child allowance. We would like to include a wage subsidy in this comparison but do not know of a carefully spelled out plan of that type. (See Kesselman [8] for a discussion of the issues.)

The several plans, briefly sketched, are as follows. To achieve comparability, we assume, following Projector, that each plan is to be financed, to the extent new tax revenue is needed, by a surtax on personal and corporate income.

Vadakin 1: $120 per year allowance per child; retain child exemption in the income tax; finance by making allowance taxable and adding a 7.4 percent surtax on personal and corporate income.

Vadakin 2: $120 per year allowance per child; finance by eliminating child exemption and making allowance taxable. (No surtax needed.)

Brazer: $1,400 per year allowance for first child, $900 for second, $600 for third, $400 for each added child; finance by eliminating child exemptions, taxing adjusted gross income by a special child allowance tax at marginal rates around 33 percent but varying both by income and family size, reducing federal contribution to AFDC, and adding a surtax of about 6 percent on personal and corporate income.

Family Assistance Plan: Benefits restricted to families with children; $500 per year for first two persons, $300 for each additional person; finance by taxing other income by a special offset tax at a zero rate on first $720 of earnings and at a 50 percent rate beyond that, eliminating federal contribution to AFDC, adding a surtax of about 2.5 percent on personal and corporate income.

Heineman: Benefits not restricted to families with children; $750 per year for each of first two adults, $450 for each other person; finance by taxing other income by a special offset tax at a 50 percent rate, eliminating federal contribution to food stamps and to all categorical

TABLE 8

Average Amount of Change in Disposable Income for Families and Unrelated Individuals, by Total Money Income, Four Children's Benefit Plans, 1967, and Heineman Plan, 1966

Total money income	Vadakin 1	Vadakin 2	Brazer	Family Assistance Plan	Heineman
Under $3,000	$ 49	$ 47	$ 260	$ 127	$ 417
$3,000–4,999	78	30	345	75	184
$5,000–6,999	78	2	139	–9	–7
$7,000–9,999	63	–15	–132	–29	–151
$10,000–14,999	3	–30	–211	–49	–246
$15,000–24,999	–159	–59	–346	–102	–457
$25,000 and over	–845	–147	–949	–347	–1,517

Source: Columns 1–4, Dorothy S. Projector [18, Table 5]. Column 5, Nelson D. McClung [13].

125

assistance programs, adding a surtax of about 12 percent on personal and corporate income. (The latter surtax is equivalent to a surtax of 18 percent on personal income only. These surtax rates are for 1966 and would be lower for 1967.)

Table 8 demonstrates the similarity in basic design of all child allowance and negative income tax plans in changing disposable income by income bracket. The break-even points differ, ranging from around $15,000 in the Vadakin 1 plan to $5,000 in the Family Assistance Plan. The amount of gain and the distribution of that gain, as well as the amount and distribution of loss, vary among the several plans. Further insight into the variations of the plans is offered by Table 9, which shows the total increases in disposable income occasioned by the introduction of the plans. It should be noted that these estimates take no account of possible reductions in work effort nor of changes in family size or composition which might result from the plan. These increases in income, which are matched by decreases above the line, vary from a low of $1.1 billion for Vadakin 2 to a high of $8.6 billion for the Heineman plan. The net benefit to the poor also is different among the plans. The Family Assistance Plan does the most for the poor per dollar transferred and in that sense may be said to be the most intensively antipoverty plan. A proponent of child allowances has commented on this point as follows: "It will be said that a child allowance wastes money on children who are not poor. . . . A child allowance designed carefully in relation to the income tax system would waste little money. In any event, that money is well wasted that purchases a sense of its rightness. . . . [Moreover] because it is not related to income it quite avoids interfering with the incentive to work" [19]. (Note, however, the high guarantee and high marginal tax rates in the Brazer plan.) None of these plans would confine its benefits to the 23 million persons who are poor. FAP would add 14 million persons to those in benefit status, some of whom already have incomes above the poverty lines. The Heineman plan would reach 36.8 million persons in 1971, almost half of whom would not be poor in the absence of the benefits.

Deciding on how to rank these plans in terms of desirability may well turn, for each citizen, on a complex set of considerations. It may lend perspective to relate the amount that would be transferred under these plans to the amount now transferred. According to Table 7, the total amount of money transfers in 1967 was $59.1 billion. So, the largest amount listed here, the Heineman plan's cost for 1966 of $8.6 billion, is about one-seventh of that total. (The amount needed to finance that plan in 1971 is estimated to be only $6 billion.) A similar consideration is

TABLE 9

Comparison of Four Children's Benefit Plans, Based on 1967 Income, and the Heineman Plan, Based on 1966 Income

Characteristic	Vadakin 1	Vadakin 2	Brazer	Family Assistance Plan	1966 Heineman
1. Amount "transferred"[a] (billions of dollars)	2.5	1.1	7.5	2.5	8.6
2. Income level above which average change in disposable income is negative (see Table 8)	15,000	7,000	8,000	5,000	6,000
3. Effect on those without children					
a. Receive benefit	No	No	No	No	Yes
b. Pay tax	Yes	No	Yes	Yes	Yes
4. Net benefit to households with under $3,000 income (billions of dollars)	0.6	0.6	3.6	1.8	5.6
5. Increase in share (was 4.1 percent) of income going to lowest fifth of households (percent)	0.1	0.1	0.4	0.3	1.2
6. Marginal tax rates below break-even income (percent)	[b]	[b]	30–40	0–50	50

Source: On the Heineman Plan [6] [13] [17]. On the other plans, calculated from data in Projector [18].

[a] In this case, "transfer" means change in disposable income. The total amount of such change below the levels shown in line 2 is matched by an offsetting amount above the line.

[b] Surtax only.

suggested by the question: how much change in the share of income going to the lowest fifth of households would follow from each plan? The most redistributive of the plans by this measure is the Heineman plan, which would change that share from 4.1 to 5.3 percent; i.e., a 30 percent increase. (See Table 9, line 5.)

There are, then, certain broad issues to be weighed. How much total transfer, how to divide transfers between cash and in-kind, how much emphasis on children, how intensely to concentrate on poverty reduction, how high a marginal tax rate, what existing transfers should be reduced to help finance any new benefit? But even after those issues are resolved, there are numerous somewhat more technical issues to be settled. A simple family allowance plan, such as Vadakin 1 or 2, does not have to contend with some of these issues, but the other three plans discussed do. We have space here only to list some of them: (1) Should the plan have a work test associated with it, as does FAP? Should the work test apply to all adults? Should the penalty for failing to work less than full time be severe? (2) Should the income subject to the special offset tax be defined broadly (as in FAP) or narrowly (as in the Brazer plan)? Should social security benefits be included and taxed? Should work expenses and child care expenses be deductible? (3) Should the family be defined so as to leave choice as to what persons, and hence whose incomes, are to be included in calculating a family's benefits? (4) What income period should be used in determining benefits? Most negative income tax analysts have assumed a year would be the period, but public assistance administrators use a month. (5) How should a new benefit be articulated with existing public assistance programs? The Heineman proposal is silent on this point, but FAP has a complicated scheme to assure maintenance of effort while discouraging increases of relatively high benefits by the states for those in the dependent children categories. It also enforces conformity with FAP upon the states in defining income and income period, family, and resource and work tests for eligibility. It also sets maximum combined tax rates for those families simultaneously on FAP and a state benefit program. (6) How should the new cash benefit be related to in-kind benefits such as food stamps and Medicaid? If food stamps are priced inversely to income, they take on the basic characteristic of a negative tax and hence have a marginal tax rate associated with them. That marginal tax rate could combine with other tax rates to raise the overall tax rate on some families to very high levels. Should the food stamp bonus be calculated after the FAP benefit but before the state supplementary payment, or after both? The Heineman Commission urges that all food stamps be dropped and that the funds be diverted to financing their more generous negative income tax.

(7) How should the plan be administered and by whom? Should it be handled by the states or by the federal government? If the latter, should it be done by the Internal Revenue Service, the Social Security Administration, or a new agency? Brazer nominates the Internal Revenue Service; FAP points to the Social Security Administration.

Those seven questions indicate the complexity of introducing a new type of income-conditioned benefit into the existing system of transfers. Economists, tax lawyers, welfare administrators, and other scholars and experts can help to inform the debate now going on concerning President Nixon's Family Assistance Plan and alternatives to it.

Regardless of how that debate comes out, economists have more to do before we fully understand the set of changing institutions by which we can and do modify the preredistribution income, the goals of redistribution (of which poverty reduction is only one), and the consequences, costs, and benefits of such redistribution.

REFERENCES

1. Barr, J. W., Secretary of the Treasury. 1969. Statement before Joint Economic Committee of the Congress, January 17.
2. Bridges, B., Jr. 1967. Current redistributional effects of old age income assurance programs. *Old age income assurance, part 2*. U.S. Congress, Joint Economic Committee, December. Washington, D.C.: U.S. Government Printing Office.
3. Brazer, H. E. 1969. The federal income tax and the poor: where do we go from here? *California Law Review*, March, pp. 442–49.
4. Fabricant, S. 1969. Philanthropy in the American economy. *Foundation News*, September–October, pp. 173–86.
5. Gillespie, W. I. 1965. Effects of public expenditures on the distribution of income. In *Essays in fiscal federalism*, ed. R. A. Musgrave, pp. 122–86. Washington, D.C.: Brookings Institution.
6. Harris, R. 1969. "Role of taxes and grants in income maintenance." Paper prepared for meeting of the National Tax Association, October. Mimeographed.
7. Johnson, H. G. 1965. Discussion on the economics of poverty. *American Economic Review*, May, pp. 543–45.
8. Kesselman, J. 1969. Labor supply effects of income, income–work, and wage subsidies. *Journal of Human Resources*, Summer.
9. Lampman, R. J. 1966. How much does the American system of transfers benefit the poor? In *Economic Progress and Social Welfare*, ed. L. H. Goodman, pp. 125–57. New York: Columbia University Press.
10. ———. 1966. Toward an economics of health, education, and welfare. *Journal of Human Resources*, Summer, pp. 43–53.
11. ———. 1969. Transfer and redistribution as social process. In *Social Security in international perspective*, ed. S. Jenkins. New York: Columbia University Press.
12. Lurie, I. 1969. "Transfer payments and income maintenance." Staff paper for the President's Commission on Income Maintenance Programs. Mimeographed.

13. McClung, N. D. 1969. "Problems in the development of data bases for the static microsimulation of income transfer program direct effects." Staff paper for the President's Commission on Income Maintenance Programs. Mimeographed.

14. Merriam, E. C., and Skolnik, A. M. 1968. Social welfare expenditures under public programs in the United States (1929–66). Research Report no. 25. Office of Research and Statistics, Social Security Administration. Washington, D.C.: U.S. Government Printing Office.

15. Morgan, J. N.; David, M. H.; Cohen, W. J.; and Brazer, H. E. 1962. *Income and welfare in the United States.* New York: McGraw-Hill.

16. Orshansky, M. 1968. The shape of poverty in 1966. *Social Security Bulletin,* March, pp. 3–32.

17. The President's Commission on Income Maintenance Programs, Report of. 1969. "Poverty amid plenty: the American paradox." Mimeographed.

18. Projector, D. S. 1969. "Children's allowance and welfare reform proposals: costs and redistribution effects." Paper prepared for meeting of the National Tax Association, October. Mimeographed.

19. Schorr, A. L. 1966. Alternatives in income maintenance. *Social Work,* July, pp. 22–29.

20. Vadakin, J. C. 1968. *Children, poverty, and family allowances.* New York: Basic Books.

VII

In-Kind Transfers and
the Size Distribution of Income

EUGENE SMOLENSKY, LEANNA STIEFEL,
MARIA SCHMUNDT, AND ROBERT PLOTNICK

INTRODUCTION

This paper is concerned with one important issue in appropriately measuring the size distribution of income—the treatment of in-kind transfers. We show first that accounting for in-kind transfers reduces income inequality compared to the distribution of cash income. Second, recognizing that recipient benefits from these transfers may be less than the cost to the government, we measure this difference and discuss its implications. Finally, a technique for measuring donor benefits from in-kind transfers is implemented and the results evaluated.

I. DEFINING AND ACCOUNTING FOR IN-KIND TRANSFERS

A reasonable definition of an in-kind transfer would be the difference between what the taxpayer would pay for a good or service in a Lindahl equilibrium and what he does pay [2]. Every program would probably then involve some transfer. In this paper only goods and services provided to clearly identifiable beneficiaries at other than marginal cost

This is an abstracted version of the articles which originally appeared in *The Distribution of Economic Well-Being*, vol. 21, ed. F. Thomas Juster. New York: National Bureau of Economic Research, forthcoming. Reprinted by permission of the authors and the National Bureau of Economic Research.

131

TABLE 1
Major In-Kind Transfer Programs, 1970 (millions of dollars)

Program	Federal expenditures	State– local expenditures	All government
Consumption transfers			
Food Stamps[a]	$ 1,577		$ 1,577
Commodity distribution[a]	321		321
Child nutrition[b]	703	$ 185	888
Public housing[c]	368		368
Rent supplements[b]	18		18
Medicare[d]	5,255		5,255
Medicaid[e]	2,548	2,260	4,808
Veterans hospital and medical care[b]	1,651		1,651
OEO Health and nutrition[b]	123		123
Legal aid[b]	51		51
Subtotal	12,615	2,445	15,060
Investment transfers			
Elementary, secondary and other education[f]	1,214	42,934	44,148
Higher education[f]	336	11,325	11,661
Manpower programs	*1,149*	*98*	*1,247*
MDTA institutional[g]	173		173
MDTA on-the-job[h]	36		36
NYC in-school[i]	41		41
NYC out-of-school[i]	21		21
Operation Mainstream[j]	9		9
Concentrated Employment[j]	82		82
JOBS[k]	82		82
Job Corps[j]	96		96
WIN[l]	50		50
Vocational Rehab.[m]	340	98	438
Other manpower[j]	219		219
Veterans education benefits[n]	991		991
Total in-kind transfer expenditures	$16,305	$56,802	$73,107

[a] Derived from [21]. Total includes administrative costs and is for FY 1971.

[b] Derived from [21]. Total excludes administrative costs and is for FY 1970.

[c] Estimated value of subsidy derived from Table 2. Contrary to our proposal, this total excludes capital consumption of the public housing stock.

[d] Data from *Social Security Bulletin Annual Statistical Supplement,* 1970, Table 117, row 2; net of SMI premium cost to recipients and adjusted slightly downward since the Current Population Survey (used to derive Table 3) counts less eligibles than did the Social Security Administration. Data exclude administrative costs and are for calendar year 1970.

[e] Total expenditure data are for calendar year 1970 and are from HEW, *Number of Recipients and Amounts of Payments under Medicaid, 1970,* Social and Rehabilitation Services publication number (SRS) 73-03153. Allocation between federal and state–local

are called transfers.[1] Even this approach implies a relatively broad view of what constitutes in-kind transfers. The programs that ordinarily are classed as in-kind transfers are included—food stamps, Medicaid and Medicare, public housing, etc. Such programs provide what we label as *consumption* in-kind benefits. Our definition also includes *investment* in-kind transfers. This category is comprised of direct expenditures on public education, subsidies and grants to students (e.g., GI Bill and manpower programs); in short, subsidized programs which principally increase the recipient's human capital. The distinction between consumption and investment transfers is not always clear-cut; health programs for example. Since we treat both types in identical ways in our analysis, the distinction is merely an expositional convenience.

In 1970 the federal government provided $16 billion in in-kind transfer benefits. State and local governments administered another $57 billion, mainly for education. The major in-kind programs (as we define them) and their costs are listed in Table 1. The dollar volume of in-kind transfers exceeded that of cash transfers, which totaled $63 billion in 1970.[2] In what follows we restrict our attention to seven major in-kind transfer programs costing $68.8 billion in 1970.[3]

[1] Since there is little reason to believe that taxes are on a marginal benefit basis, all government expenditures can be thought of as having a transfer component. In another paper, Reynolds and Smolensky have distributed all government expenditures and taxes by income size class. In that paper, however, in-kind transfers are treated in the traditional way. It would also have been consistent to enter in-kind taxes (imprisonment, compulsory school attendance, jury duty, military conscription), but no attempt was made to do so.

[2] See A. Skolnik and S. Dales [18, Table 1].

[3] The seven programs are food stamps, public housing, Medicare, Medicaid, elementary, secondary, and other public education, higher public education, and manpower programs.

---

governments is based on the average of the proportion of Medicaid expenditures found in [21], for FY 1970 and 1971; excludes administrative costs.

[f] Reynolds and Smolensky [14, appendix D, for FY 1970].

[g] Manpower Development Training Act; data are for FY 1970 and exclude administrative costs and estimated cash payments to participants. Source of data is Office of Management and Budget, *Special Analyses of the Budget,* 1972, p. 138.

[h] Same as note g, except data are on obligations basis from the *Manpower Report, 1971,* p. 299.

[i] Neighborhood Youth Corps; note and source same as in g.

[j] Note and source same as in g.

[k] Job Opportunities in the Business Sector; note and source same as in g.

[l] Work Incentive program; note and source same as in g.

[m] Same as b. Excludes estimated cash payments to participants also.

[n] Administrator of Veterans Affairs, *1972 Annual Report,* p. 166.

II. THE DISTRIBUTION OF IN-KIND INCOME

How did the provision of $68.8 billion of in-kind transfers affect average household incomes and the degree of income inequality? Table 2 shows that in-kind transfers markedly increase the average incomes of all groups (column 12). For the poorest group, the difference of $559 (column 10) increases income by 215 percent.

There is a strong positive relationship between benefits and income. Regression indicates that a rise in cash income of 1 percent is, on average, associated with a .22 percent gain in in-kind transfer income. An exception to this pattern for the range $6,000–7,999 results largely from decreased Medicaid benefits after $6,000.

Consumption transfers, nevertheless, are distributed in a strongly propoor pattern (column 5). Investment transfers, which account for 79 percent of all in-kind transfers, rise steadily with income (column 9).

Although in-kind transfers are prorich, they are more evenly distributed than cash incomes. Hence, including them in personal income decreases the degree of "inequality." The Gini coefficient for cash income was .398; adding all in-kind benefits shifts it down to .371. Similarly, including in-kind transfers raises the share of income going to the four poorest income classes—the bottom 24 percent—from 5.2 percent to 6.5 percent. A third measure of inequality, the coefficient of variation, declines from .52 to .49 percent when income includes in-kind transfers.

The high level of aggregation, and our use of averages, obscures the fact that in any given income bracket, some households receive above-average benefits by participating in many in-kind programs, while others with nearly equal cash incomes obtain few or no benefits [20]. Though the degree of equity of some individual in-kind transfer programs has been studied, [19] [5], currently available data do not permit a study of this issue for the *complete system* of in-kind transfers. National data on program enrollment and benefits at the family level are needed but nonexistent.

The data in Table 2 are meant to be illustrative of orders of magnitude only. No attempt has been made to adjust for known sources of bias (e.g., underreporting of money income in the Current Population Survey), or for inconsistencies in reporting periods (some data are for the calendar, some for the fiscal year), etc. Often, distributing benefits by income class required heroic assumptions.

One slightly less obvious caveat to note about Table 2 is that it does not measure, even conceptually, the redistribution of income due to in-kind transfers. Measuring the redistribution of income due to the fisc, or any part of it, requires a quite different accounting framework. The essential element of this framework is a counterfactual which recognizes the general equilibrium interdependence between the fisc and the distribution of earned income. What is important in Table 2 is that the sum of columns 10 and 11 represents a more complete distribution of personal income.

Finally, it should be noted that human capital investments are valued at their supply price. Two comments are in order on this procedure. Though the supply price may differ from the capitalized value of the associated future earnings stream, any such difference does not affect current income. Second, the cash equivalent of the subsidy need not equal the supply price, since human capital investments are in-kind transfers.

III.   A SIMULATION APPROACH TO BENEFIT WEIGHTS

It has been demonstrated that in-kind benefits when valued at tax-payer cost affect measured income inequality. In this section we determine if this conclusion would be altered by valuing in-kind transfers at their cash equivalence to recipients. Our procedure is to calculate a set of scalars (benefit weights) which convert taxpayers' costs to benefits as evaluated by the recipient. A range of benefit weights for a selected list of programs is obtained via simulation.

Five programs were selected for this simulation—food stamps, public housing, rent supplements, Medicare, and Medicaid. We assume each recipient family participates in a package of in-kind transfer programs, and is enrolled in at most one housing and one medical program. A utility function, a budget constraint (Y), and maximizing behavior are assumed, and the utility the family obtains is calculated. The cash income that the family would need if it were to enjoy the same level of utility but received *no* in-kind transfers, EY, is then computed. It is inferred that the bundle of in-kind benefits increased the family's welfare, measured in dollar terms, by EY. The ratio of EY to the taxpayer cost of providing this set of transfers is the benefit weight.

A.   Specifying the Utility Function

A variant of the displaced CES utility function was used in this exercise.[4] Because the five in-kind programs we are concerned with

[4] Of all the possible functional forms for a utility function, this is one of the few that is empirically tractable and yields demand functions consistent with economic theory. See A. S. Goldberger [6]. Recent work on consumer benefits from public housing lends empirical support to our choice. See M. P. Murray [11].

TABLE 2
Distribution of Average Household Benefits of Selected In-Kind Transfers, 1970

Income class	Consumption transfers					Investment transfers				(10) All in-kind transfers	(11) Average cash income[g]	(12) In-kind transfers as a percentage of cash income
	(1) Food Stamps[a]	(2) Public Housing[b]	(3) Medicare[c]	(4) Medicaid[d]	(5) Total	(6) Elem., sec. and other education[e]	(7) Higher education[e]	(8) Manpower training[f]	(9) Total			
$0–999	18	6	104	94	222	272	4	61	337	559	260	215.0
1,000–1,999	50	20	179	184	433	272	4	47	323	756	1,508	50.1
2,000–2,999	71	18	173	191	453	358	10	44	412	865	2,461	36.4
3,000–3,999	62	15	146	134	357	444	16	39	499	856	3,468	25.5
4,000–4,999	53	12	122	156	343	543	36	31	610	953	4,471	21.7
5,000–5,999	36	7	90	142	275	612	52	19	683	958	5,445	17.8
6,000–6,999	24	4	69	59	156	634	61	5	700	856	6,452	13.3
7,000–7,999	17	2	55	33	107	721	71	6	798	905	7,458	12.1
8,000–9,999	16	—	46	26	88	807	96	3	906	994	8,920	11.3

10,000–14,999	3	—	35	24	62	843	231	—	1,074	1,136	12,120	9.4
15,000–24,999	—	—	37	11	48	795	367	—	1,162	1,210	18,410	6.5
25,000+	—	—	50	—	50	744	1,171	—	1,915	1,965	35,755	5.5

[a] Assumes total food stamp subsidies equal $1,577 million as shown in Table 1. Relative distribution of benefits obtained from J. Morgan et al., *A Panel Survey of Income Dynamics*, Ann Arbor; Institute for Social Research, Survey Research Center, 1972.

[b] Distribution among income classes of public housing tenants obtained from HUD, *Statistical Yearbook, 1970*, Tables 107, 112, and 148. Average subsidy based on Smolensky–Gomery [19, Table I-B, inflated to 1970 price level].

[c] All eligible recipients are assumed to receive the same benefit, which was computed by dividing total payments (net of premium cost) by total number of Medicare enrollees. The distribution of enrollees was derived from the *Current Population Reports*, series P-60, no. 80 "Money Income in 1970 of Persons and Families," Tables 17 and 22.

[d] Table values are the sum of two separate distributions, since Medicaid recipients are divided into two groups—those receiving public assistance and those not on public assistance but qualifying as "medically indigent." For the public assistance group the percentage distribution of eligible recipients among income classes was obtained from *A Panel Survey of Income Dynamics* (see note *a*). Multiplying the percentage by total Medicaid payments gave the total benefits to an income class. Average household benefit for that class then equaled total class benefits divided by the total number of households in the class. For the "medically indigent" the same procedure was used, except that Medicaid eligibility was determined by comparing the household's income to the limits set by its state of residence. These limits were found in "Income and Resources Levels for Medically Needy in Title XIX Plans in Operation as of April 15, 1970," unpublished table of the Social Security Administration. Resource levels were not considered because of data limitations, but it is believed that no serious bias resulted.

[e] Drawn from M. Reynolds and E. Smolensky, [14, appendix D].

[f] Includes all manpower programs listed in Table 1 except "Other." For all included programs except Vocational Rehabilitation, distribution of benefits based on Tables F-5, 7, 10, 11, 12, 13, 14 of *Manpower Report*, 1971. For Vocational Rehabilitation, distribution of benefits based on Table 4 of "Characteristics of Clients Rehabilitated in Fiscal Years 1967–71," HEW, Social and Rehabilitation Services, 1973.

[g] Source is Dorothy Projector and Judith Bretz [13, Table 5].

137

involve only three commodities—food, housing, and medical insurance—the utility function has just four arguments, these three and "other." Hence, we assume:

$$(1) \qquad U = \sum_{j=1}^{4} b_j (x_j - g_j)^{(\sigma-1)/\sigma}, \qquad \text{if} \quad \sigma \neq 1.$$

$$(2) \qquad U = \prod_{j=1}^{4} (x_j - g_j)^{c_j}, \qquad \text{if} \quad \sigma = 1.$$

where

x_j = quantity of good j consumed,
g_j = displacement parameter (minimum quantity consumed),
b_j, c_j = parameters,
σ = elasticity of substitution.[5]

To proceed with the simulation, equations (1) and (2) must be given empirical content, which in turn requires identifying the c_j, g_j, b_j and σ. To show that the c_j's are the marginal propensities to consume, assume that good 4 is "other," $g_4 = 0$, and quantity units are specified so that market prices equal unity. Maximizing (2) with the constraint $Y = \sum x_j$ gives:

$$(3) \qquad x_j = g_j + c_j \left(Y - \sum_{i=1}^{4} g_i \right), \qquad j = 1, 2, 3.$$

The parameter values of the c_j, were chosen for the utility functions of five prototype families, which differ by size and/or income, from the expenditure data in the *Survey of Consumer Expenditures*, 1960–61.[6] The data themselves are observations of the money spent on $x_1, \ldots, x_4$ by family size and income, and from them we computed crude estimates of $c_1, \ldots, c_4$.

To determine the minimum consumption expenditures on each good (g_j) we solve the demand equations of (3) and obtain:

$$(4) \qquad g_j = x_j - (c_j/c_4)x_4, \qquad j = 1, 2, 3.$$

To identify the b_j maximize (1), and solve the demand equations for g_j to obtain:

$$(4') \qquad g_j = x_j - b_j^{\sigma} x_4.$$

---

[5] In equation (1), omitting the exponent $\sigma/(\sigma - 1)$ simplifies calculations and does not affect the final results.

[6] This procedure assumes identical utility functions for all families of a given size and income, but allows them to vary across income classes and by family size.

Comparing 4' to 4 shows that $b_j = (c_j/c_4)^{1/\sigma}$. Only σ remains to be identified. The simulations were run by successively assuming $\sigma = .5$, .75, and 1.

B. Maximizing Utility with the Transfer Programs

Substituting our choice of σ and our parameters into (1) and (2) produces a specific utility function for each prototype family. Assigning a particular package of in-kind benefits to a family, we maximize its utility using this estimated function, subject to the budget constraint (5), which exists when in-kind transfers are received:

$$(5) \qquad Y = \sum_{I} (1 - s_j)xp_j + \sum_{II} xp_j - \sum_{II} s_jxr_j + \sum_{III} (1 - s_j)xr_j.$$

We are assuming units are chosen such that all prices are unity and:

Y = family cash income;

s_j = subsidy rate for good j, which depends on the transfer program's features and may depend on Y;

xp_j = total amount of good j consumed when family receives the assigned set of in-kind transfers;

xr_j = quantity of good j *required* to be consumed if received as an in-kind transfer. This number is constant for each recipient and is determined by the government.

I, II, III = program categories which are defined next.

As indicated in equation (5), each commodity falls into one of three categories, depending upon the way in which the rules of the program affect the budget constraint.

Goods in category I are:

(a) nonsubsidized ($s_j = 0$) because the family does not participate in an in-kind program providing good j; or

(b) "other" goods, where no subsidy is ever available, or

(c) subsidized at rate s_j both on the margin and inframarginally. That is, there is no quantity restriction on the consumption of this transfer (e.g., Medicare), or some maximum limit has been set by the administrators which is larger than the amount actually desired at the subsidized price.

Category II contains commodities for which the subsidy ceases at quantity xr_j and the recipient must purchase at least xr_j but is free to supplement this level of consumption at market prices without losing the subsidy *and does so*. In this case the family pays $(1 - s_j)xr_j$ for the

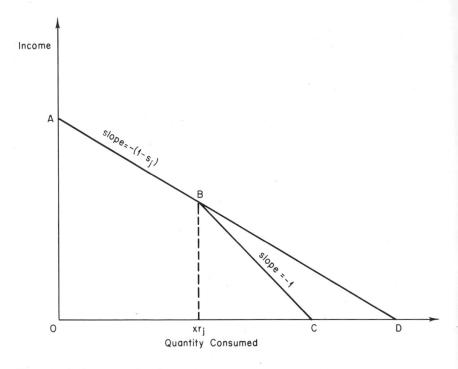

Figure 1. Budget constraints for subsidized commodities.

subsidized goods, and $xp_j - xr_j$ for the unsubsidized portion. The total cost is $xp_j - s_jxr_j$ as shown in equation (5). Note that s_jxr_j is de facto an outright cash transfer, since the subsidy does not affect the family's market behavior at the margin.[7]

Subsidized items in category III are those for which the recipient either *must* consume a prescribed fixed quantity xr_j or desires to consume this amount. Public housing, which restricts a recipient to one particular apartment, falls in this category.

Figure 1 relates the three categories to the budget constraint for a subsidized commodity. If the good is in category I, there is no relevant restraint imposed by regulation on the quantity the household can consume and the budget constraint is therefore AD. If the commodity is

[7] An example of an in-kind transfer in this category is the school lunch program, in which a student can get a 60 cent lunch for 30 cents, but not a 40 cent lunch for 20 cents nor two 60 cent lunches, but who may bring a sandwich. Of the five programs in this simulation, food stamps can fall into this category, though it may not if the family does not exceed its food stamp allotment when buying food. Similarly, rent subsidies may or may not be in this category, depending on family consumption choices.

in category II, it is subsidized up to some quantity; the household must consume at least that quantity but consumes additional units purchased at the market price. Hence the household is restricted to the segment BC. In category III the quantity the household must consume and the price it must pay are both fixed; the budget constraint collapses to point B.

Now that the budget constraint (5) has been explained, we proceed to indicate the demand functions for each category of goods obtained from maximizing utility.

(6) Category I. $xp_j = g_j + c_j(1 - s_j)^{-\sigma}(\sum_I c_i(1 - s_i)^{1-\sigma} + \sum_{II} c_i)^{-1}A$

(7) Category II. $xp_j = g_j + c_j(\sum_I c_j(1 - s_j)^{1-\sigma} + \sum_{II} c_i)^{-1}A$

(8) Category III. $xp_j = xr_j$

for all σ and where:

$$A = \left(Y = \sum_{II} s_i(xr_i - g_i) - \sum_{I,III} (1 - s_i)g_i - \sum_{III} (1 - s_i)xr_i \right).$$

The Simulations

To obtain the simulated numerical values for the xp_j from equations (6), (7), and (8), we need estimates of c_j, g_j, s_j, xr_j, Y and σ. The first two are known from the utility function, while we chose various representative values of Y and σ. We approximated the s_j and xr_j that a prototype family would face if it participated in program j by examining the specific regulations of each of the five in-kind programs and making several assumptions.[8]

The numerical values for the xp_j are substituted into (1) and (2) to compute the family's utility, U^*, given that it receives a particular set of in-kind transfers.

At this point we observe from (6)–(8) that the amount of food, shelter, and medical care (i.e., the xp_j) demanded can vary as the category in which the corresponding in-kind transfer is placed varies. In turn, this means that U^*, a function of the xp_j, is not unique. The problem is partially mitigated because one can unambiguously assign Medicare and Medicaid to category I, and public housing to III. However, food stamps may fall in category II or III, since the program permits a family's xp_{food}

---

[8] For example, federal regulations indicate that a two-person family with cash income of $2,869 in 1970 was eligible for $725 of food stamps at a cost of $583, a subsidy rate of .20. Because the family must buy all the stamps if it is to receive any, $xr = $725. (Since these estimates were made, this requirement has been changed.)

to exceed xr_{food} (II) or be equal to it (III). The actual outcome depends upon the family's demand functions for *all four* commodities simultaneously. (Rent supplements, similarly, can be in any category.)

To deal with this simultaneity problem, all permutations of categories were considered when the transfer package at hand included food stamps and/or rent supplements. Inconsistent results were eliminated; of the remainder, the one yielding the highest utility was selected for further analysis.[9]

Having determined the recipient family's utility, U^*, given its cash income and its participation in a set of in-kind transfer programs, we next compute how much money income, EY, it would need to maintain the same U^* if *no* in-kind transfers were available. We maximize (1) or (2) subject to the usual constraint that is in force when no in-kind transfers exist:

$$(9) \qquad\qquad EY = \sum_{j=1}^{4} xp_j$$

This gives the quantities demanded as a function of EY:

$$(10) \qquad xp_j^* = g_j + c_j(EY - \sum_{i=1}^{4} g_i) \qquad j = 1, \ldots, 4$$

Substituting the right hand side into (1) and (2) produces the indirect utility function $U(EY)$. Solving

$$(11) \qquad\qquad U(EY) = U^*$$

gives EY^* the cash equivalent of cash income, Y, plus in-kind transfers. Hence the transfers provide a dollar benefit of $EY^* - Y$.

The taxpayer cost is:

$$(12) \qquad TC = \sum_{I} (s_j + p_j - 1)xp_j^* + \sum_{II,III} (s_j + p_j - 1)xr_j^*$$

where market prices $= 1$ and $p_j =$ ratio of government cost price to market price. (Note that when $p_j = 1$, TC is simply the direct subsidy at market prices given to recipients.)

The benefit weight is:

$$(13) \qquad\qquad \frac{EY^* - Y}{TC}.$$

A sample of the benefit weights obtained appears in Table 3. Of the

[9] An inconsistent case exists if assigning good j to one category yields, from (6)–(8), an xp_j that contradicts the assignment. For instance, a permutation placing rent supplements in Category II (where $xp > xr$) might result in $xp < xr$; this case would be excluded.

TABLE 3
Benefit Weights for Selected Programs

| | Two-person family | | | | Four-person family | | | | | |
| | $Y = 2,869$ | | $Y = 4,883$ | | $Y = 3,414$ | | $Y = 4,706$ | | $Y = 6,572$ | |
Program package	$\sigma = .5$	$\sigma = 1$	$\sigma = .5$	$\sigma = 1$	$\sigma = .5$	$\sigma = 1$	$\sigma = .5$	$\sigma = 1$	$\sigma = .5$	$\sigma = 1$
f	1.0	1.0	na	na	1.0	1.0	1.0	1.0	na	na
p	.61	.78	na	na	.62	.80	.86	.93	na	na
r	na	na	na	na	na	na	.99	1.0	.99	.99
mr	.81	.89	.91	.95	na	na	na	na	na	na
md	.64	.76	na	na	.67	.78	.74	.85	na	na
f, p	.72	.85	na	na	.90	.95	.94	.97	na	na
f, r	na	na	na	na	na	na	.98	.99	na	na
f, mr	.88	.93	na	na	na	na	na	na	na	na
f, md	.72	.81	na	na	.86	.91	.83	.90	na	na
p, md	.74	.85	na	na	.75	.86	.87	.93	na	na
r, md	na	na	na	na	na	na	.84	.91	na	na
f, p, md	.80	.87	na	na	.91	.95	.92	.95	na	an
f, r, md	na	na	na	na	na	na	.86	.92	na	na
f, p, mr	.85	.92	na	na	na	na	na	na	na	na

Note: na = ineligible for program
  f = food stamps
  p = public housing
  r = rent supplements
  mr = Medicare
  md = Medicaid

143

five prototype families, two were two-person households and can be thought of as elderly couples. One had a low income of $2,869 and was eligible for several transfers; the other's income of $4,883 entitled it only to Medicare. We assumed these families would not receive rent subsidies. The three remaining families had four members and incomes of $3,414, $4,706, and $6,572.[10]

Several notable observations emerge from the table. Turning first to those instances in which households participate in only one program, one conclusion easily drawn is that the food stamp program is a de facto cash transfer. All families attach a weight of 1 to their benefits, because most families spend more on food than their stamp allotment even if they receive no stamps. Rent supplements can also be considered cash transfers in view of the benefit weights of .99 and 1. Public housing, in contrast, benefits the recipients less than the government's cost of providing it. For low-income households, the benefit weights in the range .6 to .8 indicate that the gain from renting public housing at, say, $500 below market prices (i.e., an in-kind transfer costing $500) is between $300–400.[11] For the middle-income family, government housing subsidies are converted into direct consumption benefits at more efficient rates (on the order of .9). Compared to food stamps and rent supplements, the lower benefit weights for public housing presumably reflect its category III nature. Recipients must purchase the housing services of the assigned apartment, no more, no less, and this rigid requirement may create a large distortion in consumption patterns. The two medical transfers also have a wide range of benefit weights. Even though Medicaid is free, its weights are not equal to one.

Many families that receive one of the five in-kind transfers also receive others. Because of this, the benefit weights for selected groups of in-kind transfers are also presented in Table 3. The weight for a two- or three-program bundle is not an easily computed weighted average of the several separate weights, but can only be derived independently. For example, the benefit weight of a low-income two-person family receiving both public housing and Medicaid is greater than the weight of either program taken singly. These outcomes arise because the addition of a

---

[10] These income figures correspond to the income classes in the *Survey of Consumer Expenditures,* 1960–1961, which are the original data but inflated to 1970 price levels.

[11] The benefit weights on public housing are more variable than our table suggest and fall as low as .24 in one instance. Packages of transfers which contain public housing also, therefore, have quite variable, and frequently quite low benefit weights. To a lesser extent, there is some greater variability in the weights than revealed by Table 4, for other housing programs as well.

new transfer changes the relative prices of all commodities and thereby affects the total pattern of consumption. The general tenor of these multitransfer benefit weights is that they are on the high side. Few dip below .8 and a number are close to 1.

To determine if our earlier conclusions on the impact of in-kind benefits on the size distribution could be affected by moving to a cash equivalent basis, we modified the entries in Table 2 based on the results of Table 3. That set of benefit weights which would yield the maximum change in Table 2's figures was chosen for this exercise.[12] Nonetheless, Table 4 indicates relatively little change when compared to Table 2, except for the three lowest income classes. A more prorich pattern than that of Table 2 (as reproduced here in column 8) results because benefit weights generally rise with income, but the change is slight. The income elasticity of unweighted transfers is .22; after the cash equivalent adjustment it is .27. For the unweighted distribution based on taxpayer cost the Gini coefficient was .371; on a cash equivalent basis it rises to .374.

Our benefit weights apply only to consumption transfers. Consequently, they have greater impact when attention is restricted to this type of transfer, as seen when columns 5 and 6 are compared. Again, of course, benefit weight calculations modestly increase the progressivity of in-kind transfers. Unweighted consumption transfers have income elasticity of $-.46$; applying the weights increases this number to $-.33$.

We have not calculated the cash equivalent transfers for education.

---

[12] Specifically, we assumed that $\sigma = .5$ and that (a) public housing tenants receive no other benefits, (b) Medicare enrollees reveive no other benefits, and (c) all food stamp recipients are on Medicaid, and vice versa. These conditions, of course, do not reflect the true pattern of program overlap in 1970. Also, a greater change in Table 2's figures could be produced by assuming, for example, that some Medicaid recipients receive no food stamps. Our choices, however, yield the largest change of any simple set of assumptions.

Since the simulations cover a limited income range, rough extrapolations were used to obtain a full set of benefit weights. Table 4 was constructed with the following weights:

Income class	Public housing	Medicare	Food stamps and medicaid
$ 0–$999	.3	.6	.5
$1,000–$1,999	.5	.7	.6
$2,000–$2,999	.6	.8	.7
$3,000–$3,999	.7	.85	.85
$4,000–$4,999	.85	.9	.85
$5,000–$5,999	.95	.95	.95
$6,000+	1.00	1.00	1.00

TABLE 4
The Distribution of In-Kind Transfers at Their Cash Equivalent Values

| Income class | Recipient (ΔY) valuation of consumption benefits | | | | | (6) Taxpayer cost of 1–4 | (7) Recipient valuation of all in-kind transfers | (8) Taxpayer cost of all in-kind transfers |
	(1) Food Stamps	(2) Public housing	(3) Medi-care	(4) Medi-caid	(5) Total			
$0–999	9	2	62	47	120	222	457	559
1,000–1,999	30	10	123	110	273	433	594	756
2,000–2,999	50	11	138	153	352	453	764	865
3,000–3,999	53	11	117	114	295	357	794	856
4,000–4,999	45	10	104	133	292	343	902	953
5,000–5,999	34	7	81	135	257	275	940	958
6,000–6,999	24	4	66	59	156	156	856	856
7,000–7,999	17	2	55	33	107	107	905	905
8,000–9,999	16	—	46	26	88	88	994	994
10,000–14,999	3	—	35	24	62	62	1,136	1,136
15,000–24,999	—	—	37	11	48	48	1,210	1,210
25,000+	—	—	50	—	50	50	1,965	1,965

That the benefit weights appropriate to education may differ from one (at least for some income classes) is plausible enough to merit testing. Conceptually the framework developed for consumption goods is applicable, but the required assumptions are strained even more, and the data requirements are more burdensome. For example, since private education is consumed even when public education is available, public and private education must be quite different goods. Appeal to budget data, therefore, will not yield a marginal propensity to consume public education directly, if at all. This and the many other problems are not insuperable, but the effort required to overcome them was beyond our immediate resources.

Any reasonable set of benefit weights for education would be expected to rise with income, thus accentuating the prorich character of education beyond that in Table 2. However, the weights would have to be very low at the bottom end to affect any conclusions of the study in a critical way. To make education benefits proportional over the income range $1,500–20,000, the benefit weight in the class $1,000–1,999 would have to be as low as .14. On the other hand, introducing benefit weights for consumption goods did reduce the income of the lowest class from those transfers by almost 50 percent. If the weights at the low end of the distribution are as low for education as they may be for Medicaid, the increase in welfare of the poor due to in-kind transfers could be substantially overstated by Table 2.[13]

Though subject to considerable qualification, we conclude that our benefit weights undercut the argument that donor benefits rationalize the existence of in-kind transfers. Since the benefit weights generally have values fairly close to 1, in-kind transfers do not greatly alter consumption choices. Thus, they cannot be justified on donor benefit grounds.

Of course, our results are hardly definitive. Some, for example, may conclude from Tables 2 and 3 that consumption choices are importantly altered. Our failure to calculate benefit weights for education, the largest in-kind transfer and the one most likely to generate external benefits, is another limitation of the study.[14] Our estimated marginal propensities to consume were crudely derived, as were our specifications of program characteristics. Only one utility function was simulated. Other valid criticisms can also be offered. Nevertheless, we believe our results will prove robust. Our utility function is fairly flexible and was simulated with a wide range of elasticities of substitution.

---

[13] However the Gini coefficient is not substantially altered when the Medicaid weights are applied to all human investment programs.

[14] See footnote 13, however.

C. Taxpayer Benefits from In-Kind Transfers: Estimating Redistribution Services

In this section we assume that the giving of in-kind transfers is a pure public good generating donor benefits. To quantify the taxpayer benefits from in-kind transfers, we shall use the methodology suggested by Aaron and McGuire [1] and Maital [10]. The effects on the size distribution of income of distributing these benefits will then be computed. (Relying on our tentative simulation results, we ignore any benefits which may result from the alteration of recipient consumption patterns.) We intend the calculations to be suggestive rather than definitive.

Maital's Methodology

Assume that for persons with income y,

$$(14) \qquad mu(g) = t(t)\lambda(y),$$

where
 $mu(g)$ = marginal utility of in-kind transfer g,
 $t(y)$ = tax price per unit of g,
 $\lambda(y)$ = marginal utility of income.

Multiplying (14) by G, the number of units of in-kind transfers, and rearranging gives:

$$(15) \qquad Gt(t) = Gmu(g)/\lambda(y).$$

Since the left-hand side is the total taxes a household with income y would be willing to pay for the benefits it receives from public goods, $Gt(y)$ is its imputed benefits, B, from giving. Making the strong assumption that all households have the same, separable utility function, $mu(g)$ is a constant across all donors, since, by definition, they consume the same quantity of redistribution. Applying (15) to donors i and j and dividing i's equation by j's produces:

$$(16) \qquad B_i/B_j = \lambda(y_j)/\lambda(y_i).$$

Hence, the imputed benefits of G vary inversely with the marginal utility of income.

To apply (16) we assume, along with Aaron and McGuire [1] and Maital [10], that $\lambda(y) = ay^{-\theta}$, where θ is the elasticity of marginal utility with respect to income. Hence (16) becomes:

$$(17) \qquad B_i/B_j = (y_i/y_j)^{\theta}.$$

As Maital explains, estimates of θ have been obtained from many econometric studies of consumption that use CES utility functions. These studies suggest that for the United States, $\theta = 1.5$.

We can compute the distribution of taxpayer benefits from equation (17), and our lower bound assumption that the sum of the B_k equals total cost, and the additional assumption that each household has the mean cash income of its class. We then have:

$$(18) \qquad B_i/B_j = (y_i/y_j)^{1.5}$$

and

$$(19) \qquad \sum_{k=1}^{12} P_k B_k = \$68.8 \text{ billion}$$

where

y_k = mean income of class k,
P_k = number of households in class k,
$68.8 billion = total spent on our selected set of in-kind transfers in 1970.

The resulting benefits per household are shown in Table 5 (column 1).

Column 1 indicates that taxpayer benefits are distributed in a steeply prorich pattern, a result which necessarily follows from our use of equation (18), with its income elasticity of benefits of 1.5.

To calculate the resulting size distribution we sum "Consumption of Redistribution," the recipient value of consumption from in-kind transfers (column 4), personal consumption, personal savings, and adjusted personal taxes. For consumption, savings and *all* personal taxes we substitute CPS cash income (column 3). An adjustment of taxes is needed because, after adding $68.8 billion of taxpayer benefits to household incomes, we must subtract an equivalent amount in taxes used to "purchase" these benefits. This reduction is distributed in column 2 ("Offsetting Tax Reduction"), according to the incidence of all personal taxes in 1970 [14, Appendix C].

With the inclusion of donor benefits (net of taxes) in personal income, the Gini coefficient is .382. This slightly exceeds the coefficient presented in the previous section (.374).[15] It appears that donor benefits add about as much to inequality as the offsetting taxes reduce it.

As a final note, we observe that the calculations in this paper permit easy analysis of a modified concept of disposable income. The conven-

---

[15] This section assumed a CES utility function that is constant for all people; earlier we explicitly allowed the function to vary across income classes and by family size. Hence combining these results in Table 5 is not strictly justifiable.

TABLE 5
Taxpayer Benefits and the Distribution of Personal Outlays per Household

	(1) Consumption of redistribution	(2) Offsetting tax reduction	(3) Cash income	(4) Recipient value of in-kind transfers	(5) (1) + (2) + (3) + (4)
$0–999	4	−67	260	457	654
1,000–1,999	53	−67	1,508	594	2,088
2,000–2,999	112	−176	2,461	764	3,161
3,000–3,999	186	−300	3,468	794	4,148
4,000–4,999	273	−441	4,471	902	5,205
5,000–5,999	366	−540	5,445	940	6,211
6,000–6,999	473	−632	6,452	856	7,149
7,000–7,999	588	−731	7,458	905	8,220
8,000–9,999	770	−879	8,920	994	9,805
10,000–14,999	1,138	−1,143	12,120	1,136	13,251
15,000–24,999	2,285	−1,654	18,410	1,210	20,251
25,000+	6,179	−6,788	35,755	1,965	37,111

tional definition of disposable income is consumption out of cash income plus savings. We further add in-kind consumption at cash equivalent value and donor benefits. The Gini coefficient for this expanded concept of disposable income is .372 compared to a coefficient of .380 for the conventional notion.

CONCLUSION

We have provided an illustrative set of numbers to show how the size distribution of income is altered when in-kind transfers, treated our way, are distributed across income classes and added to cash income. The resulting changes are, in fact, quite small. Redistribution through in-kind transfer appears to consist of shuffling a great mass of things about, mainly in the dense middle of the distribution, with those in the lower tail gaining some.

The emphasis we put on valuing recipient benefits on a cash equivalent basis for the study of income distribution seems misplaced. Our simulations, while only suggestive, yielded rather high benefit weights. Therefore, donor benefits generated by the alteration of recipient consumption patterns cannot be important.

Our results are in no sense definitive, however, and additional useful work could be done. A low-income household survey that determined the number of recipients receiving more than one in-kind transfer and the mix of benefits they receive would be especially helpful. If most low-income families are in several programs, then practical concern over recipient valuations of in-kind transfers would be ended. (Of course, why we engage in such transfers when benefit weights are 1, would emerge as an important issue in public economics.) If only a small proportion of households receive transfers from more than one source, attention to consumption of subsidized commodities by low-income families would yield better income elasticities than were available for this study. Such a survey might also help to answer a variety of horizontal equity questions not otherwise tractable.

An issue not yet amenable to household survey solutions is to better conceptualize and then to calculate the set of benefit weights appropriate for education and other human-capital-augmenting public programs.

The issues surrounding the concept of donor benefits also needs considerably more attention. It would be especially useful to contrast the results from assuming Pareto-optimal redistribution with other models such as the median voter framework.

In summary, it seems quite acceptable to continue to account for in-kind transfers at cost (including capital costs). The notion that redistribution is an activity augmenting personal income with a concomitant reduction in taxpayer burdens requires further theoretical and empirical consideration.

REFERENCES

1. Aaron, H., and McGuire, M. 1970. Public goods and income distribution. *Econometrica* 38:907–1220.
2. Behrens, J., and Smolensky, E. 1973. Alternative definitions of income redistribution. *Public Finance/Finances Publiques* 28:315–32.
3. Christensen, L. R., and Jorgenson, D. W. 1969. The measurement of U.S. real capital input, 1929–1967. *Review of Income and Wealth,* December, pp. 293–319.
4. ———. 1970. U.S. real product and real factor input, 1929–1967. *Review of Income and Wealth,* March, pp. 19–50.
5. Feldstein, M.; Friedman, B.; and Luft, H. 1972. Distributional aspects of national health insurance benefits and finance. *National Tax Journal* 25:497–510.
6. Goldberger, A. S. 1967. "Functional form and utility: a review of consumer demand theory." Mimeographed. Madison, Wis.: University of Wisconsin.
7. Hochman, H. M., and Rodgers, J. A. 1969. Pareto optimal redistribution. *American Economic Review* 59:542–57.
8. Kendrick, J. W. 1972. *Economic accounts and their uses.* New York: McGraw-Hill.
9. Lampman, R. 1972. "Social accounting for transfers." Mimeographed. Madison, Wis.: University of Wisconsin.
10. Maital, S. 1973. Public goods and income distribution: some further results. *Econometrica* 41:561–68.
11. Murray, M. P. 1974. "The distribution of tenant benefits in public housing." Mimeographed. Charlottesville: University of Virginia.
12. Nordhaus, W. D., and Tobin, J. 1973. Is growth obsolete? In *The measurement of economic and social performance,* ed. Studies in Income and Wealth, no. 38. New York: National Bureau of Economic Research.
13. Projector, D. S., and Bretz, J. S. 1975. Measurement of transfer income in the current population survey. In *The personal distribution of income and wealth,* ed. J. D. Smith, pp. 377–477. New York: Columbia Univ. Press.
14. Reynolds, M., and Smolensky, E. 1974. The post-fisc distribution: 1961 and 1970 compared. *National Tax Journal* 27:515–30.
15. Reynolds, M., and Smolensky, E. in press. *Public expenditures, taxes, and the distribution of income: the U.S., 1950, 1961, 1970.* New York: Academic Press.
16. Ruggles, N., and Ruggles, R. 1970. *The design of economic accounts.* New York: National Bureau of Economic Research.
17. Schmundt, M.; Stiefel, L.; and Smolensky, E. 1975. When do recipients value transfers at their cost to taxpayers? In *Integrating income maintenance programs,* ed. I. Lurie. New York: Academic Press.
18. Skolnik, A., and Dales, S. 1972. Social welfare expenditure, 1971–72. *Social Security Bulletin* 35:3–17.
19. U.S. Congress, Joint Economic Committee. 1973. Efficiency and equity effects in the benefits from the federal housing program in 1965. By E. Smolensky and J. D. Gomery. 92nd Cong., 2d sess. Washington, D.C.: U.S. Government Printing Office.

20. ———. 1973. How public welfare benefits are distributed in low-income areas. *Studies in Public Welfare*, no. 6. Washington, D. C.: U.S. Government Printing Office.
21. U.S. Department of Health, Education, and Welfare, Social Security Administration. 19 n.d.. "Social welfare expenditures." Unpublished tables. Mimeographed.
22. U.S. Department of Labor, Bureau of Labor Statistics. 1966. *Survey of Consumer Expenditures*, 1960–61, Supplement 3. Washington, D.C.: U.S. Government Printing Office.
23. von Furstenberg, G. M., and Mueller, D. C. 1971. The Pareto optimal approach to income redistribution—a fiscal application, *American Economic Review* 61:628–37.

VIII

The Economic Well-Being of Low-Income Households: Implications for Income Inequality and Poverty*

TIMOTHY M. SMEEDING

INTRODUCTION

The annual Current Population Survey has well-known inadequacies as a measure of the economic status of households. After these have been discussed, the first section of the paper presents an expanded concept of the size distribution of income and compares it to the theoretically appropriate "full" income definition. The second section explains the adjustments made to take into account effects of the positive tax system, income sharing within households, and underreporting. Subsequent sections outline the method used to estimate the value of in-kind transfers, derive a new method for the standardization of household income, compare the results at various stages of the process, and cite the implications of these revised estimates for the measurement of poverty.

The Bureau of the Census annually publishes its Current Population Survey (CPS) estimates of the size distribution of personal income and the extent of income poverty in the United States.[1] While the CPS figures are the most common source of poverty and income distribution

* This investigation was supported in part by grant number 57811 from the Social Security Administration, U.S. Department of Health, Education and Welfare, Washington, D.C. The author has benefited greatly from the helpful comments of Robert Haveman and Marilyn Moon.
[1] See, for example, U.S. Bureau of the Census [24] [25].

statistics, these estimates of household economic welfare are deficient in several respects. The shortcomings are particularly acute for low-income households—the group on which this paper will focus.

The first shortcoming is the underreporting of personal income. In 1972, the CPS recorded only 90 percent to have actually accrued to United States households. The degree of underreporting varies substantially by source of income. For instance, cash public assistance payments reported in the CPS totaled only about 74 percent of the amount that various government administrative agencies actually paid out in 1972. Social Security (OASDHI [Old Age, Survivers, Disability, and Health Insurance]) and railroad retirement payments were 89 percent reported.[2] When assessing the level of economic well-offness of low-income households—the major recipients of income transfers—this underreporting may lead to seriously biased estimates of actual cash incomes.[3]

In addition to problems of underreporting, the CPS contains no information on federal, state, or local tax payments. While different degrees of tax shifting may preclude estimates of the incidence of sales or property taxes, the amount of federal personal income and OASDHI payroll taxes paid could be easily obtained from CPS interview households.[4] To be sure, low-income households are often liable for both types of tax payments. Hence, the failure to include estimates of federal tax liability may lead to substantial overestimates of disposable income for some low-income units, e.g., the "working poor."

Further, the CPS provides no estimates of government noncash transfers such as subsidized food, housing, or medical care, which directly benefit low-income households. The seriousness of this particular omission cannot be overstated. As Table 1 attests, the total market value of noncash transfers directly increasing consumption of U.S. households, i.e., Food Stamps, Department of Housing and Urban

---

[2] U.S. Bureau of the Census [25, p. 149]. Bench-mark totals are derived from administrative records adjusted to eliminate population groups (inmates of institutions, military personnel living on post, etc.) not covered by the CPS.

[3] In contrast, the U.S. Bureau of the Census [25, p. 149] reports that wage and salary income was 98 percent of the bench-mark total. While the majority of low-income households have some earnings, other less well reported types of income are more important to lower-income households.

[4] In fact, because CPS respondents are asked to consult federal income tax forms and income tax withholding statements in reporting their incomes, it seems appropriate to inquire why federal personal income tax and payroll tax information is *not* collected in the CPS.

TABLE 1

The Aggregate Market Value of Selected[a] Noncash Transfer Programs and Cash Public Assistance Payments (in Billions of Current Dollars)

Type of transfer payment	Calendar year			
	1968	1972	1973	1975[d]
1. Cash public assistance[b]	$5.225	$ 9.745	$10.666	$12.100
2. Noncash transfer payments[c]	8.695	16.351	20.417	26.712
3. Difference 2.–1.	3.470	6.606	9.751	14.612
4. Percentage difference (3./1.)·100	66.4	67.8	91.4	120.8

Sources: U.S. Department of Health, Education, and Welfare, the Social Security Administration, and the Budget of the United States Government.

[a] These include only the programs specifically considered in this paper. See note c for details.

[b] These include Aid to Families with Dependent Children; State and Local General Assistance; and Old Age Assistance, Aid to the Blind, and Aid to the Permanently and Totally Disabled, which were combined in 1974 to form the new Supplemental Security Income program.

[c] These include Food Stamps; Medicare, Supplemental Medical Insurance, and Medicaid; and four federal housing programs: Low Rent Public Housing, Rent Supplements, "Section 236" rental assistance, and "Section 235" home ownership assistance.

[d] These figures are based on U.S. budget estimates and unpublished Department of Health, Education, and Welfare data.

Development public housing programs, and Medicaid, Medicare, and Supplementary Medical Insurance, exceeds cash public assistance by an ever-increasing margin.[5] For 1975 the subsidy value of these noncash transfers ($26.7 billion) is more than twice as large as the dollar volume of cash public assistance payments ($12.1 billion). Clearly a major source of economic welfare for low-income households is omitted from the CPS data.

Cash income—even after adjusting for in-kind transfers and taxes—is an inadequate measure of economic status. While income captures the market value of resources at the command of the unit in question, it does not reflect the needs to which these resources will be applied.

[5] Transfers in the form of food, housing, and medical care are assumed to add directly to household current consumption. Other types of "investment" transfers, e.g., education subsidies and manpower training programs, are omitted from this study. Cash public assistance includes needs-adjusted payments made under the following programs: Aid to Families with Dependent Children, Old Age Assistance, Aid to the Blind, Aid to the Permanently and Totally Disabled, and State and Local General Assistance.

Consumption needs vary by household size, location, and sex and age composition. Hence, in this analysis, a measure of income per unit of need—termed equivalent income—is employed to reflect both the level of household resources and claims made upon them.

Finally, to treat noncash transfers as sources of additional economic welfare for low-income households, it is important to estimate correctly the incremental welfare added by these benefits. Often the value of the food, housing, or medical care transfer is less than the cost of providing that benefit to the recipient unit. Because additional economic welfare provided by noncash transfer payments is a crucial variable in estimating household well-offness, the recipient's valuation of the transfer must be determined. Estimation of the value that a recipient places on in-kind transfers is, however, difficult. Here a simple and theoretically defensible model for estimating the cash equivalent value of these transfers is employed.

Concentrating on the CPS shortcomings noted above, I present an expanded estimate of the size distribution of personal income including the recipient value of noncash transfers, intrahousehold income sharing, federal income and payroll tax liability, and income underreporting adjustments. I also develop an equivalent income standardization procedure which adjusts my "comprehensive" household income measure for the basic needs of its members. This is my preferred welfare measure. Comparisons (1) between the CPS measure and my more inclusive measure of comprehensive household income, and (2) between the size distribution of my comprehensive household income measure and my measure of equivalent comprehensive income suggest major implications for the measurement and extent of income poverty.

I. ECONOMIC WELFARE AND COMPREHENSIVE INCOME

Many critical assumptions are necessary even to compile theoretically a comprehensive "full" income definition of household economic status. By assuming that a household has the ability to shift income flows and wealth stocks between periods and a uniform preference for allocating real consumption over its remaining lifetime, and by assuming no voluntary bequests or estates at death, we may theoretically define "full" income in any period as the annual annuitized value of the total stock of expected lifetime consumption.[6] Because income and wealth can be used to even out consumption flows, theoretical full income and full consumption are identical. Adding the assumption of full knowledge of future income flows, household position in the life cycle is unimportant because all households are assumed to evenly allocate their total stock of wealth and the present value of future income over their remaining lifetimes. Given such information, the size distribution of the average income flow of any household over *any* period of time could be gauged. This enables a partial adjustment to the inadequate distributional inferences derived from cross-sectional income data.[7] Further, given an appropriate poverty threshold index, a household's "permanent" poverty status could be estimated. For several practical reasons, however, such estimates cannot be made.

On a theoretical level, the sources of "full" income include current returns to market and nonmarket productive activities, net transfers, and wealth. However, we will not venture to estimate the net value of time spent in such productive nonmarket activities such as housework, volunteer work, acquiring an education, or home production.[8] Further, nonmarket income sources such as leisure, "donor" benefits accruing to those who transfer income, and the value of publicly provided goods and services are certainly important to a comprehensive index of economic well-being. Unfortunately they are not objectively quantifiable on a microeconomic basis. Thus, these adjustments to cash income are omitted as well. Rather, we are forced to concentrate our efforts on

---

[6] Gary Becker [3] first utilized the term "full income" in referring to the real satisfaction households receive from all productive activity, including leisure, the value of home services, work satisfaction, and the value of public goods and services received without explicit cost. Ismail Sirageldin [19] first attempted the empirical estimation of aggregate "full income" for 1964, based on Becker's work and the pioneering work of James Morgan et al. [15]. To this analysis, we add the lifetime income hypotheses of Franco Modigliani and Richard Brumberg [13] and of Albert Ando and Franco Modigliani [2]. Thus our theoretical concept of full income includes additions to and deletions from real wealth as well as current income received from market and nonmarket productive activity, and income transfers. Marilyn Moon [14] has considered such a measure of economic welfare in her work on the economic well-being of the aged. Rather than offering a complete description of these welfare measures, the discussion below combines and abbreviates these foundations in arriving at a comprehensive measure of household economic well-being, or "full income," at any point in time.

[7] For a starting point for comparisons between cross-sectional and lifetime distributions, see V. Stoikov [23] and Morton Paglin [18].

[8] One attempt at measuring these welfare components has been carried out by Sirageldin [19].

measurable market and nonmarket (tax and transfer) sources of comprehensive income.

The base for developing estimates of current household comprehensive income is annual money income. As a result, the more comprehensive welfare measure will indicate the command over marketable goods and services in each year.[9] The demographic accounting unit for income sharing will be the household. Thus we take implicit account of intrahousehold income transfers between nonrelated members of the same household.[10]

The more comprehensive income measure used here is thus defined as follows for any year t:

$$Y_t = \hat{C}_t + I_t = T_t + \hat{R}_t + E_t$$

where

Y_t = comprehensive household income,

$\hat{C}_t$ = CPS earned and property income adjusted for net underreporting,

I_t = implicit intrahousehold transfers,

T_t = estimated federal personal income tax and payroll tax liability,

$\hat{R}_t$ = cash income transfers adjusted for net underreporting,

E_t = the cash equivalent value of in-kind transfer payments.

The next two sections briefly discuss each of these income components. In the final sections of the paper, this comprehensive income value (Y_t) will be compared to the census household income estimate:

$$CSH_t = C_t + R_t + I_t$$

[9] Because the CPS contains no data on household liquid or illiquid asset ownership and no information concerning capital gains income, we are not able to use an income–net worth measure (for instance a constant annuitization scheme) to convert a households' stock of wealth into an average yearly property income flow. See Moon [14] or Burton Weisbrod and W. L. Hansen [29] for excellent treatments of income–net worth. The effect of including income–net worth on the welfare of "low-income" units is unclear. Normally one would expect that annuitized net worth would add to the previously estimated income flow of the average household. If, however, debts exceed assets, as is probably the case for many low income units, net worth may actually be negative and hence reduce economic welfare. For some discussion of indebtedness among urban households see Daniel Bell [5], and also Moon [14] on the aged poor. Nor are we able to estimate an important source of income for middle age and elderly poor, the rental income flow from owner-occupied housing. Again, see Moon [14] for an estimate of the rental value of owner-occupied housing for the aged segment of the population.

[10] This procedure is compared to the Census Bureau's standard "family" and "unrelated individual" accounting procedure in the next section of the paper. For an example of the usual Census Bureau treatment see U.S. Bureau of the Census [25].

where

CSH_t = unadjusted census money income as reported in the CPS,

C_t = earned and property income as reported in the CPS,

R_t = cash transfers as reported in the CPS,

I_t = implicit intrahousehold income transfers.

II. ADJUSTED CPS CASH INCOME: INCOME UNDERREPORTING, FEDERAL TAXES, AND INTRAHOUSEHOLD TRANSFERS

Income Underreporting: $\hat{C}_t$, $\hat{R}_t$. Current Population Survey (CPS) cash income figures for each type of reported income were adjusted for *net* underreporting and nonreporting according to a procedure based on that developed by the Urban Institute.[11] Final adjusted figures correspond closely to CPS bench-mark counts of the actual number of recipient units and aggregate dollar values for each income component.

Federal Taxes: T_t. Federal personal income and payroll taxes were estimated according to a detailed imputation procedure.[12] Statutory OASDHI payroll tax rates and earnings ceilings were used to estimate payroll tax liability for earnings and self-employment income.[13] Personal income tax payment estimates separated persons by tax filing units,

---

[11] Net underreporting of survey income information is all that can be treated without a direct record for record check between survey income respondents and their individual administrative records (personal income tax forms, welfare agency records, etc.). If in fact people often overstate different types of income for whatever reasons, any n percent net underreporting noticed in the aggregate figures most probably consists of a total x percent overreport coupled with an $x + n$ percent underreport. Short of a direct record match, there is no perfect method of adjusting for income misreporting.

See H. Beebout and P. Bonina [4] for more information on the Urban Institute income underreporting adjustment model. In brief, this adjustment model deals with both underreporting (i.e., an inadequate total dollar amount as compared with the adjusted bench-mark total) and nonreporting (i.e., an inadequate number of recipients as compared to recipient control counts). The key assumption is one of proportional underreporting of income, given the correct number of recipients for each income type. See Timothy Smeeding [20, chapter 2 and appendix 2], for a complete description of the process followed in this paper.

[12] See Timothy Smeeding [20, appendix 6].

[13] Federal government employees payroll tax contributions were estimated separately. While it may be argued the employer's share of payroll taxes are to some extent shifted back in the form of lower wages, any shifting of this type is already affected in lower before-tax wages. Hence, only the statutory employee portion of the payroll tax need be included.

calculated standardized or itemized deductions, tax credits, and personal exemptions, and applied tax liabilities from Internal Revenue Service tax tables. In this procedure, tax filing rules where chosen to minimize the tax liability of each filing unit. Taxes paid by separate filing units were then aggregated into households to determine the total liability. Estimated tax liabilities by income level correspond closely to Internal Revenue Service estimates for households with less than $12,000 of adjusted gross income. For higher income tax paying units, the broad variance in the value of itemized deductions and the CPS omission of capital gains income prohibit a more accurate estimate of the actual income tax liability of each household.

Intrahousehold Transfers: I_t. The unit of analysis employed in this study is the household. Thus, families and unrelated individuals (one-person families) are not separated as is the usual Census Bureau practice. Besides including one-person units with (family) units of two or more, the difference between the "household" and "family and unrelated individual" definitions concerns the relatedness of household members. If all members of a particular economic unit are related by blood, marriage, or adoption, the household and the family are equivalent and all members are assumed to share equally the unit's resources.[14] However, if unrelated persons share living arrangements, the census normally treats these persons as separate economic units and disregards any intrahousehold income sharing among them. While it is impossible to measure accurately the actual degree of income and resource sharing which occurs in such units, it is more appropriate to treat these individuals as a single resource sharing unit for poverty status determination, rather than as separate units.

While this realignment of units affects only a small proportion of the total number of households, it has a large impact on the estimated number of poor units. Using this realignment, it is estimated that the "official" census poverty count for 1972 is reduced 12.2 percent, from 9.958 million to 8.744 million poor households.[15] In terms of the number

---

[14] This is generally the case. In fact, household and family income are equal for more than 95 percent of all census units. See U.S. Bureau of the Census [26].

[15] The official census poverty counts are taken from U.S. Bureau of the Census [24]. Recent population trends indicate that this accounting bias in census poverty counts is growing at a rapid rate, particularly among young adults (18–30) who are increasingly living together as unrelated individuals. In 1968 household versus family–unrelated individuals accounting reduced the poverty count by only 6.5 percent. Thus the effect of the census accounting bias has roughly doubled in importance from 1968 to 1972 (see Smeeding [20, pp. 82–88]).

of poor persons, the 1972 census poverty count drops from 24.455 million to 23.160 million persons, a reduction of 1.295 million individuals, or 5.3 percent. For analyzing the degree of income inequality, there is no clear agreement on the appropriate unit of analysis. Yet the usual compilation of income distribution statistics for families implicitly omits 13.986 million unrelated individuals—thus ignoring income inequality among more than 20 percent of all households.[16] To maintain consistency and to include all income sharing units in one set of estimates, this paper establishes the household as the unit of analysis.

III.   THE CASH EQUIVALENT OF IN-KIND TRANSFERS: E_t

Noncash transfer benefits were imputed to households using adjusted income and demographic eligibility criteria and independent government agency estimates of the distribution of these benefits by age, sex, income level, geographical location, and public assistance status of recipients. The programs covered were the Food Stamp program; the Medicare and Supplemental Medical Insurance (SMI) programs; the Medicaid program; and finally four separate public housing programs: Low Rent Public Housing, Rent Supplements, "Section 236" rental assistance, and "Section 235" subsidized mortgages for owner-occupied housing. Other noncash transfers, mainly those in the form of education benefits, were not included in this study.

Medical care benefits were imputed on the basis of their insurance value rather than the amount of money paid to medical vendors on any recipient's behalf. Thus, all persons eligible for Medicare–SMI and Medicaid were assigned the fair insurance value according to their

---

[16] Source, U.S. Bureau of the Census [26, p. 5]. Essentially, we are trying to identify the income sharing unit rather than the income-receiving unit. If the former is larger than the latter we will underestimate intrahousehold transfers, and so the level of economic well-being of the household unit, by employing a family–unrelated individuals accounting framework. For more on this topic see Fiegehen and Lansley (1975). The family–unrelated individuals accounting convention implies that separate income distribution summary statistics (e.g., Gini coefficients) should be used for each type of unit, thus separating households of size 1 from households of size 2 or more. Per capita income distribution statistics ignore economies of size in providing most types of goods (e.g., food and housing) to larger income sharing units. Finally, income distribution statistics based on the household accounting procedure may in fact overstate the amount of intraunit resource sharing which actually takes place. Thus there is no clearly preferable unit for presenting income distribution statistics.

recipient category.[17] Benefit levels were further adjusted to reflect regional variations in medical care costs and deflated by the difference between the medical price index and the consumer price index to reflect the real insurance value of the coverage. Public housing benefits were imputed according to household income levels, age, household structure, and public assistance status. Imputed benefits were then roughly adjusted for geographical location and metropolitan–nonmetropolitan residence. In addition to income level, public assistance status, and household demographic structure, Food Stamp benefits were further adjusted to reflect the number of months each family participated in the program.[18]

At least three recent studies have attempted to determine a household unit's willingness to pay for noncash transfers—that is, their equivalent cash value to the family.[19] Voluntary participation in a noncash welfare program indicates that the household is in some sense better off than if it had not participated in the program. Yet whether this value is equal to the taxpayer cost of providing the service depends on the type and amount of each particular study.[20]

The methodology followed here first assumed that a family comparable to the recipient unit in terms of cash income and family size received a hypothetical cash transfer equal to the market value of the in-kind subsidy.[21] Then, the share of total consumption expenditures that this comparable household with its higher income level, would devote to the subsidized commodity was calculated. This value served as an estimate of the cash value of the transfer to the actual recipient household. If the

[17] The fair insurance value of a medical insurance subsidy is measured by all vendor payments plus administrative costs minus premiums paid by eligibles in each eligibility category, divided by the total number of eligibles in each category.

[18] For a more complete description of the imputation procedures followed by the author, see Smeeding [20, especially appendix 7].

[19] Eugene Smolensky et al. [22] is probably the best and most comprehensive treatment of this problem. Also, J. Kraft and E. Olsen [12] and Kenneth Clarkson [6] deal with cash equivalents of in-kind transfers in the form of Low Rent Public Housing and Food Stamps, respectively.

[20] If in fact the subsidy is open-ended price subsidy, it is generally true that a smaller cash payment would put the recipient family on the same indifference curve as the more expensive noncash subsidy. The problem then is to estimate how much less cash income would leave the household as well-off as the in-kind benefit. This requires measuring the shape of household indifference curves, i.e., measuring elasticities of substitution between subsidized and nonsubsidized goods. See Smolensky et al. [22] and Smeeding [20, pp. 103–40] for a further discussion of this topic.

[21] In the case of medical care subsidies, households were further differentiated according to the age of the household head. See Smeeding [20, appendix 7].

amount which the comparable household receiving the hypothetical cash transfer would have spent on the subsidized good exceeded the market value of the in-kind transfer, the cash equivalent and the subsidy cost were considered equal.[22] In this case, the household receiving the noncash transfer was presumed to be indifferent between the noncash subsidy and an equivalent cash grant. Hence, grants fulfilling this criterion are treated as perfect substitutes for cash. On the other hand, if the subsidy cost of the in-kind transfer exceeded the amount which the comparable family would voluntarily have spent on the subsidized good, the value of the subsidy was reduced by the difference between these two amounts.[23]

On average, the estimated cash equivalent values for food, housing, and medical care subsidies were 88, 56, and 68 percent of their market value, respectively. Table 2 shows the subsidy values by income class, the corresponding cash equivalents (*ce*), and efficiency ratios (the ratio of the *ce* to the subsidy value) for each type of transfer in 1972.[24] Since food, housing, and medical insurance are normal goods, household willingness to pay for noncash transfers (and hence their average *ce*) rises with household cash income. In the case of food stamps, the *ce* value approaches the subsidy cost at low income levels, indicating that food stamps are a fairly good substitute for cash. For medical care subsidies the *ce* values rise very slowly, indicating a relatively low income elasticity of medical care consumption. In the case of public housing subsidies, the efficiency ratio first rises and then *falls* at higher income levels. This result is due to the peculiar form of Low Rent Public Housing transfers and "Section 236" rental assistance subsidies, which comprise 73 percent of the market value of all public housing transfers. Essentially these two programs offer a "take it or leave it" choice to prospective public housing tenants. Either recipients accept the transfer by living in a specific public housing unit or they do not participate. As a result, many households would have consumed more housing than the

---

[22] This is not quite true in the case of some public housing subsidies, as is pointed out later.

[23] Smolensky et al. [22] directly utilize formal utility functions and then separately select elasticities of substitution (σ) between the subsidized good and other goods. Kraft and Olsen [12] utilize a Cobb–Douglas utility function where $\sigma = 1$. As distinct from these approaches, the model used here implicitly determines the value of σ, rather than choosing it on an ad hoc basis. For further information see Smeeding [20, pp. 103–40 and appendix 7].

[24] Smolensky et al. [22] refer to these as "benefit weights." One minus the "efficiency ratio" expresses the percentage of extra taxpayer cost involved in coercing recipients to consume the desired goods versus presenting recipients with equal value cash transfers.

TABLE 2
Average Food, Medical, and Housing Subsidies and Their Cash Equivalents at Various Levels of Disposable Personal Income in 1972

Level of household disposable personal income (in thousands of dollars)	Food stamps			Medicare–SMI and Medicaid			Public Housing		
	(1) Average bonus value	(2) Average cash equivalent value	(3) Efficiency ratio (2)/(1)	(4) Average medical insurance subsidy	(5) Average cash equivalent	(6) Efficiency ratio (5)/(4)	(7) Average public housing subsidy	(8) Average cash equivalent	(9) Efficiency ratio (8)/(7)
$0–.999	$659	$481	.73	641	373	.58	$912	621	.68
1. 0–1.999	343	295	.86	863	468	.54	913	683	.74
2. 0–2.999	297	261	.88	661	393	.59	1032	666	.65
3. 0–3.999	355	316	.89	525	335	.64	1060	605	.57
4. 0–4.999	344	310	.90	484	326	.67	987	554	.56
5. 0–5.999	334	309	.93	474	328	.69	763	395	.52
6. 0–7.499	344	325	.95	485	336	.70	768	344	.45
7. 5–9.999	325	323	1.00	440	339	.77	783	275	.35
10. 0 +	375	375	1.00	375	317	.85	831	214	.26
Aggregate market value in billions and overall average efficiency ratio[b]	$1.922	$1.692	.88	$12.916	$8.828	.68	$1.513	$.854	.56

[a] Cash income after adjusting for federal payroll and personal income taxes and income underreporting.
[b] The overall average efficiency ratio equals the total market value of each subsidy divided by the total cash equivalent value of that subsidy.

public housing unit provided if presented with an equal value cash transfer or if presented with a flexible rent-subsidy.[25]

IV. EQUIVALENT INCOME

As indicated above, the level of economic welfare of an income sharing unit is better represented by its comprehensive income per unit of economic need than by the cash value of comprehensive income. Hence, the household welfare measure employed here is defined as:

$$W_t = \gamma Y_t$$

where

W_t = equivalent comprehensive household income,

Y_t = comprehensive household income as previously defined,

γ = income standardization factor.

The income standardization factor, γ, is a household equivalence scale ratio relating the number of adults in a four-person nonfarm household to the actual number of adults in any given household.[26] Hence, each

---

[25] In estimating the ce's for public housing programs, 34.1 percent of all Low Rent Public Housing and "Section 236" public housing recipients (408,000 household units) would have consumed more housing than was provided by their public housing unit if presented with an equal cash payment. In other words, the form of the subsidy discouraged the consumption of extra housing for 408,000 public housing beneficiaries. In this case, the value of the subsidy to the household is reduced by the difference between the desired consumption share of our comparable household and the market value of the housing subsidy. One interpretation of this phenomenon (see Smolensky and Gomery [21] and Smeeding [20, p. 124]) is that not only does the average taxpayer desire that transfer recipients consume housing per se, but also that they live in the particular physical location of the housing unit. This particular cost can be estimated by subtracting our 56 percent average efficiency ratio from a 72 percent average efficiency ratio estimated by Smolensky et al. [22] which did not take account of the quantity restrictions of low rent public housing. Hence 16 cents of each public housing dollar discourages the consumption of additional housing. This extra cost can be attributed to the restrictive form in which the majority of public housing benefits are offered. The remaining 28 percent efficiency cost may be attributed to satisfying the paternalistic preferences of the average "donor" taxpayer for housing consumption and/or other motives.

[26] Equivalence scales are a method of accounting for economies of scale in providing economic goods to different types of households. Equivalence scales then seek to find the level of disposable cash income which would make each family with a set of given demographic characteristics as well-off as any other family with different size, location, and compositional characteristics. See Milton Friedman [8] for a general discussion of the equivalence scale methodology. The equivalence scales utilized in this study are implicit in the U.S. Bureau of the Census poverty lines developed by Mollie Orshansky [16]. For

family's income is standardized to that of a four-person family. In general, equivalent income levels of smaller families exceed their cash income levels, while the reverse is true for higher income units. For a nonfarm family of four persons, cash and equivalent income are identical.

V. THE SIZE DISTRIBUTION OF INCOME AND THE TAX TRANSFER SYSTEM

The degree of inequality in economic status is affected by the income definition employed. This section examines the effect of adjusting pretransfer income for underreporting of taxes, cash transfers, and noncash transfers on measured inequality. Tables 3 and 4 show the degree of inequality for a number of income definitions in both 1972 and 1968.[27]

Table 3 shows the size distribution of household income (1) before taxes and transfers, (2) after personal income and payroll taxes but before transfers,[28] (3) after taxes and cash transfers, and, finally, (4) after taxes and cash and in-kind transfers (i.e., "comprehensive income"). All of these distributions include adjustments for underreporting.[29] The final column presents the distribution of reported CPS money income. Covering these same income types, Table 4 gives the cumulative percentage of households with income less than selected bench-

[27] In order to show interyear changes in income distributions, we have included a set of statistics for the 1968 income year as well. Thus we are able to compare figures for the 1972 focal year with a similarly adjusted set of income distribution statistics from an earlier year.

[28] This provides some estimate of the distribution of pretransfer income. Yet to the extent that the availability of income transfers affects the distribution of pre- and posttax income, "posttax but pretransfer" income cannot be taken to represent the distribution of income in the absence of transfers.

[29] Reported census income does not take account of federal taxes paid, income underreporting, or the cash equivalent value of in-kind transfers, as previously mentioned.

---

each household i:

$$W_{ti} = \frac{\bar{T}_t}{T_{ti}} \cdot (Y_{ti}) \qquad \text{where } \bar{T}_t \text{ is the poverty threshold in year } t$$

for a nonfarm family of four persons ($4,275 in 1972), while T_{ti} is the poverty threshold for the given household. Because both T's change yearly with the consumer price index, the equivalent income standardization is identical in 1968 and 1972. See Smeeding [20, appendix 1].

TABLE 3
Size Distribution of Personal Income, 1972 and 1968

Percentage of households	Cumulative percentage distribution of:				
	$\hat{C}_t + I_t$ [a]	$\hat{C}_t + I_t - T_t$ [b]	$\hat{C}_t + I_t - T_t + \hat{R}_t$ [c]	$\hat{C}_t + I_t - T_t + \hat{R}_t + \hat{E}_t = Y_t$ [d]	CSH_t [e]
1972					
10	.2	.2	1.6	1.9	1.2
20	.9	.8	4.9	5.6	4.0
30	3.7	4.0	9.8	10.7	8.5
40	9.3	9.8	16.4	17.1	14.9
50	17.3	17.9	24.9	25.5	22.5
60	27.0	27.8	34.5	34.8	32.2
70	38.8	40.0	45.3	45.8	43.4
80	53.3	54.2	58.8	58.9	56.8
90	72.8	72.0	75.2	75.2	74.6
100	100.0	100.0	100.0	100.0	100.0
1968					
10	.2	.3	1.4	1.7	1.1
20	1.1	1.2	5.0	5.4	4.0
30	4.8	5.2	10.1	10.5	8.5
40	11.0	11.7	16.9	17.4	15.0
50	19.2	20.2	25.2	25.7	23.0
60	29.5	30.4	35.4	35.9	33.0
70	41.3	42.5	46.2	46.6	44.3
80	55.3	56.5	59.5	60.0	57.8
90	72.5	73.4	75.3	75.7	73.9
100	100.0	100.0	100.0	100.0	100.0

[a] Earnings plus property income and other minor sources of taxable income, adjusted for income underreporting.

[b] Income after federal personal income taxes and OASDHI payroll taxes, adjusted for income underreporting.

[c] Income after taxes plus public and private cash transfers, adjusted for income underreporting.

[d] Income after taxes plus public and private cash transfers, adjusted for income underreporting, plus in-kind food, housing, and medical transfers measured at their cash equivalent to value.

[e] Original census income as reported in the *Current Population Survey*, March Supplement. Underreporting adjustments, noncash transfers, and federal tax payments are not accounted for.

169

TABLE 4
Personal Income Distribution by Income Class, 1968 and 1972

Upper bound of income brackets (in current dollars)	$C_t + I_t$ [a]	$C_t + I_t - T_t$ [b]	$C_t + I_t - T_t + R_t$ [c]	$C_t + I_t - T_t + R_t + E_t = Y_t$ [n]	CSH_t [o]
			Percentage of households with incomes less than upper bound of given income classes		
			1972		
$1,000	16.8	17.2	2.0	1.3	2.8
2,000	21.0	21.7	6.5	4.1	8.1
3,000	24.5	25.5	12.4	10.1	14.3
4,000	27.8	29.4	18.0	16.3	20.0
5,000	31.3	34.2	24.4	22.9	25.5
6,000	35.0	39.2	30.8	29.6	30.8
7,500	41.6	47.7	40.8	39.8	38.1
10,000	52.6	61.4	56.5	55.9	51.1
12,500	64.0	73.6	70.2	69.8	64.1
15,000	73.9	83.0	80.6	80.4	73.6
20,000	87.1	92.8	91.7	91.6	87.9

	a	b	c	d	e
$ 1,000	15.7	17.2	3.1	2.4	4.5
2,000	20.2	21.7	9.7	8.5	11.7
3,000	24.0	25.5	16.2	15.2	18.1
4,000	28.7	29.4	23.8	22.9	24.8
5,000	33.7	34.2	31.4	30.7	31.1
6,000	39.5	39.2	39.4	38.8	37.8
7,500	49.0	47.7	52.7	52.1	48.8
10,000	64.7	61.4	71.4	71.0	65.8
12,500	77.3	73.6	84.1	83.8	79.4
15,000	86.2	83.0	91.2	91.0	87.4
20,000	94.6	92.8	96.8	96.8	95.1
Gini coefficients	.4368	.4312	.3562	.3476	.3852

[a] Earnings plus property income and other minor sources of taxable income, adjusted for income underreporting.

[b] Income after federal personal income taxes and OASDHI payroll taxes, adjusted for income underreporting.

[c] Income after taxes plus public and private cash transfers, adjusted for income underreporting.

[d] Income after taxes plus public and private cash transfers, adjusted for income underreporting, plus in-kind food, housing, and medical transfers measured at their cash equivalent to recipient households.

[e] Original census income as reported in the *Current Population Survey*, March Supplement. Underreporting adjustments, noncash transfers, and federal tax payments are not accounted for.

mark income levels. The income figures on which the first four columns of each table are based reflect the adjustments made for income underreporting.[30] Finally, Table 4 also displays the Gini coefficients for each income definition, based on computed mean incomes within each decile.[31]

All three tables emphasize the overall income-equalizing effect of the combined U.S. tax and transfer system on the personal income. Table 3 reveals that the share of the bottom 20 percent of all households rises from .9 percent of earned plus property income to 5.6 percent of comprehensive income. This corresponds to the census estimate of a 4.0 percent share of reported CPS income. After the adjustments undertaken here, the income share of the bottom quintile is 40 percent greater than that indicated by the census estimates. A similar pattern is also apparent for 1968.

[30] Because the data revisions incorporated in this paper have primarily concentrated on deriving a more comprehensive measure of economic well-being for "low-income" groups, and, further, due to the difficulties involved in correcting for these deficiencies, two additional sources of income which largely accrue to middle- and higher-income groups have been ignored. First, dividend income, which was 55 percent underreported on the original CPS data file, was not adjusted. Thus, in 1972 approximately $10.1 billion of income accruing primarily to upper income classes was omitted. Second, the CPS income data makes no allowance for the $18.1 billion of realized capital gains income reported to the Internal Revenue Service in 1972, and again accruing primarily to higher-income classes. Yet it does not seem that these omitted figures would make a great deal of difference to the results of this study. For instance, the bottom 20 percent of households receive only 5.63 percent of the total comprehensive income of $722.5 billion. Now assume that the bottom quintile of households receive *none* of the omitted $28.2 billion of realized capital gains and underreported divident income. Further, assume that *none* of this additional income is liable for personal income taxation. This extra income would reduce the share of the bottom quintile of households to 5.42 percent of the new $750.7 billion income total. More reasonably, if one-quarter of this extra $28.2 billion is paid in personal income taxes, the share of the bottom quintile is reduced by only .016, to 5.47 percent of total income. From Internal Revenue Service figures, we calculate that the bottom quintile receives roughly 1.2 percent of these omitted payments, or $32 billion. If this is actually the case, the income share of the bottom quintile falls by only .1 percent, to 5.53 percent of total income. Hence, we conclude that the omission of these income sources makes little, if any, difference in the accuracy of our estimates.

[31] This provides a lower bound estimate of actual Gini coefficients. While the upper bound estimate may be derived by distributing the income so as to maximize the spread within each income grouping (decile in this case), Gastwirth's experimentation with Internal Revenue Service tax return data for 1967 indicates that the difference between bounds is less than .006. See J. L. Gastwirth [10, p. 306]. The availability of micro income data allows us to use the actual mean income within each fractile, rather than being forced to use income bracket midpoints in computing the Gini coefficient, as is often the case with grouped data.

However, the income share of the bottom quintile falls slightly in 1972 when federal personal income and payroll taxes are subtracted from earned plus property income. This is in contrast to 1968, when the same comparison reveals that federal taxes slightly increased the share of income accruing to the bottom quintile. In part, this reflects the increasingly regressive nature of the OASDHI payroll tax, which rose from 4.4 percent to 5.2 percent of earnings over this period. While some households in the lowest earnings-plus-property income quintile probably paid personal income taxes in 1968, by 1972 no one in that quintile was liable for personal income taxation.[32] Yet, despite the offsetting effect of progressive changes in the personal income tax law, the increasingly regressive payroll tax actually *lowers* the percentage of after-tax income accruing to the bottom quintile.

When comparing the distributions of comprehensive and census-reported CPS income (Y_t and CSH_t) for 1968 and 1972, the degree of interyear stability is substantial. For instance, the size distribution of "comprehensive income" in 1968 differs from that of 1972 by no more than 1.1 percentage points in any decile. The distribution of census-reported income shows much the same interyear pattern, differing by 1.0 percentage point or less in any decile between 1968 and 1972. Thus, despite demographic population shifts, rising unemployment rates, and rapidly rising cash and noncash income transfers, only a minor amount of change in the yearly size distribution of personal income is realized between these years. Comparing 1972 and 1968 comprehensive income distributions, the income share of the bottom 30 percent of all households increased by about .2 percentage points, while the income share of the top 60 percent of all households decreased by about the same amount. Thus there was a minor amount of income redistribution from

---

[32] In both 1968 and 1972 the lowest quintile of households had an upper income bound of slightly less than $2,000 before taxes and transfers. In 1972, a single person's adjusted gross income (AGI) needed to be above $2,050 to be liable for personal income taxation. Due to personal exemptions, the AGI point below which personal taxes are zero rises with household size. Thus no households in the bottom quintile were liable for personal income taxes in 1972. In 1968, however, single persons with an AGI of more than $900 were liable for income taxes. Thus some households in the lowest quintile probably paid personal income taxes in 1968. Failure to account for these "standardizing" items yields biased comparisons of the inequality of economic welfare if there are large differences in average size and family structure among high- and low-income households. It is important to note that families are reranked by deciles in computing each separate distribution in Table 5. Thus households move from decile to decile depending on the concept and measure of income which is employed.

the middle and high comprehensive income groups to the lowest comprehensive income deciles.

In Table 4, we find the lowest income groups increasing their dollar level of economic well-being mainly because of income transfers. For instance, in 1972, 5.1 percent fewer households had comprehensive incomes below the $3,000 level, yet in both years, 25.5 percent of all households were below the $3,000 mark after taxes but before transfers. Thus, the cash and in-kind transfer system reduced the number of households with incomes below $3,000 by just over one-third between 1968 and 1972. Adjusting for the 20.2 percent change in consumer prices between 1968 and 1972, about 13.2 percent of households had comprehensive income under $3,000 in the latter year. As a result, the difference in percentage of households with real incomes less than $3,000 is about 2.0 percent. Hence, for the lowest-income households, real income rises at a slower rate. A comparison of the final two columns indicates the effect of the data adjustments on the percentage of households below any given income level. For instance, our estimate of the proportion of households with incomes less than $3,000 is 10.1 percent versus the census estimate of 14.3 percent.

Finally, the Gini coefficients in Table 4 display a slightly more unequal income distribution in 1972 than in 1968 for all of the income measures. The final column, however, indicates that the transfer system in 1972 had a substantial equalizing effect. The 1968 and 1972 Gini coefficients are similar for comprehensive income but vary substantially for the earned plus property income distributions. Thus, we conclude that the system of taxes and cash and in-kind transfers has contributed a great deal to the maintenance of observed interyear equality.

VI. THE SIZE DISTRIBUTION OF COMPREHENSIVE INCOME AND EQUIVALENT INCOME

In Table 5, both comprehensive income ($) and original census income ($) are compared to their equivalent income counterparts ($e) for 1968 and 1972. As indicated above, the equivalent income measure standardizes any absolute income measure into a measure of income per unit of economic need.

Several types of comparisons seem useful. First, the distribution of comprehensive income is compared with its standardized equivalent income distribution in the top half of Table 5, for 1968 and 1972. In 1968, the distributional differences between these two measures are very

TABLE 5
Two Size Distributions of Cash Income and Equivalent Income in 1968 and 1972

Percentage of households ranked by $ or $e as appropriate[a]	Cumulative percentage distribution of *comprehensive* income: Y_t			
	1968		1972	
	Cash income ($): Y_t	Equivalent income ($e): W_t	Cash income ($): Y_t	Equivalent income ($e): W_t
10	1.7	2.0	1.9	2.5
20	5.4	6.0	5.6	6.9
30	10.5	11.4	10.7	12.4
40	17.4	18.2	17.1	19.2
50	25.7	26.2	25.5	27.3
60	35.9	35.4	34.8	36.6
70	46.6	46.2	45.8	47.5
80	60.0	59.0	58.9	60.2
90	75.7	74.7	75.2	76.0
100	100.0	100.0	100.0	100.0
Gini coefficients	.3476	.3479	.3522	.3287

Percentage of households ranked by $ or $e as appropriate[a]	Cumulative percentage distribution of *original* CPS income: CSH_t			
	1968		1972	
	Cash income ($): CSH_t	Equivalent income ($e)	Cash income ($): CSH_t	Equivalent income ($e)
10	1.1	1.5	1.2	1.6
20	4.0	4.9	4.0	5.0
30	8.5	9.8	8.5	9.9
40	15.0	16.3	14.9	16.2
50	23.0	24.0	22.5	23.9
60	33.0	33.2	32.2	33.1
70	44.3	44.2	43.4	44.0
80	57.8	57.2	56.8	57.3
90	73.9	73.7	74.6	73.7
100	100.0	100.0	100.0	100.0
Gini coefficients	.3852	.3780	.3890	.3781

[a] That is, in each separate column households are ranked according to the particular type of income (comprehensive or original CPS) and measure of economic welfare (cash, $, or equivalent, $e, dollars) under consideration.

small. The income share of the lowest quintile increases by about 11 percent, from 5.4 to 6.0 percent, while that of the highest quintile decreases from 41.1 percent to 39.8 percent. Moreover, comprehensive income per unit of need is more equally distributed than the absolute amount of comprehensive income: the Gini coefficient for the latter is .3522, while that for the former is .3287. The lower panel of Table 5 shows the distribution of reported census income in cash and equivalent income terms, indicating a pattern similar to that of comprehensive income. From 1968 to 1972 the dollar share of the lowest quintile rises from the absolute to the equivalent income distributions. Thus, a slightly more equal equivalent income distribution, with a larger share accruing to lower-income units, is apparent. The Gini coefficients for 1968 and 1972 confirm this result.[33]

A second comparison concerns the interyear changes in the distributions. In the upper panel, there appears to be some equalization of comprehensive income from 1968 to 1972 in $\$$ terms. For both $\$$ and $\$e$, the share of the lowest-income groups has increased. This difference is most pronounced in the $\$e$ figures—the share of the lowest quintile rises from 6.0 to 6.9 percent of total equivalent income. Thus, we conclude that the distribution of income per unit of need is less unequal in 1972 than in 1968. The changes in the $\$e$ Gini coefficients also confirm this relationship. The CPS income distributions, however, present a different picture—the share going to any decile changes by less than one percentage point for absolute income and by only .2 percent for equivalent income. Thus, an analysis based on "official" reported Census Bureau figures would indicate no equalization between the two

[33] The fact that the distributions of comparable types of cash and equivalent income are similar in 1968 and 1972 is *not* to say that there has been no change in shifting from one concept to another because households do change positions depending on the type of income used to rank them. In order to show this difference we have computed income distributional figures whereby families were ranked by *cash* comprehensive income ($\$$) and then their shares of *equivalent* comprehensive income ($\$e$) were determined. The difference between these distributions and those presented in Table 5 are quite significant. For instance, the Gini coefficients for 1972 comprehensive income in Table 6 are .3287 for $\$e$ and .3522 for $\$$. When ranked by $\$$ and then distributing $\$e$, however, the Gini falls to .2897, an 11.9 percent drop in the former and a 17.7 percent change in the latter figure.

The correct method of presenting comparable income size distributional statistics is presented in Table 5. However, what these alternate statistics do show, when compared to the distribution of comprehensive cash income in Table 5, is that ranking households by cash income can often belie the fact that the distribution of income per unit of need ($\$e$) is much more equal than the distribution of cash income alone ($\$$) *when families are ranked in an identical order*. That is, the income share of the bottom 20 percent of households ranked by cash income in 1972, i.e., 5.6 percent, is 2.2 percentage points less than the 7.8 percent of equivalent income which these same households received in that year.

years. However, an analysis based on the more comprehensive income definition suggests a substantial equalization between 1968 and 1972 in terms of equivalent income and a rise in the income share of the lowest deciles by absolute income.

Finally, the distributions of comprehensive and original CPS income can be compared. Comprehensive income is more equally distributed than reported CPS income in both $ and e terms, in both 1968 and 1972. This trend will continue as the volume of federal income taxes and cash and noncash transfer programs increases, providing the structure of these programs remains constant. In 1968 and 1972 the Gini coefficients for original CPS income, expressed in e terms, were .3780 and .3781 respectively. The Gini coefficients for comprehensive income, again expressed in e terms, were .3479 in 1968 and .3287 in 1972. Thus a difference of .0301 between the Gini coefficients for comprehensive and original income in 1968 expands to a difference of .0494 by 1972. Similarly, in 1968, households in the bottom quintile of the e distributions of comprehensive and original CPS income received 6.0 and 4.9 percent of all income, respectively. For 1972, the two estimates for the bottom quintile were 6.9 and 5.0 percent of comprehensive and original equivalent income. Thus, by 1972 the variation between the two measures had nearly doubled.

It seems, therefore, that published census income distribution statistics relying on reported CPS income consistently overstate the actual degree of income inequality in any given year. These statistics also understate the degree of income equalization between 1968 and 1972. Comparing the comprehensive income distributions in $ and e terms between 1968 and 1972, cash income shows a slight increase in overall inequality as measured by the Gini coefficient but income per unit of need is substantially more equally distributed in 1972 compared to 1968. Thus, comparisons of income per unit of need reveal a very different and much more equal interyear trend than comparisons of cash income alone, which lead to the opposite conclusion over this same period.

VII. THE DISTRIBUTION OF EQUIVALENT INCOME: IMPLICATIONS FOR MEASURING THE INCIDENCE OF INCOME POVERTY

In Table 6, the distribution of income by equivalent income class is presented for 1968 and 1972. The significance of these figures can be illustrated by reference to the equivalent income standardization tech-

178   Timothy M. Smeeding

TABLE 6
Two Estimates of the Distribution of Equivalent Income by Income Class of Recipient

Upper bound of equivalent income bracket[a]	Percentage of households with income less than upper bound of equivalent income class:	
	Comprehensive income: W_t	Original census income[b]
1972		
$e 1,000	.9	1.9
2,000	1.8	3.7
3,000	3.4	7.1
4,000	6.2	11.6
4,275	6.6	12.8
5,000	11.1	16.5
5,558	14.4	19.2
6,000	17.0	21.3
7,500	26.4	28.7
10,000	42.0	41.0
12,500	56.5	53.5
15,000	68.7	64.1
20,000	84.3	79.6
1968		
$e 1,000	1.6	2.5
2,000	4.2	5.7
3,000	8.9	11.3
3,553	10.8	14.7
4,000	14.9	17.3
4,316	15.7	19.1
5,000	21.9	23.3
6,000	29.3	29.6
7,500	41.4	40.0
10,000	60.2	56.1
12,500	73.8	69.4
15,000	83.1	78.9
20,000	93.0	90.4

[a] Upper bounds of each bracket are presented in terms of current dollar equivalent income.

[b] These figures are based on the distribution of original census household income. See Table 7, note b.

nique. Because this procedure transforms cash income for a given family into income equivalent to that of a nonfarm four-person family, and because the equivalency ratios of the census poverty lines were also employed, the percentage of poor households can be estimated directly from Table 6.[34] The underlining in Table 6 indicates two common poverty income thresholds: the official government poverty line for a nonfarm family of four persons ($4,275 in 1972 and $3,553 in 1968) and one-half median family income ($5,558 in 1972 and $4,316 in 1968).[35] The equivalent income standardization technique yields a poverty count identical to that obtained from a matrix of poverty lines varying by household size, location, age, and sex structure compared with household cash income. In short, the equivalent income technique standardizes income and compares it to a single poverty line, while the census technique adjusts the poverty lines and compares them to household income.

From the data in Table 6, the implications of the adjustments described above for the measurement of income poverty are unmistakable. For instance, assuming the official poverty lines best represent a true income–needs standard and using the household definition which presumes income sharing among unrelated individuals living together, about *half* as many poor households are observed when basing poverty status determination on a comprehensive income measure (6.6 percent) as when basing our estimates on the census income measure (12.8 percent). The extent of the census overcount is even more serious if intrahousehold income sharing among unrelated individuals is ignored. Table 7 indicates the census estimates of 14.6 percent of all families and unrelated individuals in poverty in 1972. In this case, the comprehensive income concept yields less than half as many poor units (i.e., 6.6 percent versus 14.6 percent). In 1968, this difference was 31.6 percent. Thus, the

---

[34] Alternatively, the same result can be obtained by utilizing cash income alone and adjusting poverty lines according to the same equivalence scales. That is, if Y_i is some given income level and $\bar{T}$ the poverty line for a nonfarm family of four persons, the census method of determining poverty, i.e., $Y_i < T_i$, is identical to the equivalent income method, i.e., $Y_i \cdot (T/T_i) < \bar{T}$, since multiplying both sides of this last equation by $1/\bar{T}$ yields $Y_i (1/T_i) < 1$, which is identical to $Y_i < T_i$.

[35] The official census poverty lines were developed by Orshansky [16] for 1963 based on a 1955 U.S. Department of Agriculture Survey. Since 1963 these thresholds have been held constant in real terms, only changing annually with the Consumer Price Index. For a more detailed analysis of this (and alternative) poverty needs standards see Smeeding [20, chapter 2]. For the most recent estimate of poverty incidence, see U.S. Bureau of the Census [27]. For references to the relative income standard, see Frank Ackerman et al. [1], D. M. Gordon [11], V. Fuchs [9], and Smeeding [20]. Finally, these figures are based on one-half median family income (MFI) as reported in the CPS statistics. Interpolating between the equivalent income brackets presented in Table 6, we would estimate the equivalent comprehensive income of the median household in 1972 to be about e 11,180, in which case one-half median household comprehensive income would be e 5,590, only $32 away from the published one-half MFI figure.

TABLE 7
Estimates of the Incidence[a] of Income Poverty, 1968 and 1972

	Percentage of all units that are poor		
Poverty line	(1) 1968	(2) 1972	(3) 1968–1972 percentage change ((1) − (2))/(1)
Official poverty line			
Census estimate	15.8[b]	14.6[b]	7.6
Revised estimate	10.8	6.6	38.9
Percentage difference:			
(census − revised)/census	−31.6	−54.7	
One-half median family income			
Original census income	19.1	19.2	−0.5
Comprehensive income	15.7	14.4	8.3
Percentage difference:			
(census − revised)/census	−18.2	−25.0	

[a] The incidence of poverty is here defined as the percentage of all households that are poor in a particular year.

[b] These figures are taken from U.S. Bureau of the Census [24] and not from Table 6. The figures in Table 6 show a lower percentage of poor people because they take account of household income sharing while the official figures ignore intrahousehold transfers and treat families and unrelated individuals separately. Thus the official figures shown above are the sum of all poor families and all poor unrelated individuals divided by the total number of U.S. families and unrelated individuals.

extent of bias in the official measure is growing over time. While census figures show only a 7.6 percent drop in poverty incidence between 1968 and 1972, our estimates show 38.9 percent fewer poor in 1972.

The one-half median family income threshold varies with "average" income, hence it is a relative measure of poverty. In order to reduce poverty by this definition, the income distribution must become more equal.[36] Some economists suggest that with a relative poverty definition there would have been no change in poverty incidence over the past thirty years.[37] The figures in Tables 6 and 7 bear this out if the census income definitions are used. Indeed, using this definition, Table 7 suggests an increase in poverty of .5 percent from 1968 and 1972.

[36] Conversely, a reduction in poverty may be achieved by the census definition if family income rises faster than prices, the inequality of the income distribution remaining unchanged.

[37] See Ackerman et al. [1] or Fuchs [9].

However, if we accept the comprehensive income definition rather than the census measure, there has been a modest reduction in the incidence of poverty, from 15.7 percent of the nation's households to 14.4 percent. In fact, if the census were to switch to the comprehensive income definition presented here and to accept the one-half median income poverty measure, there would be fewer poor households in both 1972 and 1968. Further, between 1968 and 1972, poverty would have decreased at a greater rate.

CONCLUSION

This paper presented a comprehensive estimate of the level of economic well-being of low-income households. A comprehensive income measure was used to develop a more accurate estimate of the incidence of income poverty than that provided by the official government estimates. By incorporating federal income and payroll taxes paid, net income underreporting, the cash equivalent of in-kind transfer benefits, and intrahousehold transfers into the comprehensive income measure, the lowest quintile's income share became 5.6 percent of total income, rather than the 4.0 percent estimate provided by the census. In addition, the concept of "equivalent income"—an index of income per unit of need, varying by the household's size, location, and age and sex composition—was introduced. Ranking families according to equivalent comprehensive income, we found that the share of the bottom quintile rose to 6.9 percent—23 percent above this group's share of cash comprehensive income. A comparison of equivalent comprehensive income to original cash income raised the share of the bottom quintile from 4.0 to 6.9 percent, a 78 percent increase.

Based on the comprehensive income indicator, 6.6 percent of all households fell below the official poverty lines in 1972. This is less than one-half of the census poverty estimate. By utilizing the comprehensive income measure of well-being, the census could have raised its poverty lines 30 percent—to one-half median family income—and still had fewer poor households and a greater rate of poverty reduction between 1968 and 1972 than was officially estimated.

REFERENCES

1. Ackerman, F., et al. 1971. Income distribution in the United States. *Review of Radical Political Economics*, Summer.

2. Ando, A., and Modigliani, F. 1963. The "Life cycle" hypothesis of saving: aggregate implications and tests. *American Economic Review* 53:55–84.
3. Becker, G. 1965. A theory of the allocation of time. *Economic Journal* 75:493–517.
4. Beebout, H., and Bonina, P. 1972. TRIM: A microsimulation model for evaluating transfer income policies. Working Paper. Washington, D.C.: Urban Institute.
5. Bell, D. 1974. Indebtedness in black and white families. *Journal of Urban Economics* 1:48–60.
6. Clarkson, K. 1975. *Food stamps and nutrition.* Washington, D.C.: American Enterprise Institute for Public Policy Research.
7. Fiegehen, G. and Lansley, P. 1975. Household size and income unit in the measurement of poverty. Paper presented at the 14th General Conference of the International Association for Research in Income and Wealth, Aulanko, Finland, August.
8. Friedman, M. 1952. A method of comparing incomes of families differing in composition. In *Studies in income and wealth* no. 15. New York: National Bureau of Economic Research.
9. Fuchs, V. 1969. Comments on measuring the low-income population. In *Six papers on the size distribution of wealth and income*, ed. Lee Soltow, pp. 198–202. New York: National Bureau of Economic Research.
10. Gastwirth, J. L. 1972. The estimation of the Lorenz curve and Gini index. *Review of Economics and Statistics* 54:306–16.
11. Gordon, D. M. 1972. *Theories of poverty and unemployment.* Lexington, Mass.: D.C. Heath.
12. Kraft, J., and Olsen, E. 1974. The distribution of benefits from public housing. Paper presented at the Conference on Research in Income and Wealth, May. Ann Arbor: National Bureau of Economic Research.
13. Modigliani, F., and Brumberg, R. 1954. Utility analysis and the consumption function: an interpretation of cross-section data. In *Post-Keynesian economics*, ed. K. K. Kurifara, pp. 388–436. New Brunswick: Rutgers Univ. Press.
14. Moon, M. 1975. The economic welfare of the aged and income security programs. Discussion Paper no. 266–75. Institute for Research on Poverty, University of Wisconsin.
15. Morgan, J.; David, M.; Cohen, W.; and Brazer, H. 1962. *Income and Welfare in the United States.* New York: McGraw-Hill.
16. Orshansky, M. 1965. Counting the poor: another look at the poverty profile. *Social Security Bulletin,* January, pp. 3–29.
17. ———. 1969. Statement before the House Committee on Education and Labor, Special Subcommittee on Education. Washington, D.C.: November.
18. Paglin, M. 1975. The measurement and trend of inequality: a basic revision. *American Economic Review* 65:598–609.
19. Sirageldin, I. 1969. *Non-market components of national income.* Ann Arbor: University of Michigan, Survey Research Center.
20. Smeeding, T. M. 1975. Measuring the economic welfare of low-income households, and the anti-poverty effectiveness of cash and non-cash transfer programs. Ph.D. dissertation, University of Wisconsin—Madison.
21. Smolensky, E., and Gomery, J. 1973. Efficiency and equity effects in the benefits from the federal housing program in 1965. In *Benefit Cost Analyses of Federal Programs,* Washington, D.C.: Joint Economic Committee Print.
22. Smolensky, E.; Stiefel, L.; Schmundt, M.; and Plotnick, R. 1974. Adding in-kind transfers to the personal income and outlay account: implications for the size

distribution of income. Discussion Paper no. 199–74. Institute for Research on Poverty, University of Wisconsin—Madison.

23. Stoikov, V. 1975. How misleading are income distributions? *Review of Income and Wealth,* Spring, pp. 239–50.

24. U.S. Department of Commerce, Bureau of the Census. 1973a. Characteristics of the low-income population 1972. *Current Population Reports,* series P-60, no. 91.

25. ———. 1973b. Money income of families and persons in the United States 1972. *Current Population Reports,* series P-60, no. 90.

26. ———. 1973c. Household and family characteristics, March 1973. *Current Population Reports,* series P-20, no. 258.

27. ———. 1975. Money income and poverty status of families and persons in the United States 1974. *Current Population Reports,* series P-60, no. 99.

28. U.S. Department of Labor, Bureau of Labor Statistics. 1965. *Consumer Expenditures and Income,* no. 273–93.

29. Weisbrod, B., and Hansen, W. L. 1968. An income–net worth approach to measuring economic welfare. *American Economic Review* 58:1315–29.

IX

The Iso-Prop Index:
An Approach to the
Determination of Differential
Poverty Income Thresholds*

HAROLD W. WATTS

INTRODUCTION

This article is concerned with the problem of finding levels of income which can be used to attribute equivalent levels of poverty to families in different demographic circumstances. An index is developed which incorporates these demographic characteristics as components. It can be used to deflate family income so that it is comparable for all families. It can also be used to provide appropriately differentiated threshold values or "poverty lines" from an initial value which is not differentiated by family type—such as the $3,000 per family used by the Council of Economic Advisers in 1964.

I begin by reviewing some of the history of attempts to provide an inventory of poverty. I then develop an index by using the share of income devoted to particular categories of consumption as the basis for defining equivalence. That is, families which spend an equal fraction on necessities are taken to be equally poor. This enables me to derive a poverty index from estimated Engel curves. I conclude by applying the method thus developed to data from the 1960 Survey of Consumer Expenditures.

Reprinted by permission of the *Journal of Human Resources* and the author from *Journal of Human Resources* 2 (Winter 1967):3–18. The introduction has been added.

* The name Iso-Prop is an abbreviation for iso-proportional, suggested from the general category of index numbers based on equivalence in terms of the fraction of income (or some other total available for disposition) allocated to a class of expenditures (or subset of possible dispositions). The author would like to acknowledge here the assistance and support of Mr. David Horner who has been in charge of the statistical processing.

185

Given an initial, essentially arbitrary specification of a poverty income threshold which is intended for a particular family situation, we almost immediately face the problem of determining "equivalent" thresholds for families in different situations. The original $3,000 threshold used for the initial, admittedly crude, inventory of poverty was roughly intended to be applied to a nonfarm family of four persons. The $1,500 threshold for an individual living alone was the first attempt at a differential threshold for a contrasting situation. The intent, in rather vague terms, was to determine the level of income that would allow a single individual to live no better than the average person in a four-person family receiving $3,000.

The next level of refinement, carried out by Mollie Orshansky [3], provided a more complete set of family size differentials and an adjustment for the particular situation faced by farm families. The family size differentials were essentially based on food budgets providing adequate nutrition for use on an "emergency" basis which had been proposed for alternative family sizes (and composition). These budgets were priced out and multiplied by three, on the grounds that a poor family typically must spend as much as one-third of its income on food. This latter assumption implies that the other components of a minimum standard follow the same scale economies as does food, a proposition that has little theoretical or empirical support.

A paper by Elliot Wetzler of the Institute for Defense Analysis [5] explored a slightly different approach to the determination of family size differentials. His index was based on the notion that families spending equal fractions of their income on food are, on the average, equally poor. This approach follows the general line of reasoning used by the Bureau of Labor Statistics in establishing equivalence scales for family size classes.[1] It is also a special case of a procedure considered by Milton Friedman in 1935.[2] Given this proposition, Wetzler is able to infer equivalent income levels from Engel curves estimated for different family sizes. The basic rationale can be illustrated as follows. In Figure 1, hypothetical Engel curves for four-person families and five-person families are drawn along with a line through the origin corresponding to, say, 30 percent of income. According to the Engel curves, four-person families spend 30 percent of their income on food when their income is $Y(4)$. Similarly, five-person families with an income of $Y(5)$ spend 30

[1] See Marsha Froeder [2].

[2] Milton Friedman [1]. A more recent investigation of equivalence scales is found in S. J. Prais and H. S. Houthakker [4].

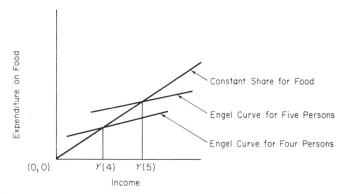

Figure 1

percent of it on food. We infer, then, that $Y(5)/Y(4)$ is an appropriate
index for changing a given four-person threshold into an equivalent
threshold for a five-person family. Wetzler's application of this method
resulted in family size differentials which were roughly consistent with
those provided by Orshansky. This is not surprising, in one sense,
because they are both based on food expenditures and on constant
expenditure shares across family sizes. On the other hand, the two
methods do not combine the ingredients in the same manner, and they
could have produced quite different results.

A current need for guidance in establishing poverty threshold differentials for regions and for the urban and rural segments of the nonfarm
population has motivated further research along these lines. On an
intuitive basis, it seems obvious that a family of four living on $3,000 in
Harlem is poorer than a family of four with the same money income
living near Canton, Mississippi. This does not imply that the Southern
rural family is affluent or even comfortable, but it does imply that a flat
nationwide poverty threshold will include some rural Southern "near-
poor," while excluding some urban Northern families who are relatively
much worse off. In order to obtain a more accurate assessment of the
location and other characteristics of the poverty population, it is
necessary to seek differential thresholds which correspond more closely
to "equivalent" levels of welfare.

Price discrepancies are an important component of the geographical
differentials, but it should not be assumed that they are the only reason
for distinguishing poverty thresholds by location. Other features of the
environment, such as climate, predominant patterns of product distribution, availability and quality of publicly provided goods and services,

transportation facilities, etc., all bear upon the quality of life at the $3,000 level. A differential that allowed only for price deviations would probably be an improvement over the flat nationwide standard, but it would leave out a large category of important, possibly offsetting, determinants of the "welfare value" of a given money income.

In the theoretical and empirical analysis which follows, the Wetzler–BLS–Friedman approach is examined as a method for arriving at geographic differentials. It is probably impossible to give an entirely rigorous or even convincing argument that this procedure adequately reflects all the factors which relate to locational differentials. The method proceeds from the proposition that expenditure fractions change as the "level of life" changes, advanced by Engel himself, to the use of such fractions as indicators of living levels. To the extent that the expenditure category covers a fairly broad range of goods and services, allowance is made for substitution according to local variation in taste, need, and relative prices. Moreover, as will be seen below, the procedure does yield results that are stable and in accord with one's a priori notion.

The procedure's most certain advantage lies in its objectivity—it can be calculated directly from measures of observable household behavior as reflected in available data. Its most serious deficiency, in the view of those who prefer to base equivalence on technically prescribed levels of minimum adequacy (e.g., for nutritional intake), is that it may not produce threshold levels which admit the possibility of attaining all such minimum levels.

I. THEORETICAL DEVELOPMENT

Stated in general terms, we wish to construct an index, I (family size, location, . . .), which can be multiplied into a basic poverty threshold, Y_0, defined for a particular (roughly typical) family situation, in order to obtain "equivalent" poverty thresholds for a wide range of situations. The arguments of I can include any number of descriptors of a family situation, but availability of data, both for estimation and for application, provides practical limitations, and there are probably a fairly limited number of variables which make a noticeable difference in the poverty levels.

Symbolically, let N and L denote family size and location, respectively. Then

$$Y(N, L) = I(N, L) \cdot Y_0$$

where

$$I(N_0, L_0) = 1.0,$$

and Y_0 is the basic threshold for location L_0 and family size N_0. We will further seek an index $I(N, L)$ that can be factored into two indices, i.e.,

$$I(N, L) = I(N) \cdot I_2(L),$$

and further, an index I_2 that can be factored into a regional index and a rural–urban component, i.e.,

$$I_2(L) = I_3(R) \cdot I_4(r).$$

In other words, the adjustment factor for a rural resident is constant, regardless of region or family size. The family size and region indices are similarly independent of other circumstances.

Consider now a general caregory of Engel curves:

$$E = E(Y, N, L),$$

where

E = expenditure on some group of goods and services,
Y = total income,
N = family size,
L = location (perhaps represented by binary variables).

The proportion of Y spent on E can easily be obtained from such a function and can be written as:

$$\lambda = E/Y = P(Y, N, L).$$

Assuming that P is monotonic in Y (decreasing if the goods are necessities), this function can be "solved" to yield Y explicitly as a function of λ, N, and L. This form of the relation can be written:

$$Y = Y(\lambda, N, L).$$

The Iso-Prop Index can now be defined very easily as the ratio of the relation above to the same function evaluated for a base family size and location, where both functions use the same expenditure proportion.

$$I(\lambda^*, N, L) = \frac{Y(\lambda^*, N, L)}{Y(\lambda^*, N_0, L_0)}.$$

A commonly encountered family of Engel curves is characterized by constant income elasticities. Such curves are usually estimated by "double-log" linear regressions. With allowance for variation according to family size and location, this family can be expressed as:

$$E = Y^b \cdot f(N, L),$$

where b = the income elasticity of expenditures. The corresponding P-function is:

$$\lambda = E/Y = Y^{(b-1)}f(N, L).$$

Solving for Y produces:

$$Y(\lambda, N, L) = \left[\frac{f(N, L)}{\lambda}\right]^{(1-b)^{-1}}$$

The Iso-Prop Index is simply:

$$I(\lambda^*, N, L) = I(N, L) = \left[\frac{f(N, L)}{f(N_0, L_0)}\right]^{(1-b)^{-1}}$$

In this case the index is independent of the choice of λ. This is a consequence of the constant elasticity property and does not hold in general. The independence implies that the index would be equally valid for poverty thresholds or affluence thresholds. In the empirical analysis which follows, constant elasticity functions will be used, but some attention will be given to evaluating their suitability and to avoiding the consequences of incorrectly assuming constancy.

If $I(N, L)$ is to be factorable into family size and location components, then the logarithm of $f(N, L)$ above must be composed of additive parts. That is:

$$\ln[f(N, L)] = g_1(N) + g_2(L), \text{ etc.}$$

The index for family size will then be simply:

$$I(N) = \exp\left[\frac{g_1(N) - g_1(N_0)}{1 - b}\right]$$

and for location:

$$I(L) = \exp\left[\frac{g_2(L) - g_2(L_0)}{1 - b}\right].$$

As with the income part of the Engel curve, the empirical analysis will use very simple forms for the g functions. For $g_1(N)$, a simple log-linear form is used, i.e., $g_1(N) = \rho \ln N$. This implies a constant elasticity of expenditure with respect to variations in family size. Some tests of this restriction are made. For $g_2(L)$ a binary-coded representation of region and urbanization is introduced.

II. ESTIMATION PROCEDURES AND DATA

Application of the ideas described above has been carried out for two categories of expenditure: food and a group of expenditures roughly corresponding to necessities—food, housing, clothing, and transportation. Preliminary regressions were carried out using income before tax and income after tax as alternative income measures. Because the results were quite similar in qualitative terms for both measures, and because the officially recognized Orshansky thresholds are in terms of total money income before tax, only the pretax income regressions are reported here.

In addition to the variables already mentioned, the age of the household head and a binary variable for homeowners were introduced into the expenditure function. The intent, at present, is only to provide an appropriate control for these variables. In principle, such variables could also be used as further arguments of a more detailed Iso-Prop Index, but that would require more careful consideration of the appropriate form for the age function.

The basic regression function can be written:

$$\ln E = a + b \ln Y + c \ln N + d_1 R_1 + d_2 R_2 + d_3 R_3 + d_4 r + fA + gH + U$$

where

E =   expenditure on food or necessities,

Y =   income before tax,

N =   family size (number of persons),

$R_1 = \begin{cases} 1 \text{ for North Central Region,} \\ 0 \text{ for other regions,} \end{cases}$

$R_2 = \begin{cases} 1 \text{ for South Central Region,} \\ 0 \text{ for other regions,} \end{cases}$

$R_3 = \begin{cases} 1 \text{ for West Central Regions,} \\ 0 \text{ for other regions,} \end{cases}$

$r = \begin{cases} 1 \text{ for rural (nonfarm),} \\ 0 \text{ for urban,} \end{cases}$

A =   age of household head in years,

$H = \begin{cases} 1 \text{ for homeowners,} \\ 0 \text{ for others,} \end{cases}$

U =   error term.

The data were taken from the tabulated summaries of the 1960 Survey of Consumer Expenditures. Mean values of the variables listed above were available for households jointly classified by income (intervals), family size, region, and urban–rural. Each set of mean values was weighted by the sample frequency in the corresponding cell; then the regression was carried out according to the usual procedure for fitting by least-squares to grouped data.

The use of grouped data leads to a minor loss of efficiency for coefficients of the variables defining the groups. Since nonlinear transformations have been used on linear aggregations of the expenditure, income, and family size variables, some biases should be expected relative to the ungrouped data. For variables such as age and home ownership, the grouped data are likely to obliterate a major part of the basic variation.

Two kinds of variations on the basic regression have been tried. First, the regression has been fitted to different subsets of the data, on the grounds that constant elasticity restriction will introduce less distortion over limited ranges. Second, additional terms were introduced to measure and test for departures from constant elasticity. These variations will be specified in detail as the results are discussed below.

III. THE EMPIRICAL RESULTS

The regression coefficients obtained by fitting the basic equation above to alternative sets of observations are displayed in Table 1. The three upper rows pertain to the "basic necessities"—food, housing, clothing, and transportation. The lower three are for food alone. In all cases, the income elasticities are well below unity, being somewhat lower for food than for the more inclusive expenditure category.[3] The family size elasticity is also substantially less than one, but shows a larger elasticity for food than for all necessities.

The regressions denoted by I used the full range of the data. More than 95 percent of the variance of expenditures in the grouped data was accounted for by the regression. The average deviation from the regressions was around 5 percent in both cases. The II regressions were limited to the income classes between $1,000 and $5,000 and family size classes from 3.0 to 5.9 persons. With the more limited range, the

---

[3] The excluded uses of income are saving and expenditures on personal care, recreation, reading, education, medical care, and other items totaling less than 2 percent of the budget.

TABLE 1
Regression Coefficients for Alternative Estimates of Engel Curves

		Constant term	Income (log)	Family size (log)	Locational binaries				Age	Home ownership
					North Central	South	West	Rural		
Expenditure on necessities (log scale)	I[a]	.201 (.057)	.595 (.010)	.186 (.013)	-.083 (.012)	-.131 (.013)	-.043 (.014)	-.077 (.012)	-.041 (.009)	.103 (.033)
	II	.018 (.187)	.652 (.038)	.238 (.063)	-.067 (.031)	-.078 (.029)	-.035 (.038)	-.030 (.032)	-.028 (.028)	.018 (.096)
	III	.252 (.102)	.522 (.030)	.230 (.029)	-.072 (.023)	-.172 (.022)	-.058 (.027)	-.058 (.021)	-.042 (.016)	.069 (.061)
Expenditure on food only (log scale)	I	-1.044 (.062)	.458 (.011)	.412 (.014)	-.131 (.014)	-.190 (.014)	-.073 (.015)	-.090 (.014)	.024 (.010)	.033 (.037)
	II	-1.187 (.196)	.489 (.040)	.472 (.066)	-.134 (.032)	-.162 (.030)	-.136 (.040)	-.050 (.034)	.031 (.029)	.010 (.101)
	III	-1.029 (.127)	.376 (.037)	.466 (.036)	-.109 (.028)	-.192 (.028)	-.080 (.033)	-.082 (.026)	.018 (.019)	.107 (.076)

Variable (estimated error in parenthesis)

[a] I: regression carried out for all income and family size classes.
II: regression carried out for income class $1,000–$5,000 (four classes); and family sizes 3–5 (three classes).
III: regression carried out for selected income classes in proximity to poverty threshold for each family size class (see footnote 4).

193

multiple R^2 dropped to .88 for basic necessities and .83 for food, but the average deviation also fell to 4.5 percent, indicating some improvement in fit for the narrower range. The regressions in case III attempt a compromise. A different range of income classes was selected for each family size, so as to include only income classes in the "neighborhood" of the current poverty thresholds.[4] The reasoning behind this tactic was that the constant elasticity assumption is more defensible at and around a given level of welfare. Here the R^2's are around .95, and the average deviations are 5 and 6 percent for basic necessities and food, respectively. In general, the relations fit quite closely and seem to be reasonably stable.

Iso-Prop Indices for region based on the North East (i.e., $I(NE) = 100$) can be computed quite readily from the regression results. According to the theory developed above, the index for the North Central region derived from the first row in Table 1 is:

$$I(NC) = \exp(-.083/.405)$$

$$= \exp(-.205)$$

$$= .815$$

or 81.5 (on a scale with base 100). Similarly, the index for rural areas is 82.7 relative to urban areas at 100. According to the logic by which the index was constructed, the index for North Central rural areas relative to North East urban areas would be:

$$\frac{81.5 \times 82.7}{100} \quad \text{or} \quad 67.3$$

One further step is needed to eliminate the arbitrary choice of North East urban areas as the basis of comparison. Clearly, the index could be based on any other choice of location by a simple process of renormalization. It is also possible to obtain an "average" location which can be defined as base and assigned an index value of 100. Such a procedure is adopted here. We will want to apply the index to prevailing national threshold levels, and these presumably represent some base considered

---

[4] Selected income classes are as follows for respective family sizes:

1 person	$ 0–2,000
2 persons	1,000–3,000
3 persons	1,000–4,000
4 persons	1,000–5,000
5 persons	2,000–6,000
6 persons or more	2,000–7,500

to be an "average" location. Consequently, the choice of base determines the average level of the resulting thresholds and ultimately affects
the number of persons below the poverty line. While it is impossible to
infer from available data just how the index should be normalized to
maintain a constant total number in poverty, it is clear that some
weighted (geometric) average of the index values must equal 100. The
following weights have been used to provide an approximate normaliza-
tion base:

North East	20%
North Central	25%
South	40%
West	15%
Urban	75%
Rural	25%

These weights were chosen on the basis of the current distribution of the
poverty population and notions as to how it would shift if a locational
index were to be applied.

Tables 2 and 3 contain normalized index values for the regressions in
Table 1, as well as for several others not reported in regression form.
The index values corresponding to I, II, and III are shown in lines 1, 4,
and 6, respectively. Lines 2, 3, and 5 are all from similar regression
equations fitted to different truncations of the data base, as explained in
the stub heads.

The index values in line 7 were derived from a regression which
allowed for different family size elasticities for the range below 2.5
persons, between 2.5 and 5 persons, and more than 5 persons. For both
food and basic necessities, the elasticity tended to increase in the
midrange and decrease for larger families (for given income levels). Only
in the case of necessities did these variations in slope, or "kinks," prove
to be statistically significant. The locational index values were only
slightly affected by this modification, as can be seen comparing lines 6
and 7 in the two tables.

Comparison among the lines in Tables 2 and 3 shows substantial
variation in the index, depending on which subset of data was used for
estimation. To the extent that the all-inclusive regressions were influ-
enced by the behavior of the affluent part of the sample, we would
prefer the more limited regressions based on behavior at and around the
poverty line. Tests, carried out by introducing "kinks" into the log-
linear regression, rejected the hypothesis that income elasticity is
constant. This further supports the notion that the more limited data

TABLE 2

Iso-Prop Indices Based on Constant Ratio of Expenditure on "Necessities" to Pretax Income, Normalized Indices[a]

Data base for estimation	North East		North Central		South		West	
	Urban	Rural	Urban	Rural	Urban	Rural	Urban	Rural
1. All income classes, all family sizes	1.277	1.055	1.039	0.959	1.020	0.843	1.148	0.948
2. Income classes 1–4,[b] all family sizes	1.305	1.094	1.077	0.903	0.870	0.730	1.210	1.014
3. All income classes, family sizes 3–5	1.206	1.079	0.995	0.890	0.958	0.857	1.066	0.954
4. Income classes 1–4, family sizes 3–5	1.192	1.094	0.982	0.901	0.951	0.873	1.078	0.989
5. Income classes 0–6,[c] all family sizes	1.326	1.097	1.078	0.892	0.876	0.725	1.188	0.983
6. Selected data regression without kinks	1.259	1.115	1.081	0.958	0.878	0.777	1.115	0.988
7. Selected data regression with kinks	1.253	1.096	1.086	0.950	0.885	0.774	1.114	0.974

[a] Based on the following arbitrary distribution of poor by region: North East 20%, North Central 25%, South 40%, West 15%; Urban 75%, Rural nonfarm 25%.

[b] Income classes 1–4, ranges from $1,000–5,000 per year family income.

[c] Income classes 0–6, ranges from $0–7,500 per year family income.

TABLE 3
Iso-Prop Indices Based on Constant Ratio of Expenditure on Food to Pretax Income, Normalized Indices[a]

Data base for estimation	North East		North Central		South		West	
	Urban	Rural	Urban	Rural	Urban	Rural	Urban	Rural
1. All income classes, all family sizes	1.300	1.101	1.021	0.864	0.917	0.776	1.130	0.962
2. Income classes 1–4,[b] all family sizes	1.307	1.196	1.042	0.953	0.857	0.785	1.136	1.039
3. All income classes, family sizes 3–5	1.285	1.099	0.983	0.841	0.959	0.820	1.069	0.914
4. Income classes 1–4, family sizes 3–5	1.294	1.172	0.995	0.901	0.942	0.853	0.991	0.898
5. Income classes 0–6,[c] all family sizes	1.323	1.093	1.058	0.874	0.897	0.741	1.151	0.951
6. Selected data regression without kinks	1.245	1.091	1.045	0.915	0.915	0.802	1.096	0.960
7. Selected data regression with kinks	1.242	1.082	1.047	0.912	0.918	0.800	1.095	0.954

[a] Based on the following arbitrary distribution of poor by region: North East 20%, North Central 25%, South 40%, West 15%; Urban 75%, Rural nonfarm 25%.
[b] Income classes 1–4, ranges from $1,000–5,000 per year family income.
[c] Income classes 0–6, ranges from $0–7,500 per year family income.

base may provide results that are more appropriate for the poverty population.

Figure 2 represents graphically the values of the index in line 7 for the "selected income classes" with "kinks" in the family size relation. The left-hand bars are based on basic necessities; the right-hand on food. The dollar scale shows the levels that are equivalent to $3,000 for an "average" family of four. At these income levels, such a family with a 40-year-old head and renting its dwelling would spend approximately 80 percent of its income before taxes on the four components of basic necessities. Close to 32 percent of total income would be spent for food alone, according to the estimates of the food relation. At the same income, the expenditure fractions would be about 10 percent higher for homeowners, i.e., 88 and 35 percent, respectively.

The same regressions provide family size adjustments based on the same rationale as the regional differentials. Although the emphasis here has been on the regional analysis, it may be of some interest to examine

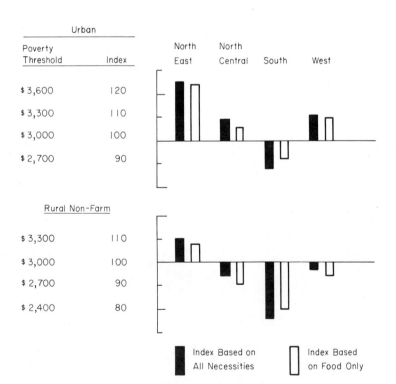

Figure 2. Index for family size differentials. (Poverty threshold is based on $3,000 for a nonfarm family of four persons.)

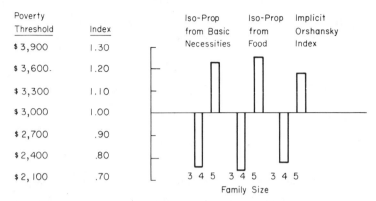

Figure 3. Iso-Prop Index values for adjusting poverty thresholds by region and urbanization. (Family of 4 = 100.)

the Iso-Prop Index for family size. Figure 3 displays the index values of family sizes 3, 4, and 5 for the "central" segment of the regressions, which included the variable slopes for family sizes. For comparison, the index implied by the Orshansky thresholds is also presented. An adjacent scale indicates the threshold levels based on $3,000 for a family of four.

CONCLUDING REMARKS

On the basis of the analysis above, the Iso-Prop Index appears to be a promising approach to the problem of equivalent income levels. It is based on observable behavior; it does not limit itself to price variations alone; and it produces results which are both consistent with a priori notions and, in the case of family size, similar to the equivalence scales estimated by others.

The locational differences appear to be reasonably well estimated in the various regressions. The resulting index values can be taken as a reasonable approximation to the "true" ratios of incomes that equalize expenditure shares. However, the index, even if it is approximate for the adjustment of poverty lines, does not provide a complete solution to the problem of localized poverty thresholds. In particular, the border between the North East and the South separates the highest and the lowest areas. Probably no one would assert that crossing the Mason-Dixon line implies an abrupt change of $1,000 in equivalent levels of poverty. As an average, and for making general interarea comparisons, the index would be appropriate. For purposes of detailed local administration, e.g., eligibility tests, it would perhaps lead to improvements, on the average, but would produce individual injustices as well.

Further empirical work is needed to explore the Iso-Prop Index for intercity variations. This would provide a more convenient way of graduating the equivalence scales at the borders. For this it would be desirable to use the individual observations from the Consumer Expenditure Survey, instead of the grouped data used here. The city tabulations provide means for income classes *or* family size classes, but they are not cross-classified.

In view of the nonconstancy of income elasticities, it would also be useful to carry out further research on other forms of the Engel curve. When the elasticity is not constant, the income and expenditure data should be deflated by an equivalence index before the relation is estimated. Perhaps an iterative scheme could be used here to obtain successive approximations to an appropriate index.

REFERENCES

1. Friedman, M. 1952. A method of comparing incomes of families differing in composition. In *Studies in Income and Wealth,* vol. 15, pp. 9–24. New York: National Bureau of Economic Research.
2. Froeder, M. 1960. Technical note: estimating equivalent incomes or budget costs by family type. *Monthly Labor Review,* November, pp. 1197–1200.
3. Orshansky, M. 1965. Counting the poor: another look at the poverty profile. *Social Security Bulletin,* January, pp. 3–29.
4. Prais, S. J., and Houthakker, H. S. 1955. *The analysis of family budgets.* New York: Cambridge Univ. Press.
5. Wetzler, E. 1965. Determination of poverty cut-off levels. Institute for Research Analysis, Poverty Research Project, Working Paper no. 6.

X

The Distributional Effects of Inflation and Higher Unemployment

JOHN L. PALMER AND MICHAEL C. BARTH

INTRODUCTION

Enlightened debate and decision-making on the issues of inflation and unemployment require a good sense of the magnitude and distribution of the economic costs they impose across various income-demographic groups. This paper provides a synthesis of available evidence in this area.

The first section examines the effects of inflation. The second assesses the impact of the higher unemployment which is frequently a consequence of attempts to reduce inflation.

The possible detrimental effect of high rates of inflation on the well-being of various groups in the population is a subject of current concern. And anti-inflation policies are likely to result in increases in unemployment which will create additional hardships, perhaps among groups that are already poor. As a result, there is once again a growing debate on the two related policy concerns: the extent to which higher rates of inflation should be traded off—if they can be—against lower rates of aggregate unemployment; and the feasibility, desirability, and shape of

A slightly different version of this paper originally appeared as Technical Analysis Paper no. 2, Office of Income Security Policy, Office of the Assistant Secretary for Planning and Evaluation, Department of Health, Education, and Welfare, 1974.

Although the chapter was written under the general direction of Palmer and Barth, substantial contributions to the writing were made by staff coauthors, Peter Gottschalk, Denton Marks, Florence Setzer, and Larry Thompson. We also wish to acknowledge the editorial assistance of Naomi Salus and the research assistance of Gregory Mills.

possible policy actions designed to alleviate hardship imposed by high rates of inflation and/or unemployment.

While there is general agreement that nearly everyone is bearing some cost of the current situation (Fall 1974), there is little information on the precise dimensions of the loss among specific groups. And even if the burdens of inflation and unemployment were equally distributed, some groups would be less able to bear real income losses than others. For this reason, this paper pays particular attention to those groups—the elderly and low-income populations—generally thought to be most vulnerable to the effects of inflation or anti-inflation policy and, therefore, of the greatest policy concern.

I. EFFECTS OF INFLATION

In this section, the effects of inflation on the economic status of various income–demographic households are examined in four categories: cost of living, wealth, taxes, and income sources. A synthesis of the overall effects of inflation is then presented.

A. Cost-of-Living Effects

In looking at the effects of inflation on different economic or demographic groups, it is essential to focus not only on income changes but also on increases in the prices of the commodities bought by different groups. This is important when differences exist in the price increases of commodities and in the composition of consumption expenditures across income or demographic groups. Suppose, for example, that food prices go up disproportionately and that the poor spend a disproportionately large share of their income on food. The result is a larger increase in prices paid by the poor than the nonpoor.

The measure of overall price increase commonly used is the Consumer Price Index (CPI). This index is based on the goods typically bought by families headed by an urban wage earner or clerical worker. Though this group includes some poor, the index is heavily weighted by the goods bought by middle-income families. To the extent that poor families spend a larger share of their income on food and housing, goods whose prices recently have risen disproportionately fast, the CPI understates the true impact of inflation on the group. Table 1 indicates the expenditure patterns of poor, middle-income, and higher-income fami-

TABLE 1

Allocation of Consumption among Major Categories: Percentage Spent on Each Category

	Poor	Middle income	High income
Food	34.9	22.4	21.9
Housing	35.6	33.2	27.8
Apparel	7.8	10.6	11.8
Transportation	5.1	13.8	16.0
Medical care	5.8	5.7	6.2
Personal care	3.3	2.7	2.7
Recreation	3.4	5.9	7.7
Other	4.1	6.7	5.9
Total	100	100	100

Source: Survey of Consumer Expenditures, 1960–61.

Note: Poor families are those with income less than the poverty line. Middle-income families are urban wage earners and clerical workers. This is the CPI household and includes some below the poverty line. The mean income of this group was $6,230 in 1961. High-income families are those with incomes in excess of $10,000, placing them in the top 15 percent of the income distribution in 1960.

lies.[1] The disproportionate impact of rapidly rising food prices on the relative well-being of the poor is shown by the fact that they spend nearly 35 percent of their consumption dollar on food. This compares with 22 percent for both the middle- and higher-income groups. Housing, too, accounts for a larger share in the market basket of the poor, comprising nearly 36 percent. Middle- and higher-income families allocate about 33 and 28 percent of their expenditures to housing, respectively.

A useful technique for examining the extent to which the living costs of different groups are affected by differential price increases because of their differential expenditure patterns (as shown in Table 1) is to

[1] Though the 1961 SCE (Survey of Consumer Expenditures) weights are the most recently available data, they may be out of date for two reasons: (1) people with the same real incomes may consume a different mix of goods in 1974 than they did in 1961, (2) people holding the same relative position in the income distribution will have higher absolute real incomes in 1974. Both potentially vitiate the appropriateness of 1961 weights for constructing current cost of living indices for the upper- and middle-income units. However, since poverty is defined in terms of real income levels, the second objection is not a problem with respect to the appropriateness of the 1961 weights for the poor person's price index. If anything, the poor are likely to have an expenditure pattern that is even more differentiated from the nonpoor in 1974 that it was in 1961.

construct a separate price index for different broad income groups.[2] Using data on consumption patterns, a properly weighted index[3] of prices paid by a poor person (referred to as the Poor's Price Index, PPI) and a high income person (the High Income Price Index, HPI) was constructed. The widely known Consumer Price Index (CPI) then serves as an index of the prices paid by middle-income families.

Table 2 represents indices based on the weights in Table 1. From 1967 to 1972, a period of mild inflation, the three price indices moved together closely, never differing by more than half a point. The prices of the consumption components making up the indices moved closely together as well, making their relative weighting of minor importance. Where there were divergences these tended to cancel out, with the result that the CPI could serve as a good proxy for the PPI or HPI.

The monthly series from June 1973 to July 1974, and the changes in the yearly series between 1972 and 1973, indicate that during the new period of rapid inflation the old patterns were broken.[4] Between 1972 and 1973 the PPI rose 9.6 points, the CPI rose 7.8 points and the HPI rose 7.6 points. This is a direct result of the large increases in the price of food and housing, two items which comprise a disproportionately large share of the poor person's budget and a relatively low proportion of the high-income budget. By February 1974, the PPI was 3.8 points above the CPI. As the price increase of other goods gained momentum the gap decreased, leaving a 2.8 point gap in July 1974. As the inflation becomes less concentrated in particular sectors, this gap is likely to close even more.

There is no reason to presume that the cost of living for the low-income population would rise less or more rapidly than for other groups during inflationary periods. These relationships depend upon the particular nature of the inflation at any given time. It is important to note, however, that even a lower than average increase in the cost of living of

[2] This approach was first utilized in Robinson G. Hollister and John L. Palmer [8].

[3] A "weighted" price index values the price of each good or service by its relative importance or "weight" in consumers' market baskets. It uses percentages such as those in Table 1 to weight differentially prices paid by the poor and the rich. Ideally, one should use the most disaggregated expenditure weights and consumption prices possible since even within the categories shown in Table 1 there are likely to be considerable differences in price movements of particular items. Doing so might alter somewhat the data shown in Table 2, but not the general relationships. A fixed weight, or Laspayres, price index is used.

[4] The Bureau of Labor Statistics' budgets for urban families indicate the same pattern. Between fall 1972 and fall 1973 the "Lower Budget" increased in cost by 11 percent while the "Higher Budget" escalated by only 10 percent. Before the dramatic rise in food prices, all budgets increased at approximately the same rate.

TABLE 2
Price Indices for Three Income Groups

	Poor Person's Price Index	CPI	High Income Person's Price Index
1967	100.0	100.0	100.0
1968	104.2	104.2	104.2
1969	110.0	109.8	109.7
1970	116.6	116.3	116.1
1971	121.3	121.3	121.0
1972	125.7	125.3	124.9
1973	135.3	133.1	132.5
June 1973	134.3	132.4	131.9
July	134.8	132.7	132.2
August	138.2	135.1	134.4
September	138.5	135.5	134.8
October	139.5	136.6	135.8
November	140.7	137.6	136.9
December	141.7	138.5	137.7
January 1974	143.1	139.7	138.9
February	145.3	141.5	140.6
March	146.7	143.1	142.2
April	147.4	144.0	143.1
May	148.8	145.6	144.8
June	150.1	147.1	146.3
July	151.1	148.3	147.5

the poor as indicated by the type of price indices constructed here may result in a greater hardship for the poor. Since necessities comprise a larger share of their budget and they are already subsisting on the margin, they are less able to ameliorate the impact of higher prices of their normal consumption purchases by either substituting lower price and lower quality items or entirely forgoing certain types of purchases.

B. Wealth Effects

One way in which inflation imposes differential costs on different households is through its impact on the real value of the "net worth" (i.e., assets owned less debts owed) of each household. The precise effect of inflation on the net worth of any particular household is a function of the composition of that household's assets and liabilities.

In general, the current value of "tangible assets"—physical things owned by a household, including homes, automobiles, and the like— rises in tandem with increases in the general price level, so that inflation tends to leave the real value of this component of net worth unaffected. Similarly, "intangible" ownership claims—shares of common stock, mutual funds, and the like—also tend in the long run to increase at the rate of inflation, although these assets may not increase in price until two or three years after the occurrence of the general price increases.[5] Thus, those holding these assets who have an investment horizon of more than three or four years will probably find the real value of their net worth unaffected.

Since the prices of both tangible and intangible assets tend to rise when prices in general rise, the major impact of inflation will be on two remaining components of net worth: (1) fixed dollar financial assets, such as cash, bank accounts, bonds, and the like, whose value is specified as being a fixed number of dollars; and (2) liabilities (debts).

The impact that inflation has on the real value of fixed dollar financial assets and on the real (negative) value of liabilities depends on the degree to which the inflation is anticipated and, if anticipated, the degree to which the asset holders are able to adjust so as to protect themselves. To the extent that the inflation is not anticipated and adjusted to, its effect is to reduce the real net worth of those whose holdings of fixed dollar assets exceed their holdings of fixed dollar liabilities and to have the opposite effect on those whose position is the reverse. With inflation, the purchasing power of the fixed number of dollars that persons in debt (those with liabilities) must pay to the persons who lent them the money (those with the fixed dollar assets) declines.

Several recent studies have examined the effect that unanticipated inflation is likely to have on the distribution of real net worth among households. These studies attempt to discern the exact patterns of variation of asset holdings among households and to estimate which households are likely to be net losers and which are likely to be net gainers during an unanticipated inflation.[6] The results of these studies suggest the following:

- When households are grouped according to the level of their current income, declines in real net worth occur among both the lowest-income groups and the highest-income groups. Low-income

---

[5] Indeed, to the extent that during an inflationary period there is the expectation that anti-inflation policies will cause short-run declines in corporate profits, there can be temporary price declines among this kind of asset. Historically, however, these prices have recovered as soon as the economy recovered and have thereafter risen by more than enough to offset any inflation.

[6] See G. L. Bach [1]; G. L. Bach and J. B. Stevenson [2]; E. Budd and D. Seiders [4]; Hollister and Palmer [8]; and John L. Palmer [12, chapter 9].

households especially have relatively small liabilities and the assets of both are relatively heavily concentrated among the fixed dollar financial variety. Increases in net worth occur among the middle and upper-middle groups where debts are relatively large and most holdings are of tangible assets (e.g., houses and automobiles).

- When households are grouped according to the level of their net worth, declines in real net worth occur almost exclusively among those groups with the highest net worth per household, while increases occur among those groups with the lowest net worth.

- When households are grouped according to age of head, the largest declines in real net worth occur in the group having the oldest heads, while the largest increases occur among the group having heads aged 25–34. The aged appear, as a group, to be relatively free from debt and to hold an unusually large percentage of their assets in fixed dollar financial form, while the young appear, as a group, to be heavily in debt and to have most of their assets in variably priced assets.[7]

- When the analysis is restricted to families having incomes below the poverty line, on the average, both those with aged heads and those with nonaged heads experience declines in the real value of their net worth, but the value of these asset holdings and magnitude of their declines are generally small. Moreover, among the poor, those households headed by aged persons appear less vulnerable to inflation than those headed by younger persons.

Evidence on the net worth distribution among the poor suggests that it is extremely skewed—that a few individuals hold most of the aggregate net worth for this group.[8] Similarly, there is evidence that the distribution of asset income among the aged is also significantly skewed, implying that the middle- and upper-income aged hold most of the assets

---

[7] Indeed, one of the classic beneficiaries from inflation is the relatively young, middle-income household whose net worth is dominated by the holding of one asset, the home, that increases in value during inflationary times and the holding of one liability, the mortgage on the home, that does not increase in value. For these people, inflation can produce a rapid increase in the real value of the household's equity in its home.

[8] For instance in 1961 the median net worth of poor families headed by nonaged persons was only one-third of the mean net worth of such families, while the median income for this group was only about 20 percent below the mean income [8]. Undoubtedly, most of the nonaged poor households with sizable net worth are among the so-called transitory poor, for whom an equivalent loss in net worth would not be nearly as severe as for a household of longer-term low-income status.

of the aged as a group, while the lower-income aged hold relatively few.[9] Taken together with the evidence noted above, the following conclusions about the effect that unanticipated inflation has on the distribution of real net worth can be drawn:

- Inflation will, in general, redistribute away from the poor and the very rich, and toward the middle- and upper-middle-income households, but that the losses among the poor will be concentrated among a relatively small number of the poor. For most of the poor, the lost net worth will be negligible. The net gainers among the poor are likely to be those with temporarily, rather than chronically, low incomes.

- Inflation will, in general, redistribute away from older households and toward younger households, but the losses among the older households will be concentrated among those with moderate to high incomes. For most of the aged poor, the lost net worth will be negligible.

As noted previously, these conclusions are based on the assumption that the inflation was neither anticipated by debtors and creditors nor adjusted to in credit markets. To the extent that the inflation was anticipated and adjusted to at the time that debts were contracted, the analyses described above will represent something of an overstatement of the redistributional impact of inflation.

Recent evidence suggests that, at least in the major money markets, inflationary expectations tend to be translated rapidly into changes in the market rate of interest.[10] To the extent that these inflationary expectations are fulfilled, the losses in the real value of the fixed dollar assets sold in major money markets will be offset by the increase in the interest rate earned on such assets. As a consequence, holders of these assets will lose only to the extent that the actual inflation turns out to be more than the market's expectation. To the extent that the actual inflation turns out to be less than the expected inflation, these asset holders will gain and the persons to whom these assets represent fixed dollar liabilities will lose.

Even when inflations are fully anticipated, though, there are some serious limitations on the ability of asset holders with only moderate

---

[9] The 1970 Survey of Newly Entitled (Social Security) Beneficiaries revealed that the 6,000 married couple beneficiaries with the lowest annual incomes received only 4 percent of their income from assets, while the 10,000 with the highest incomes received 16 percent of their income from assets. Alan Fox [5, Table 22]. However, it must be kept in mind that a substantial number of the aged poor own homes requiring very little debt service.

[10] See W. Gibson [6].

amounts of liquid assets to adjust fully. Small investors do not normally deal in the major money markets. Instead, they hold their assets in the form of deposits in commercial banks and in savings and loan associations. And, while interest rates in the major money markets can rise to offset the expected inflation, legal restrictions can prevent the interest rates paid by these financial intermediaries from rising by comparable amounts. In a period when the interest rate necessary to offset all anticipated inflation exceeds about 5 percent, only those households with substantial amounts of cash and some sophistication regarding credit markets can find reasonably safe, inflation-adjusted methods of holding their savings.

C. Tax Effects

In determining the economic well-being of persons in any specified group, it is important to consider not only the income they receive and the prices they face but also the taxes that they must pay.[11] It is after-tax income that is relevant in determining the resources available to any group for its private consumption needs.

While it is obvious that under the American tax system rising income leads to higher tax payments, a distinction should be made between tax increases induced by increases in real income and tax increases induced by inflation. For example, under the current federal and state income tax laws and Social Security regulations, an increase in a family's money wage income often leads to a corresponding increase in its real tax liability, regardless of whether or not the wage increase represents an increase in real income. Nor do the tax laws distinguish between additional wages received as a result of across-the-board cost-of-living increases or additional dollars received from more hours worked or promotions.[12]

Whether a cost-of-living pay adjustment results in a higher real tax burden depends on the structure of the tax system and the base to which the cost-of-living adjustment is applied. If the tax is strictly proportional, and if the cost-of-living adjustment is applied to pretax income, then there is no additional real tax burden. However, if the tax is progressive,

---

[11] This section focuses on the effect of taxation on the individual tax unit. In conformity with discussion in other sections, it deals with micro effects of taxation. It does not treat aggregate demand aspects and potential links between taxes collected and government expenditures.

[12] The discussion throughout this section is framed in terms of a wage increase all of which is assumed to enter into the family's tax base; the points made are equally valid for increases in any source of income, provided they fully enter into the tax base.

either due to an increasing marginal tax rate structure or due to exempted income, spendable income will increase by less than the cost-of-living adjustment.

Most studies of aggregate tax incidence conclude that across a wide spectrum of the income distribution the entire federal, state and local tax system is roughly proportional with respect to income, with the progressive incidence of personal income taxes being offset by the regressive aggregate incidence of the other taxes. As we have argued, inflation-induced wage increases can lead to greater than proportionate increases in personal income tax liabilities. Unfortunately, in the case of income gains that serve only to offset inflation, there is no reason to believe that this greater than proportionate increase in personal income tax liabilities will be offset by a less than proportionate increase in other tax liabilities, since most of these other taxes are either direct ad valorem consumer taxes or taxes whose incidence is the functional equivalent. Their regressive nature derives not from an intentionally regressive schedule of rates, but from the natural consequences of variations in the consumption behavior of families at different places in the income distribution. Inflation-related wage increases differ from real wage increases in that, ceteris paribus, the former will not alter the consumption behavior of the household receiving them. Therefore, as the prices of the goods these households purchase rise by the same percentage amount as their income rises, the dollar amount of most of the consumption taxes they pay will also increase by the same percentage amount.

Table 3 indicates the impact of the federal income tax system on after-tax income when a 10 percent cost-of-living increase is granted. The

TABLE 3
Effects on Federal Personal Income Taxes of a Ten Percent
Cost-of-Living Increase

Adjusted gross income	Percentage increase in taxes	Percentage increase in after-tax income
$ 5,000	71	8.7
7,000	29	8.9
10,000	18	9.2
20,000	18	8.7
60,000	16	7.0
100,000	14	6.9

Note: The numbers reflect the effect on the taxes paid by married couples filing jointly who use the standard deduction and claim four exemptions.

main point to be drawn from Table 3 is that all tax units,[13] no matter what their incomes, realize after-tax increases in income which are *less* than the increase in the cost of living.[14] They not only pay taxes on their cost-of-living increases but pay a higher percentage in taxes on the increase than they pay on the base income, leaving them with spendable income which does not grow concomitantly with the increase in the cost of living. While prices go up by 10 percent, spendable income grows by no more than 9.2 percent and in some cases as little as 6.9 percent. The redistributional consequences of the effect, which favor middle-income taxpayers, are not strong; however, lower-income taxpayers suffer the greatest proportional increases in their tax burden (i.e., the ratio of taxes to income).

The extent to which inflation-induced tax increases are likely to occur for the low-income person depends on the source of that unit's income and its income tax status. Since federal income tax and state income taxes are not levied on Social Security, unemployment compensation, and public assistance, inflation-induced increases in these forms of income will not enter into the tax base and therefore will be fully realized by the recipient. On the other hand, as indicated in Table 3, low-income workers who pay income taxes on wages earned are less fortunate, in that their cost-of-living adjustments are partially absorbed by increased taxes.

It is not the progressivity of the tax, per se, which produces this result, but rather the fact that the parameters of the tax system (deductions, exemptions, and tax brackets) are set in money terms. This, along with the progressivity of the tax system, is what leads to less than full cost-of-living increases in after-tax income.[15]

D. Effects on Income Sources

Inflation can be expected to affect different sources of income in different ways. For example, some public transfer programs such as OASDI (Social Security) and the federal portion of SSI (Supplemental Security Income for the aged, blind, and disabled) have benefit levels that are indexed so that they rise with the CPI. On the other hand many

[13] Though the table and text deal exclusively with nonitemizers, the same conclusions would follow for itemizers, as long as the cost-of-living increase is taxable, i.e., not covered by additional deductions.

[14] Persons who do not pay taxes will, of course, receive the full cost-of-living increase.

[15] The poor are always better off with a progressive tax than with a proportional tax. The point is that during a period of inflation they would be even better off with a progressive tax system whose parameters were defined in real rather than in money terms.

private pension schemes pay fixed dollar amounts to retirees, and the real value of these pensions can be severely eroded during inflationary periods. Wages and salaries generally increase during inflation, but not necessarily across the board or at a rate commensurate with that of inflation.

In order to understand the potential effects of inflation on the income of various demographic and income groups, it is necessary to examine the relative importance to each of these groups of various sources of income such as welfare, pensions, and wages. This is done in the first half of this part. The second half documents the likely effects of inflation on these various sources of income. Wage and salary income is not considered explicitly in this context for two reasons:

- Deviations in the real value of wage and salary income from its long-run trend are primarily associated with changes in the aggregate unemployment rate and not with inflation, per se.

- Holding employment and productivity effects constant, inflation may affect real earnings levels through a temporary lag of money wage increases behind price level increases in some or all sectors of the economy or through a widening or narrowing of occupational wage differentials. These effects are not pursued here because they are neither well documented nor very important relative to the employment effects just mentioned.

The information on the effects of inflation on various sources of income and the relative importance of these sources to different types of households is not integrated into an impact statement for households in this part. Rather, this is left to the final part of Section I, where evidence on cost-of-living, wealth, tax, and income effects are integrated in assessing the overall effects of inflation.

Income Sources of Various Demographic Groups

For numerous reasons, such as categorical eligibility requirements for various public programs, the relative importance of various income sources depends primarily on the age and sex of the household head as well as the income level of the household unit. Older families might be expected to be more dependent upon Social Security, Old Age Assistance,[16] and various types of pensions. High-income aged families could be expected to depend more heavily upon earnings and private nonwage sources such as rent, interest, dividends, and pensions, since most

---

[16] The Old Age Assistance program was subsumed by the Supplemental Security Income (SSI) program as of January 1, 1974.

public sources of income are bounded by some upper limit on income. Younger units, especially those headed by a male, could be expected to derive most of their income from earnings or earnings replacement programs, such as Unemployment Insurance and Workmen's Compensation and, at higher income levels, from private nonwage sources to some extent. Nonaged female-headed units, on the other hand, might be more likely to receive public welfare payments and alimony as well as other nonwage income, although earnings would also be expected to be important to this group.

Tables 4 and 5, which demonstrate the importance of income from various sources for units with heads of different sexes and ages and at different income levels, confirm these expectations and also indicate other interesting patterns. These two tables present three types of income information in 1972 for each household type.[17] They disaggregate the population, first according to the age of the head of the household (Table 4 gives ages 14–64, Table 5 gives age 65+), then by the household's income level in terms of multiples of the poverty-level income, and finally by the sex of the head of the unit. For each such age–income level–sex group the following are presented: (1) the percentage of all households who receive income from each of the sixteen[18] sources listed down the left side of the tables; (2) for the recipients of any given source of income, the percentage of their total income received from that source; and (3) the share of average total income for the age–income level–sex group as a whole that comes from each of the sources, as well as average total income for the group.

Examination of the tables indicates, for example, how the age–sex composition of the recipient population and the relative magnitude of various sources of income change as income levels change. Receipt of various types of income also differs among different age groups (e.g., Social Security benefits are more important the older one gets) and for household heads of different sexes (e.g., AFDC is more important to female-headed families). Moreover, the tables indicate the relative importance of a given income source to recipients in a given group and how this importance changes as age, sex, and income level change.

The important points to be drawn from these tables are as follows.

[17] A household is defined as a family or an unrelated individual, as these terms are used by the Census Bureau.

[18] The major omission form these tables is an accounting of income from the Food Stamps, Housing, and Medicare and Medicaid programs. Unfortunately, the CPS does not collect data on them. This is not a serious omission for the purposes of these tables, which concern themselves less with levels of income and more with patterns. Conclusions drawn about the latter would be unlikely to differ if in-kind transfer benefits were also included.

TABLE 4

Profile of Income Sources for Households Headed by Nonaged (Fourteen–Sixty-Four) Individuals, 1972[a]

Income (multiples of poverty line): 0.0–1.0[b]

Source of income	Male head			Female head		
	Percentage of households receiving any such income	Average share (%) of total income of recipient households	Average share (%) of total income of all households	Percentage of households receiving any such income	Average share (%) of total income of recipient households	Average share (%) of total income of all households
Wage						
Wages	67.4	83.0	65.1	47.4	59.7	31.8
Self-employed, nonfarm	12.4	35.7	4.5	2.5	33.3	0.8
Self-employed, farm	6.6	41.7	2.3	0.4	30.7	0.1
Total receiving any wage income	77.1	83.7	71.9	49.3	59.9	32.7
Nonwage						
Welfare	17.1	54.8	10.3	42.0	77.4	44.3
AFDC	6.7	48.3	4.8	33.0	74.4	37.8
AB, APTD, OAA	8.9	42.8	3.8	9.1	47.2	4.7
Other welfare[c]	4.2	42.4	1.7	3.8	74.1	1.8
Pensions	6.1	53.3	3.4	3.7	49.0	2.2
Veterans	4.1	47.2	2.1	2.5	42.6	1.4
Government	1.4	64.9	0.9	0.7	69.7	0.5
Private	0.7	65.4	0.4	0.6	55.5	0.4
Social insurance	19.5	48.5	11.2	17.7	62.9	12.8
Unemployment Insurance	6.7	25.7	2.4	1.6	26.1	0.5
Workmen's Compensation	1.6	30.4	0.6	0.4	25.1	0.1
Social Security	12.1	62.9	8.1	16.0	66.4	12.2
Rent	3.3	12.5	0.4	2.7	21.8	0.5
Interest	9.1	9.3	0.7	8.6	12.7	0.9
Dividends	2.3	21.8	0.4	2.2	19.8	0.?

214

					Income (multiples of poverty line): 1.0–2.0	
Total receiving any nonwage income	49.0	55.2	28.1	69.1	80.9	67.3
Average total income of all households	$2,358		100.0	$1,771		100.0
Wage						
Wages	89.0	88.8	81.3	81.7	76.3	64.4
Self-employed, nonfarm	12.4	49.3	6.3	3.2	32.0	1.1
Self-employed, farm	5.0	36.5	1.7	0.9	27.0	0.2
Total receiving any wage income	95.1	92.1	89.3	83.5	76.5	65.7
Nonwage						
Welfare	7.1	23.8	1.7	21.0	43.6	10.3
AFDC	2.6	24.3	0.7	15.4	42.3	8.1
AB, APTD, OAA	2.4	21.6	0.5	5.5	27.5	1.6
Other welfare[c]	2.7	18.0	0.5	2.1	49.6	0.7
Pensions	8.7	26.7	2.1	8.5	33.4	2.8
Veterans	6.0	23.7	1.3	4.8	25.2	1.4
Government	1.3	31.2	0.4	2.2	38.4	0.8
Private	1.7	28.4	0.4	2.1	41.9	0.7
Social insurance	20.1	26.1	5.0	28.4	39.6	11.6
Unemployment Insurance	9.3	14.4	1.3	6.6	16.4	1.1
Workmen's Compensation	2.1	18.9	0.4	1.3	26.7	0.4
Social Security	9.9	36.2	3.2	21.9	44.3	10.1
Rent	4.3	5.8	0.3	4.3	15.3	0.6
Interest	16.7	3.1	0.5	18.0	8.3	1.3
Dividends	3.1	5.5	0.2	3.5	17.2	0.5
Other[a]	5.0	20.9	1.0	15.3	39.2	7.0
Total receiving any nonwage income	46.4	23.5	10.7	66.5	49.8	34.3
Average total income of all households	$6,538		100.0	$5,608		100.0

(continued)

TABLE 4 (Continued)

| | Income (multiples of poverty line): 2.0–3.0 | | | | | |
| Source of income | Male head | | | Female head | | |
	Percentage of households receiving any such income	Average share (%) of total income of recipient households	Average share (%) of total income of all households	Percentage of households receiving any such income	Average share (%) of total income of recipient households	Average share (%) of total income of all households
Wage						
Wages	94.9	91.2	87.5	92.9	83.6	78.3
Self-employed, nonfarm	11.3	43.9	5.2	3.9	49.8	2.2
Self-employed, farm	4.6	32.3	1.4	1.5	17.9	0.2
Total receiving any wage income	98.8	94.8	94.1	94.8	84.6	80.7
Nonwage						
Welfare	2.1	11.1	0.2	5.4	20.6	11.4
AFDC	0.5	10.6	0.1	3.6	17.4	0.9
AB, APTD, OAA	0.8	10.4	0.1	1.7	10.9	0.2
Other welfare[c]	0.9	9.9	0.1	1.0	32.2	0.3
Pensions	9.5	18.7	1.7	10.7	26.8	3.1
Veterans	6.3	14.3	0.9	5.0	18.5	1.1
Government	1.7	26.7	0.4	2.6	36.7	1.1
Private	1.9	23.0	0.4	3.6	29.5	1.0
Social insurance	17.6	14.2	2.4	23.5	28.1	7.3
Unemployment Insurance	8.8	8.9	0.8	5.9	12.6	0.8
Workmen's Compensation	2.4	8.7	0.2	2.0	11.7	0.2
Social Security	7.4	20.4	1.4	18.0	30.7	6.2
Rent	5.8	3.1	0.2	5.7	11.3	0.6
Interest	30.1	2.1	0.7	28.1	5.1	1.4
Dividends	6.3	3.5				

				Income (multiples of poverty line) 3.0+		
income	51.5	11.3	5.9	38.2		100.0
Average total income of all households	$10,196	$18,365	100.0	$6,563	$11,587	100.0
Wage						
Wages	95.9	88.0	83.7	95.7	86.5	82.3
Self-employed, nonfarm	13.8	49.6	8.6	5.6	47.4	3.6
Self-employed, farm	4.4	30.9	1.4	1.4	15.9	0.3
Total receiving any wage income	99.5	94.0	93.7	97.7	88.1	86.0
Nonwage						
Welfare	0.7	7.5	0.1	1.7	14.3	0.3
AFDC	0.1	6.8	0.0	0.5	10.7	0.1
AB, APTD, OAA	0.3	6.2	0.0	0.8	12.7	0.1
Other welfare[c]	0.3	9.1	0.0	0.5	17.9	0.1
Pensions	10.5	14.3	1.5	10.5	14.0	1.6
Veterans	6.0	9.3	0.5	5.3	8.3	0.6
Government	3.1	21.1	0.7	2.9	21.5	0.6
Private	2.0	14.4	0.3	3.1	15.2	0.5
Social insurance	13.2	8.3	1.0	19.3	15.0	3.4
Unemployment Insurance	6.0	5.8	0.3	3.2	8.8	0.3
Workmen's Compensation	1.8	6.1	0.1	1.5	10.2	0.2
Social Security	6.2	9.9	0.6	15.9	15.4	2.9
Rent	9.4	5.1	0.6	9.0	11.2	1.1
Interest	49.2	3.1	1.6	49.6	5.9	3.1
Dividends	17.0	4.9	1.1	17.4	10.4	2.1
Other[d]	3.8	9.5	0.4	11.2	19.9	2.5
Total receiving any nonwage income	65.4	9.1	6.3	68.4	19.5	14.0
Average total income of all households	$18,365				$11,587	100.0

(continued)

Source: 1973 Population Survey with income information for the 1972 calendar year.[e]

[a] Households here include families and unrelated individuals. According to the Bureau of the Census, low-income or poverty levels were as follows during 1972:

Size of household	Nonfarm		Farm	
	Male head	Female head	Male head	Female head
Unrelated individual	$2,207	$2,046	$1,824	$1,723
Two-person family	2,734	2,670	2,302	2,197
Three-person family	3,356	3,234	2,838	2,702
Four-person family	4,277	4,254	3,644	3,598

These levels are adjusted annually for changes in the Consumer Price Index.

[b] This income level excludes units which reported negative total income.

[c] Other welfare included General Assistance and any local welfare programs.

[d] Other income includes annuities, alimony, child support, regular contributions from persons not living in the household, and other periodic income such as insurance and military family allotments.

[e] The underreporting of income in the Current Population Survey must be considered in interpreting CPS data. Comparisons between reported income and aggregate bench-mark estimates provide some indication of the extent of underreporting. For the March 1973 CPS data (covering income year 1972), the Census Bureau calculated reported income as a percentage of bench-mark figures compiled from data provided by the Bureau of Economic Analysis, Social Security Administration, Veterans Administration, and other agencies. These percentages are as follows:

Total income	90%
Wages and salaries	98%
Non-farm self employment	99%
Farm self-employment	69%
Social Security and railroad retirement	92%
Property income	45%
Public assistance	74%

Unfortunately, such percentages are not available by age, sex, or income class.

In general, for households headed by an aged individual:

- Not surprisingly, less than one-fifth of *low-income* households have earnings, and, for those that do, earnings comprise only one-fourth of their total income on the average. OASDI and SSI benefits are of greatest importance to the aged poor; most income is from one or both of these sources. About 10 percent receive pension income, primarily veterans' pensions, which comprises about half of their total income. Another 25 percent receive property income, primarily interest, which comprises a fifth or less of their total income. The income profiles of households headed by low-income males and low-income females are similar, except that the latter depend even less on earnings.

- At higher, but still less than median income levels, these households depend increasingly upon earnings, pensions, and property income. They also receive OASDI benefits at a higher level than the aged poor, but these benefits comprise less of total household income than they did for the aged poor. At higher levels of income, reliance upon earnings, property income, and pensions (particularly private) continues to increase, while OASDI loses importance.

In general, for households headed by a *nonaged male*:

- Seventy-seven percent of all *low-income* households receive earned income, which comprises about five-sixths of their total income. Two other important sources of income are welfare benefits, which are received by 17 percent of such households (primarily the disabled), and OASDI, which is received by 12 percent (primarily the disabled). Where received, each of these sources of income comprises, on the average, about half of total household income. Veterans' benefits are of importance to fewer households (about 5 percent depend heavily on them) and Unemployment Insurance is of even less importance.

- The major difference between low-income households and households between one and three times the poverty level is an increased reliance upon earnings and a decreased reliance upon welfare by those at higher income levels. At the higher end of the income scale almost all income is from earned sources.

In general, for *households headed by a nonaged female*:

- Among *low-income households* there is considerably less reliance upon earnings and more upon welfare (primarily AFDC) relative to

TABLE 5

Profile of Income Sources for Households Headed by Aged (65+) Individuals, 1972[a]

	Income (multiples of poverty line): 0.0–1.0[b]					
	Male head			Female head		
Source of income	Percentage of households receiving any such income	Average share (%) of total income of recipient households	Average share (%) of total income of all households	Percentage of households receiving any such income	Average share (%) of total income of recipient households	Average share (%) of total income of all households
Wage						
Wages	15.4	32.4	6.5	8.3	37.8	4.2
Self-employed, nonfarm	4.5	22.7	1.1	1.7	8.0	0.1
Self-employed, farm	6.0	-7.7	-0.4	2.2	-23.5	-0.5
Total receiving any wage income	24.0	25.6	7.2	11.9	26.6	3.8
Nonwage						
Welfare	24.0	49.4	13.4	21.0	52.6	12.2
AFDC	2.9	25.8	1.5	1.3	31.0	0.9
AB, APTD, OAA	23.9	43.9	11.9	21.0	48.8	11.3
Other welfare[c]	0.0	0.0	0.0	0.0	0.0	0.0
Pensions	9.0	46.3	4.4	9.4	49.1	5.5
Veterans	4.5	49.2	2.4	5.4	47.1	3.2
Government	1.3	34.4	0.5	2.3	59.1	1.5
Private	3.1	47.2	1.6	1.8	40.7	0.8
Social insurance	82.1	79.3	69.9	84.5	81.2	72.3
Unemployment Insurance	0.0	0.0	0.0	0.0.	0.0	0.0
Workmen's Compensation	0.0	0.0	0.0	0.0	0.0	0.0
Social Security	82.2	79.3	69.9	84.5	81.2	72.3
Rent	7.4	9.2	0.8	7.8	12.6	1.0
Interest	16.0	16.8	2.9	22.5	14.9	3.5
Dividends	4.7	22.6	1.1	4.1	18.4	0.8

	94.4	94.1	92.8	96.1	96.8	96.2
Average total income of all households	$1,799		100.0	$1,417		100.0
			Income (multiples of poverty line): 1.0–2.0			
Wage						
Wages	23.2	42.0	11.2	16.3	50.5	10.0
Self-employed, nonfarm	5.9	22.8	1.5	2.6	26.1	0.7
Self-employed, farm	6.4	17.2	1.1	2.4	28.0	0.7
Total receiving any wage income	32.0	38.9	13.8	20.5	47.9	11.4
Nonwage						
Welfare	9.1	32.5	3.1	13.6	41.0	5.8
AFDC	0.7	17.5	0.2	0.9	21.2	0.4
AB, APTD, OAA	9.1	30.1	2.8	13.6	38.5	5.4
Other welfare[c]	0.0	0.0	0.0	0.0	0.0	0.0
Pensions	32.8	30.5	10.5	27.8	33.9	9.7
Veterans	12.5	32.3	4.1	11.9	28.8	3.5
Government	4.2	34.9	1.6	5.7	43.5	2.5
Private	17.6	25.1	4.8	11.4	30.4	3.8
Social insurance	95.6	67.6	64.3	93.8	62.6	58.4
Unemployment Insurance	0.9	13.9	0.2	0.6	18.2	0.2
Workmen's Compensation	0.4	18.8	0.1	0.6	52.8	0.3
Social Security	95.5	67.4	64.1	93.8	62.1	57.9
Rent	13.4	15.3	2.1	16.1	19.7	3.3
Interest	37.1	12.7	4.9	44.5	16.7	7.4
Dividends	7.1	11.5	0.9	14.0	16.7	2.4
Other[d]	1.9	19.1	0.5	3.7	35.6	1.5
Total receiving any nonwage income	98.4	87.9	86.2	98.5	90.0	88.6
Average total income of all households		$3,753	100.0		$2,916	100.0

(continued)

TABLE 5 (Continued)

<table>
<tr><th rowspan="3">Source of income</th><th colspan="6">Income (multiples of poverty line): 2.0–3.0</th></tr>
<tr><th colspan="3">Male head</th><th colspan="3">Female heads</th></tr>
<tr><th>Percentage of households receiving any such income</th><th>Average share (%) of total income of recipient households</th><th>Average share (%) of total income of all households</th><th>Percentage of households receiving any such income</th><th>Average share (%) of total income of recipient households</th><th>Average share (%) of total income of all households</th></tr>
<tr><td>Wage</td><td></td><td></td><td></td><td></td><td></td><td></td></tr>
<tr><td>Wages</td><td>42.1</td><td>51.1</td><td>23.9</td><td>38.8</td><td>62.3</td><td>28.4</td></tr>
<tr><td>Self-employed, nonfarm</td><td>7.6</td><td>33.0</td><td>2.6</td><td>3.6</td><td>38.0</td><td>1.6</td></tr>
<tr><td>Self-employed, farm</td><td>7.2</td><td>23.9</td><td>1.6</td><td>3.8</td><td>27.0</td><td>0.9</td></tr>
<tr><td>*Total receiving any wage income*</td><td>51.6</td><td>50.7</td><td>28.1</td><td>44.9</td><td>60.3</td><td>30.9</td></tr>
<tr><td>Nonwage</td><td></td><td></td><td></td><td></td><td></td><td></td></tr>
<tr><td>Welfare</td><td>1.6</td><td>11.3</td><td>0.2</td><td>3.3</td><td>16.8</td><td>0.7</td></tr>
<tr><td>AFDC</td><td>0.2</td><td>25.5</td><td>0.1</td><td>0.7</td><td>8.4</td><td>0.1</td></tr>
<tr><td>AB, APTD, OAA</td><td>1.5</td><td>8.9</td><td>0.2</td><td>3.4</td><td>14.2</td><td>0.6</td></tr>
<tr><td>Other welfare[c]</td><td>0.0</td><td>0.0</td><td>0.0</td><td>0.0</td><td>0.0</td><td>0.0</td></tr>
<tr><td>Pensions</td><td>50.1</td><td>31.5</td><td>15.8</td><td>39.1</td><td>37.2</td><td>14.0</td></tr>
<tr><td>Veterans</td><td>8.3</td><td>22.2</td><td>2.0</td><td>6.2</td><td>22.8</td><td>1.5</td></tr>
<tr><td>Government</td><td>9.2</td><td>38.8</td><td>3.7</td><td>13.5</td><td>46.0</td><td>6.2</td></tr>
<tr><td>Private</td><td>37.0</td><td>28.0</td><td>10.1</td><td>22.6</td><td>29.5</td><td>6.3</td></tr>
<tr><td>Social insurance</td><td>91.4</td><td>48.0</td><td>43.4</td><td>91.9</td><td>36.1</td><td>33.3</td></tr>
<tr><td>Unemployment Insurance</td><td>2.3</td><td>15.5</td><td>0.4</td><td>2.5</td><td>6.7</td><td>0.2</td></tr>
<tr><td>Workmen's Compensation</td><td>1.0</td><td>18.8</td><td>0.2</td><td>1.2</td><td>38.1</td><td>0.4</td></tr>
<tr><td>Social security</td><td>90.9</td><td>47.6</td><td>42.8</td><td>91.7</td><td>35.6</td><td>32.7</td></tr>
<tr><td>Rent</td><td>17.3</td><td>15.6</td><td>2.6</td><td>20.9</td><td>21.1</td><td>4.0</td></tr>
<tr><td>Interest</td><td>58.5</td><td>12.8</td><td>7.3</td><td>60.4</td><td>18.4</td><td>10.6</td></tr>
<tr><td>Dividends</td><td>16.9</td><td>11.0</td><td>1.8</td><td>24.1</td><td>18.4</td><td>4.2</td></tr>
</table>

Total receiving any income	96.1	75.1	71.9	97.1	70.8	63.1
Average total income of all households	$6,457		100.0	$5,633		100.0

Income (multiples of poverty line): 3.0+

Wage						
Wages	61.6	62.9	41.4	53.9	70.9	40.6
Self-employed nonfarm	13.9	48.0	9.2	6.3	40.1	2.7
Self-employed, farm	10.2	30.4	2.9	5.9	30.0	2.0
Total receiving any wage income	75.0	66.6	53.5	61.6	69.0	45.3
Nonwage						
Welfare	0.8	10.1	0.1	2.0	13.5	0.3
AFDC	0.0	0.0	0.0	0.2	4.7	0.0
AB, APTD, OAA	0.8	10.1	0.1	2.0	12.6	0.3
Other welfare[c]	0.0	0.0	0.0	0.0	0.0	0.0
Pensions	47.8	26.9	12.2	41.1	27.9	10.6
Veterans	6.9	15.7	1.0	7.0	16.0	1.2
Government	13.3	29.7	3.8	15.2	31.1	4.3
Private	33.7	22.7	7.3	23.1	23.9	5.1
Social insurance	79.8	20.5	15.5	82.9	16.3	13.4
Unemployment Insurance	3.5	10.5	0.3	2.7	11.8	0.3
Workmen's Compensation	0.7	6.5	0.1	0.8	28.6	0.1
Social Security	79.3	20.1	15.1	82.6	15.9	13.0
Rent	22.8	13.7	3.3	20.8	16.3	3.3
Interest	68.9	12.8	9.3	72.0	20.9	15.3
Dividends	33.4	14.0	5.7	40.2	23.9	10.6
Other[d]	3.9	13.8	0.6	6.6	16.1	1.3
Total receiving any nonwage income	95.3	48.6	46.5	96.9	56.4	54.7
Average total income of all households	$15,348		100.0	$12,607		100.0

Source: 1973 Current Population Survey with income information for the 1972 calendar year.[e]

[a]–[e] See footnotes to Table 4.

their male counterparts. About 10 percent of these households receive, on the average, one-half of their income from the "other" category, which includes alimony, child support, and other private transfers.

- The major difference between low-income households and those at one to three times the poverty level is a sharp drop-off in reliance upon welfare benefits at increased income levels and an equally sharp increase in the importance of earnings. "Other" income also becomes important for an increasing percentage of households. For high-income households, no source of income other than earnings is important to a sizable proportion.

Inflation and Nonwage Income

The important points to be noted about the likely effects of inflation on nonwage income are summarized below:

- *Social Security, SSI,* and *Food Stamps* all have provisions for automatic increases in benefits which coincide with publication of changes in the CPI or the Department of Agriculture Economy Food Budget. However, in states which supplement federal SSI benefits, automatic increases in federal SSI benefits may not be realized by recipients, since states are not obliged to pass them along and may simply reduce their supplements by an offsetting amount. It should also be noted that even these adjustments will not protect recipients perfectly. Each automatic adjustment offsets only the inflation that occurred prior to the adjustment, not that inflation which will occur prior to the effective date of the next adjustment. When adjustments are performed annually, as in OASDI and SSI, as long as prices continue to rise, all recipients will suffer some real income loss as a result of this adjustment lag.

- *AFDC benefits* are indexed in only three states, and consequently increases in money benefit levels do not necessarily match increases in the cost of living for most recipients of this important public transfer program. At best, AFDC payment levels are usually adjusted by legislative review and match price increases with a long lag (legislative changes may depend on price level changes from as long as two years ago). Statistical analysis of the forces that affect changes in AFDC benefits indicates that, holding other effects on benefit levels constant, changes in average AFDC benefits per recipient reflect only 70–90 percent of changes in the CPI. Moreover, even though some states do provide adjustments that keep benefits up with or ahead of inflation, there are wide variations in states' actions; in some states, average money benefits have not increased at all over long periods of inflation.

- *Unemployment Insurance* payments have been keeping up with inflation until recently. Twenty-eight states do have an annual or semiannual recomputation of the maximum weekly benefit amounts based on wages paid within the state, so that, to the extent that wages in these states are keeping up with inflation, UI benefits are partially adjusted for inflation.

- In general, benefits from *private pensions* represent decreasing real income, since they do not keep up with changes in the cost of living and recipients have no legal right to expect any increases in their payments. However, some funds do provide a limited cost-of-living increase which follows the CPI up to a maximum of 3 or 4 percent. Most of the larger plans for salaried workers have adjusted for price level changes within the last 3 or 4 years, at the initiative of individual employers. However, such adjustments are generally inadequate to maintain real benefits and only occur with a long lag.

- Whether income from *interest* rises during an inflation depends upon the type of asset held at the time the price increases begin. Interest rates on new investments tend to increase during an inflationary period, so that, during inflation, persons whose investments are in short-term assets are usually able to reinvest at an interest rate high enough to offset the effect of the inflation. However, persons who hold long-term assets at the time price increases ensue will not be able to increase their interest income to offset inflation. In order to reinvest at a higher rate these persons would have to sell their long-term assets at a substantial loss.

- During an inflationary period, income from *rents* behaves in much the same manner as does income from interest. If the rental income is received from a short-term lease, the lease can be renegotiated when it expires to reflect the higher rental charges usually associated with an inflation. But if the rental income is received from a long-term lease, no such renegotiation is possible.

- The behavior of income from *dividends* depends upon the behavior of corporate profits. There is no reason to believe that, by itself, inflation will affect the real value of corporate profits or dividends—they should rise by the same amount as prices rise. Profits and dividends can be affected, however, by anti-inflation policies.

To the extent these policies cause a decline in the level of aggregate production, they will probably cause declines in the real value of corporate profits.

- *Federal government employee pensions* are also indexed. The CPS is examined every three months and whenever it has increased by 3 percent or more since the time of the last adjustment, all pensions are increased by an amount equal to that CPI increase plus one percentage point.

- *Veterans' pensions,* although not indexed, have been changed historically with Social Security benefits. Legislation to index these benefits has been proposed.

F. Overall Effects of Inflation

Using the building blocks developed in the first four parts of this section, it is possible to assess the overall effects of inflation on different types of income–demographic households at a very detailed level. Results which seem to characterize large proportions of the household types examined are listed below. (Households with income greater than three times their poverty level are not examined.)

For those households headed by an *aged or disabled* person:[19]

- The incomes of those who are *poor* are fairly well protected against inflation since they are comprised largely of transfer payments (primarily OASDI and SSI) which rise with the general price level. They are not fully protected because adjustments in these transfers frequently occur after a considerable lag, and some states may not raise the SSI income of recipients by the full percentage increase of the CPI. Inflation-induced increases in real tax burdens are not significant in this group since less than one-fifth have earnings and those that do are below the taxable level. Private pension income, which is likely to erode in real value, is received by only 2 percent, and these 2 percent are likely to suffer. Wealth losses will be substantial for a few, but negligible for most.

- Those at *modest* income levels (one to three times the poverty level) generally receive income from other than government programs (frequently in addition to public sector transfers). Inflation will affect many of them substantially because of a high degree of

[19] The definition of disability being used here is one which would qualify a person for OASDI or SSI. It is, therefore, limited to those who have a substantial long-term handicap which severely restricts their ability to work.

dependence on a source of fixed money income (such as most private pensions). Inflation-induced increases in real tax burdens will be felt primarily by the one-half of these households who depend heavily upon earned income. (Nearly 52 percent of aged males with income of between two and three times their poverty lines had earnings, and, for those persons, earnings comprised 51 percent of total income. The comparable figures for aged females are 45 and 60 percent, respectively. These numbers rise sharply at higher income levels for males and somewhat more slowly for females.) There will be some substantial wealth losses among those who have not adjusted their asset holdings to protect themselves from inflation, but it is not possible to be precise about the characteristics of this subgroup.

For households headed by a *nonaged, nondisabled male*:

- About three-fourths of *poor* households depend heavily upon earnings, which comprise 84 percent of their total incomes. These families will likely experience increases in their real tax burden during inflationary periods. Depending upon the particular characteristics of the inflation, they may also experience additional losses of purchasing power due to falling real wage rates. The remainder of these poor households, who depend primarily upon welfare, social insurance, or veterans' pensions, will not experience increased tax burdens and will have their incomes reasonably well cushioned from inflation. Wealth losses are not likely for most, but some with modest savings will find it difficult to protect their real value.

- Except for the 10–15 percent of *lower-middle-income households* who receive social insurance or welfare benefits at some time during the year due to unemployment, retirement, or disability, most are dependent entirely upon earnings. (Over 95 percent of all male-headed families with incomes between one and three times the poverty level received about 93 percent of their income, on the average, from earnings.) Those dependent upon earnings will have an increased real tax burden, although proportionately less than low-income workers. The households dependent upon social insurance or welfare benefits will have their incomes reasonably well protected (subject to caveats already stated) and are unlikely to face increased tax burdens. Those who own their own homes will probably realize an increase in net worth. Those who do not, but have some savings, may have difficulty protecting their net worth if they are not financially sophisticated.

For those households headed by a *nonaged, nondisabled female*:

- About half of those who are *poor* depend primarily upon earnings as a source of income. Inflation will affect them much as it does their male counterparts. The other half rely primarily upon welfare (mostly AFDC), OASDI, or "other" transfers (presumably alimony, child support, and private or family charity). As noted earlier, the protection offered those on welfare will differ from state to state, although on the average and over time AFDC benefits have adjusted for 70–90 percent of CPI with some lag. It is likely that the 10 percent depending upon "other" income will be affected detrimentally by inflation. The protection of OASDI benefits from inflation has been noted earlier. An increased tax burden is not likely to be experienced by any of these households, and wealth effects are similar to those noted for poor male-headed households.

- The primary difference between *lower-middle-income households* and those who are poor is the increased dependence of the former on earnings and OASDI and decreased dependence on AFDC. This is likely to offer them greater protection of real income but increased vulnerability to tax burdens. As a group, these households are far less wealthy than their male-headed counterparts and are, therefore, less likely to have any equity in tangible assets. Thus, any wealth effects are more likely to be detrimental.

II. THE IMPACT OF HIGHER UNEMPLOYMENT

The first part of this section examines at a general level the manner in which anti-inflation policies operate. The second part focuses on the distribution of the unemployment and earnings losses which are the likely accompaniments of anti-inflation policies and the third part examines the extent to which existing transfer programs provide a cushion against these losses. Finally a brief summary is presented.

A. Anti-Inflation Policies

The most widely known and commonly employed anti-inflation tactic is to reduce the aggregate demand for goods and services.[20] The two

[20] Other important anti-inflation policies are: increasing the supply of goods and services; attacking the ability of producer and labor groups to use their market power to contribute to or induce the inflation; and increasing the efficiency with which the economy operates.

primary tools of aggregate demand management are fiscal and monetary policy. Fiscal policy refers to the government's management of its necessary taxation and expenditure functions. Aggregate demand for goods and services may be reduced by raising taxes so that consumers and businesses have less to spend and/or by the federal government reducing its own expenditures.

The impact on the incomes and employment of various groups will depend on the mix of these options adopted by the executive and the Congress. For example, a given tax increase may be levied evenly across the income spectrum or it may be progressive, so that lower income groups pay no more or only a little more in taxes. Or, for example, a given reduction in federal expenditures may be concentrated in the defense area or spread evenly across the entire range of federal programs. The former would, to some extent, concentrate hardship in particular industries and geographic areas.

Monetary policy refers to the Federal Reserve System's management of the growth of the money supply and resulting alterations in the cost of borrowing money (i.e., the levels of interest rates) and the availability of credit. There is less flexibility in the targeting of monetary policy. "Tight money" hits first at the construction industry and other industries dependent on installment credit. Because it is more difficult to borrow money, fewer purchases are made and fewer buildings are built, thus reducing demand for goods and services.

Restrictive and contractionary fiscal policy and tight monetary policy will have similar general effects, although initially perhaps not upon the same groups. As less money is spent, either by consumers or by the government, and whether because of higher taxes, higher interest rates, or lower federal expenditures, fewer goods and services are demanded. Producers of these goods and services notice the slackening of demand and eventually begin to cut back on production. They order fewer raw materials, reduce the hours worked of their labor force, and/or lay off workers. The raw materials industries soon begin to feel the slackening of demand and they too reduce their demand for workers and other inputs to production, and so on.

The manner in which employers respond to reductions in the demand for their goods and services is complex, but it is clear that they reduce their use of labor by offering fewer jobs and, for those who continue to work, fewer hours of work. Slackening labor markets do not go unnoticed by job seekers, and the inability to find a job often leads a discouraged job seeker simply to drop out of the labor force. Thus the supply of labor itself adjusts to slack labor demand.

B.   Distribution of Earning Losses Due to
Higher Unemployment

Economists have for years measured and studied the fluctuations in aggregate output and employment known as the business cycle. Until very recently, however, relatively little effort has gone into measuring the distribution of these fluctuations within American society. That is, when the aggregate unemployment rate rises from, say 5 to 6 percent, what happens to the employment and earnings of the poor relative to the well-off, of blacks relative to whites, of males relative to females, and so on?

Discussions of this subject generally focus on the direct and immediate effects of unemployment in terms of reduced incomes. As we shall see, these can be substantial. There are, however, more subtle longer-term effects, which are difficult to measure but should be mentioned. There is considerable evidence that earnings throughout one's lifetime depend upon work experience and on-the-job training. When labor demand is slack, fewer persons work and obtain such experience. In addition, those who continue working in slack periods are likely to find fewer opportunities for promotion. The point is that reductions in labor demand reduce not only employment but also the opportunities for low-income workers to advance. Thus, not only is hardship felt immediately as income declines, but the potential for lifetime income gains is also reduced. And such losses may be irretrievable. Unfortunately, despite the importance of this point, there is little evidence on the likely lifetime earnings effects of a given increase in unemployment.[21]

The direct effects operate in the following manner. As the growth of the economy slackens, the number of unemployed workers increases. This increase is not, however, evenly spread across various groups, as is demonstrated by the fact that, as the aggregate unemployment rate rises, the rates for teenagers and blacks rise by more and that for white males (particularly family heads) rises by less. Moreover, an estimate of the reduction in hours worked due to unemployment will underestimate the total reduction in hours worked associated with a cyclical contraction in economic activity and thus underestimate the total impact on earnings. It has been estimated that the reduction in hours worked by family heads is about 40 percent greater than the reduction accounted for by measured unemployment.[22] This differential principally reflects the fact that some of those who remain employed during a downswing work less, as overtime and even normal working hours are cut back. For example,

---

[21] For one attempt see Arthur M. Okun [11].
[22] See Edward M. Gramlich [7].

average weekly overtime hours of manufacturing workers fell from 3.6 in the high-employment year of 1969 to 2.9 in the recession year of 1971. Over the same period, the index of aggregate weekly man-hours of durable goods production workers fell by over 14 percent.

Another reason why hours unemployed would understate the loss in working hours attributable to slackening demand for labor is that some workers become discouraged and leave the labor force when the job search proves continually unproductive. They are not reflected in this estimate. Finally, even though movements in the employment and earnings of both male and female family heads are of primary importance because of their greater contribution to family income, the employment of secondary earners must also be considered in measuring cyclical variation in family well-being.

The Gramlich study [7] used data from the six-year Michigan Longitudinal Panel Study on Income Dynamics to provide empirical estimates of the distribution of the effects of higher unemployment by family type, race, and income.[23] As with any inferential study based on sample data, these results cannot be considered definitive, nontheless they are virtually the only such results available.[24]

In brief, the most pertinent findings are:

- The unemployment of those with the lowest incomes is the most cyclically sensitive. For example, a white male head of a poor family is one and one-half times as likely to become unemployed as a similar person with family income at three times the poverty line. Holding income constant, the unemployment of males rises more than that of females while the unemployment of blacks rises more than that of whites.

- A one percentage point increase in the unemployment rate is estimated to decrease the aggregate earnings of secondary earners in white male-headed families by 2 percent and of secondary earners in black male-headed families by 3 percent, but it does not alter aggregate earnings in female-headed families.

[23] In interpreting the results of this study, one important caveat should be borne in mind: the recession period covered, 1970–1972, was a peculiar one in that the unemployment was relatively concentrated among higher-income workers (e.g., aerospace workers). Thus the effects on lower-income groups are, if anything, understated.

[24] There are, however, a number of studies which have attempted to examine the distributional effects of the business cycle, although none of them speaks as directly to the particular topic of this section as does Gramlich's. The results of these studies, when comparable, are usually quite consistent and in no cases inconsistent with those cited in the text of this section. See, for example, Chalres E. Metcalf [9]; and Thad W. Mirer [10]; Michael C. Barth, George J. Carcagno, and John L. Palmer [3, Table 4, p. 25].

- Turning to total family earnings, it was found that, on average, poor families headed by black males suffer, as a result of earnings reductions, almost a 4 percent reduction in family personal income for each one percentage point increase in the unemployment rate. The comparable figures for families headed by white males and by all females are about 3 percent and 1 percent, respectively. The lower labor force activity of females tends to make their incomes less susceptible to changes resulting from employment fluctuations. (These relationships are portrayed graphically for the entire income distribution by the solid lines in Figure 1. For example, to find the predicted percentage decline in the income of a family headed by a black male with an income of three times the poverty line, one would read up from "3.0" on the horizontal axis to the solid line for black males and then read over to the scale at the left. All of the lines in Figures 1 and 2 are read in similar fashion.)

- At higher levels of family income the expected losses due to unemployment fall steadily for the male-headed families and at first increase and then fall for the female-headed families. The

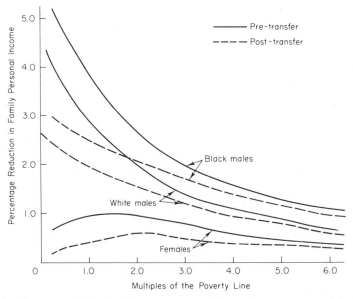

Figure 1. Percentage loss in family personal earned income due to a one percentage point increase in the unemployment rate. (Race and sex refer to race and sex of family head.) (From Edward M. Gramlich [7].)

latter phenomenon probably reflects the fact that labor income of poor female-headed families is a relatively small fraction of total family income.

The above results are averages across the entire population and thus mask the fact that, while most poor persons do not lose their jobs, those who do have income losses far greater than the average. By examining the income losses to only those families which experience unemployment, it is possible to get a better picture of the extent to which some families experience greater hardship.

- For families with incomes less than their poverty lines whose male heads experience unemployment, the average earnings loss due to a one percentage point increase in the unemployment rate is nearly 8 percent of income (see the solid line in Figure 2). In contrast,

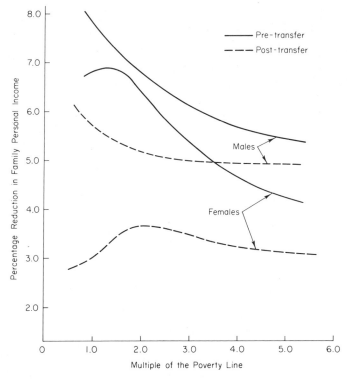

Figure 2. Percentage loss in family personal earned income due to a one percentage point increase in the unemployment rate, for those experiencing unemployment. (Sex refers to sex of family head.) (From Edward M. Gramlich [7].)

male-headed families at five times the poverty line experience a 5.4 percent income loss.

- The earnings of female-headed families are again seen to be less affected by cyclical fluctuations than those of male-headed families, although not a great deal less. Lower-income female-headed families whose heads become unemployed experience a 6.8 percent decline in income due to a one percentage point increase in the unemployment rate, while higher-income female-headed families face a 4.2 percent reduction.

Of course these income loss figures are also averages across a large number of families. Depending upon the duration of the unemployment experienced by members of one of these families, its income loss may be more or less than the average. Fortunately, these losses are cushioned to some extent by existing transfer programs, which are examined next.

C. Cushioning Effects of Transfer Programs

Reductions in family personal income reported in the previous section will be offset to some extent by public transfer programs and also by certain private transfers. The sensitivity of these sources of income to losses in earned income has been analyzed under the following four categories. (a) Unemployment Insurance (UI); (b) Aid to Families with Dependent Children (AFDC); (c) Food Stamps; and (d) other transfers: that portion of Social Security benefits which goes to the nonaged (primarily to the disabled), all other transfers resulting from other government programs, private pension benefits, help from relatives, alimony, and child support payments. The following discussion is based on the behavior of transfer incomes in 1971, as analyzed in the Gramlich study [7].

Unemployment Insurance. For eligible workers, unemployment compensation statutes provide for replacement of about 55 percent of gross wages lost through unemployment; since unemployment insurance benefits are not taxable, this would amount to 70 or 80 percent of previous disposable income. But large numbers of workers are not covered by unemployment insurance because they have been employed in uncovered occupations, have quit their prior job voluntarily, or have not worked long enough to be eligible.

In the Michigan survey data for 1971, only 52 percent of males and 22 percent of females who experienced unemployment were eligible for unemployment compensation. And unemployment insurance does not compensate for the considerable loss of income due to decreased hours of work of those who remain employed. It is estimated that in the aggregate (i.e., averaging across all families whether or not covered by UI) unemployment compensation replaces from 6 to 12 percent of the income losses of male-headed families and from 14 to 18 percent of income lost by female-headed families. The lower the family income, the greater is the income replacement. These relatively low UI income replacement percentages are the result of a number of factors: (1) the incomplete coverage of the system; (2) the fact that unemployment is, as noted above, not the only cause of reduced earnings; (3) the fact that, because of waiting periods, UI benefits do not begin as soon as some unemployment is experienced; and (4) the fact that maximum benefits frequently cause actual benefits to be less than one-half of prior wages.

Aid to Families with Dependent Children. The AFDC program in principle provides an income floor for all low-income single-parent (primarily female-headed) families, but, according to a recent analysis, 17 percent of poor female-headed families receive no benefits [3, Table 4, p. 25]. Since AFDC benefits decrease as other unearned income increases, they respond less to a decline in employment income if unemployment insurance or some other countercyclical transfer is present. On average, AFDC appears to replace about 20 percent of cyclical income losses for female-headed families who receive incomes of less than 150 percent of the poverty line.

The *AFDC–Unemployed Parent (UP) program,* which covers male-headed families and operates in only twenty-three states, has many of the limitations of unemployment insurance, in that it compensates only for income losses due to unemployment and does not cover many of the unemployed. Families must pass stringent eligibility tests: among other things, the father must have been unemployed for thirty days, must not work more than 100 hours per month, must have six or more quarters of work within a given thirteen-quarter period, and must be ineligible for unemployment insurance. The exclusion of recent labor force entrants and those eligible for unemployment insurance eliminates many who would be eligible for benefits on the basis of income. As a result, AFDC–UP replaces only about 12 percent of income losses for male-headed families with incomes of up to 150 percent of the poverty line.

The difference in the cushioning effect of AFDC–UP as between those covered and participating and those not is quite striking. As just noted, across the entire population AFDC–UP replaces about 12 percent of income losses. For those poor and near-poor families covered and participating, however, the average annual benefit in 1971 was $2,173.

This was 122.5 percent of wages lost due to unemployment (suggesting that AFDC–UP benefits exceed the pay of many low-wage jobs). About 36 percent of the unemployed male-headed families in the sample received AFDC–UP benefits.

Food Stamps. The Food Stamp program is the most comprehensive of the transfer programs, extending eligibility to all AFDC households and to other lower-income households depending on income, assets, and family size. Recent expansion has increased the number of recipients from less than 2 million in 1968 to 13 million in 1973, and the expansion is likely to continue. While in 1971 food stamp bonuses covered only about 8 percent of income lost, the program potentially may replace as much as 30 percent of cyclical income losses for low-income persons who participate.

Other Transfers. Other transfer payments to families with heads under 65, including Social Security, various pension plans, and such transfers within the private sector as alimony and child support, together compensate for less than 4 percent of cyclical losses in income for males and about 9 percent for females. The proportion remains constant across income classes.

The average percentage of lost income which is replaced by transfers can be estimated by adding the effects of all transfer programs. For male-headed families in 1971, this ranged from less than 10 percent for the highest-income group to about 36 percent for families at the poverty line. For female-headed families the amount ranged from 25 to 55 percent. Because of the recent growth of the Food Stamp program and exclusion of other in-kind benefit programs, these calculations underestimate the income cushion currently provided by transfer programs. It should be noted that these "replacement percentages" are averages across the entire population, as indicated particularly in the section on UI. Thus they understate the cushioning effect of the transfer system for those covered persons who participate. At the same time they overstate the effect of transfers in reducing hardship for those who are ineligible for one or another transfer program.

It is now possible to examine the total effect of an increase in unemployment on the distribution of income, including the effects of changes in unemployment, hours worked, employment of secondary workers, and, finally, transfer income. These relationships are portrayed graphically for the entire income distribution by the dashed lines in Figure 1, which should be compared to the solid lines in the same figure for a view of the effect of transfers on cushioning cyclical income losses. The greater the vertical distance between the solid (pre-transfer) and dashed (post-transfer) lines, for any race–sex group, the greater the cushioning effect of transfers for that group. Figure 2 may be read in the same way.

Averaging across all families, regardless of whether or not they experience any unemployment:

- An increase in unemployment of 1 percent causes an income loss of about 2 percent for white male-headed families and about 2.5 percent for black male-headed families with incomes in the neighborhood of the poverty line. The loss falls to about 1 percent at five times the poverty line, though declines in income are observed at every income level.

- Female-headed families experience a much smaller loss: about .5 percent at the low and high ends of the income distribution and slightly higher in the middle of the distribution.

Since these figures are for the entire working population, it is again useful to look at the loss in family personal income, after transfer program benefits are taken into account, for only those who experience some unemployment.

- For poor male-headed families, the average income loss due to a one percentage point increase in the unemployment rate is 5.7 percent after transfer program benefits are accounted for (see the dashed lines in Figure 2). Those male-headed families with incomes five times their poverty lines experience on average a 4.9 percent income loss.

- The incomes of poor female-headed families decline on average by 3 percent as a result of a one percentage point increase in the unemployment rate, compared with a 3.1 percent reduction for higher-income female-headed families. The similarity in income loss percentages for female-headed families at different income levels (3.0 and 3.1 percent at one and five times the poverty line, respectively) suggests that transfer programs may have a significant redistributive effect.

It should be noted that even within the group of those who experience some unemployment, there is likely to be an uneven "distribution of hardship" around the averages given, because of the wide distribution of duration of unemployment and the uneven coverage of the transfer system which cushions earnings losses. This may be seen by examining hypothetically the income loss to a four-person family living in a state which does not have the AFDC–UP program. Assume that all family income, $5,000 per annum, is earned by the male family head who, either because of his industry of employment or because of his recent employment history, is ineligible for UI. Upon becoming unemployed the family would probably get state General Assistance benefits of $125 per month and Food Stamps benefits of $135 per month. Thus about 60 percent of the family's income loss would be covered by transfers. Generalizing from this example, which is based on realistic assumptions and probably does not portray an atypical case, it appears that some of the unemployed could suffer income losses of as much as 40 percent of preunemployment income.

D. Summary

Anti-inflation policies have the effect of increasing unemployment and reducing hours worked, and thereby causing incomes to fall. In general, lower-income families experience greater percentage earnings losses than do families at higher income levels. For those low-income families whose heads experience some unemployment, these losses average 7–8 percent. In addition to this direct effect, important opportunities for gaining job experience and on-the-job training may be irretrievably lost.

On the other hand, existing public transfer programs provide a substantial cushion against earnings losses. After transfer program increments to family income are accounted for, a 1 percent increase in the unemployment rate results in a 2.5 percent average loss in income for all black male-headed families at the poverty line. White male-headed families suffer a 2 percent loss and all female-headed families a 5 percent loss on the average. Looking only at those families whose heads actually experience a spell of unemployment, one sees a picture of somewhat greater hardship. Lower-income male-headed families whose heads become unemployed suffer an average loss in income of 5.7 percent, while for similar female-headed families, the comparable figure would be 3 percent.

Anti-inflation policies have the effect of visiting the greatest hardship on those least able to bear it. And while public transfer programs prove to be a significant mitigating force for those eligible, some families will nevertheless suffer substantial income losses, perhaps ranging up to as high as 40 percent of preunemployment income.

REFERENCES

1. Bach, G. L. 1974. Inflation: who gains and who loses? *Challenge* 17:48–57.
2. ———, and Stevenson, J. B. 1971. Inflation and the redistribution of wealth. *Review of Economics and Statistics* 56:1–13.
3. Barth, M. C.; Carcagno, G. J.; and Palmer, J. L. 1974. *Toward an effective income support system: problems, prospects, and choices.* Madison, Wis.: Institute for Research on Poverty.
4. Budd, E., and Seiders, D. 1971. The impact of inflation on the distribution of income and wealth. *American Economic Review* 61:128–52.
5. Fox, A. 1973. Income for newly entitled beneficiaries, 1970. Washington, D.C.: Department of Health, Education, and Welfare, Social Security Administration.
6. Gibson, W. 1972. Interest rates and inflationary expectations: new evidence. *American Economic Review* 62:854–65.
7. Gramlich, E. M. 1974. The distributional effects of higher unemployment. *Brookings Papers on Economic Activity*, no. 3. Washington, D.C.: Brookings Institution.
8. Hollister, R. G., and Palmer, J. L. 1972. The impact of inflation on the poor. In *Redistribution to the rich and the poor: the grants economics of income distribution*, ed. K. Boulding and M. Pfaff. Belmont, Calif.: Wadsworth.
9. Metcalf, C. E. 1972. *An econometric model of the income distribution.* Institute for Research on Poverty Monograph Series. Chicago: Markham.
10. Mirer, T. W. 1973. The distributional impact of the 1970 recession. *Review of Economics and Statistics* 55:214–24.
11. Okun, A. M. 1973. Upward mobility in a high-pressure economy. *Brookings Papers on Economic Activity*, no. 1. Washington, D.C.: Brookings Institution.
12. Palmer, J. L. 1973. *Inflation, unemployment, and poverty.* Lexington, Mass.: Lexington Books.

Institute for Research on Poverty
Monograph Series

A
B 7
C 8
D 9
E 0
F 1
G 2
H 3
I 4
J 5